Society and its M

Society and its Metaphors

Language, Social Theory and Social Structure

JOSÉ LÓPEZ

continuum
NEW YORK • LONDON

For my father Marcelino (a tireless amateur sociologist)
and my mother Angelines

Continuum
The Tower Building, 11 York Road, London SE1 7NX
370 Lexington Avenue, New York, NY 10017-6503

Material in the *Introduction* and *Chapter Two* was reworked from a previously published article: 'Metaphors as Principles of Visuality' in *Journal of Classical Sociology*, Vol. 1 (1), 69–94, 2001. I am grateful to Sage Publications for permission to use this material.

First published 2003

British Library Cataloguing-in-Publication Data
A catalogue record for this book is available from the British Library

ISBN 0-8264-6384-3 (hardback)
     0-8264-6385-1 (paperback)

Typeset by Aarontype Limited, Easton, Bristol
Printed and bound in Great Britain by Bookcraft (Bath) Ltd, Midsomer Norton, Somerset

Contents

Acknowledgements

At the moment, it would appear that there is a consensus that it is debt which is keeping the world economy afloat, a worrisome thought for many. Less frightening is the recognition that it is impossible to engage in academic work without securing extensive intellectual and emotional overdrafts. Unlike economic debt, intellectual and emotional debt makes the debtor unequivocally richer. This book is the product of a cluster of debts that defy representation on any balance sheet. Nonetheless, it would be wrong not to try.

First and foremost I am in debt to the diffuse, heterogeneous, contradictory, problematic and immensely rich body of texts we call social theory. The arguments presented in this book began to emerge in the course of my doctoral work in the Department of Sociology at the University of Essex. I am grateful for the Fuller Bequest Studentship and the lively intellectual atmosphere that made this work possible. However, before Essex in the department of Sociology and Anthropology at the University of Windsor Alan Sears, Tanya Basok and Seymour Faber provided me with an indispensable introduction to both social theory and sociology. Among the people at Essex, I want to particularly acknowledge Ted Benton, John Scott and Anthony Woodiwiss but others include (at least and in no particular order) Rob Stones, Ian Craib, Miriam Glucksmann, Larry Barth, Chetan Bhatt, William Outhwaite, Damian White, Fethi Acikel, Cengiz Yaniklar, Jonathan Clarke, David Ford, Christian Clesse, Christine Rogers, Pam Higham, Tabitha Freeman, Sue Aylott, Brenda Corti, Mary Girling, Diane Streeting and especially Chiaki Hihara.

I wrote the manuscript while enjoying a very early and generous study leave shortly after my arrival at the School of Sociology and Social Policy in the University of Nottingham. I am extremely grateful to all of my colleagues for their support. However, I have a debt with Alan Aldridge that as he well knows could never be cancelled. Other people which I would like to acknowledge cannot be categorized in terms of time or place: they include Angie López, Garry Potter, my adopted sister Oonagh Corrigan, Nao Hoshino and very specially Telsing Andrews. Finally, a very special thank you to Tristan Palmer at Continuum Books.

Nottingham, April 2002

INTRODUCTION

Social Theorizing as a Language-borne Practice

Every critique comes up empty-handed if it proceeds all too hastily with the assumption that we could if we only wanted to, and so it reaches for the rod of moral admonition. It might therefore be wise to begin communication with the communication of ignorance instead of linking communication . . . to the maintenance of an 'illusion of control'. (Luhmann, 1998: 108)

INTRODUCTION

One looks in vain for a book that deals with 'doing social theory'. The most obvious place to look is, of course, the ever expanding market for introductory social theory texts. However, a perusal of these texts quickly reveals that they are not so much concerned with exploring social theory as such, but rather with introducing students to the work of particular theorists, traditions, schools or debates. In other words they are texts about social theories but not social theory. Implicit in these texts is the idea that the commentary of existing theories is the best way to teach or introduce students to the practice of social theory.

A second assumption contained in these texts is the, in my opinion correct, assumption that theoretical practice should not be understood as a self-referential activity. Social theory is a crucial component in the explanatory enterprise that seeks to make the social world intelligible; however, it is not, in and of itself, sufficient. As important as doing social theory are the processes and procedures by which the hypotheses which theories generate are put to empirical tests, however these might be understood. In other words, social theories are also connected with practices and methods for researching the social world. Interestingly, where it is nearly impossible to find texts about 'doing social theory', this is not the case with 'doing research'.

Notwithstanding the different perspectives adopted by the authors of 'doing research' texts, these texts frequently share the assumption that it is possible to teach research techniques as a practice. Of course, these texts often draw on substantive pieces of research in their discussion, but the texts are not limited to commentaries on existing pieces of research. Moreover, these texts frequently include the injunction that students should be doing research from the very beginning. This points to a curious difference between how 'research' and 'theory' are taught. In the former, students are asked to begin by doing research; in the latter, they are asked to read and to engage critically with existing theories. In other words, students are rarely asked 'to theorize' whereas students are always asked 'to research'! The assumption being that one must absorb the 'going canon' before one can speak. Given the sheer size of the field of classical and contemporary social theory, it is not surprising that very few undergraduate and graduate students identify themselves as 'theorists'.

If one scans the opening sections of introductory texts on 'Social Theory(ies?)', it quickly becomes apparent that the most frequent tropes invoked to describe social theory are visual metaphors. Social theories are represented as conceptual maps, lenses, beams, etc., that allow us to see certain 'dimensions' or 'aspects' of the social world. Implicit in the deployment of these tropes are at least two things. First, that our experience of the social world is always mediated. There is no such thing as a 'pure' and 'natural' contact with the social world. Vision is never innocent: it contains assumptions, ways of seeing and knowing. Second, in social theory 'vision' is mediated by conceptual systems. Of course everyday knowing and acting are also embedded in conceptual systems, however social theories are meant to be 'rigorous', 'coherent', 'self-conscious', 'purposive' and 'self-reflexive' accounts of the functioning of the social world.

Given that social theory is prefaced in this way, it is not surprising that two general types of critical engagements usually follow. The first draws more heavily on the visual metaphor by asking students to consider what is excluded from the conceptual vistas opened up by particular theoretical positions. What is it that theories should allow us to 'see' but do not? Thus a theory is criticized for failing to provide us with an understanding of gender, race, sexuality, culture, class, etc. These absences can in turn be explained in terms of the historical development and social location of the texts and their authors. Thus the failure of Marx's theory of class is due to the fact that he did not, maybe could not, know about how contemporary capitalism has diminished the importance of class as a co-ordinate for political mobilizations; but also, perhaps, because Marx's vision of the social world was gendered such that his understanding of agents excluded about half of the people that it should have included, namely women. In terms of my own experience of teaching social theory, the most common conclusion drawn by students, when they are engaged in this modality of critique, is that the social world is far too complex to be understood by a single theory, hence the desirability of using a variety of different theoretical frameworks, or theoretical visions, to investigate the social world. I am in principle committed to the democratic element of theoretical pluralism, but the decision to include all theoretical 'visions' leads to the well-known problem of uncritical synthesis. Unbridled eclecticism does not necessarily produce unclouded theoretical judgement.

The second modality of critical engagement also develops from the social theory as vision metaphor: the notion that social theories are conceptual maps. Here, however, the idea is not so much to stress what is included, or excluded, but to highlight the conceptual 'architecture' of a social theory itself. Social theorizing is represented as an attempt to produce a logical and coherent network of concepts that can be used to map social reality. Thus, the important thing is to investigate the logic and coherence underpinning the connections between concepts and propositions. The fundamental problem with this type of analysis is its impracticability when it is conceived in global terms, and this applies not only for students. As Turner quite rightly suggested in a discussion of critiques of Parsonian theory, to argue that global coherence is the only criterion by which social theory should be judged is, at the very least, excessive:

> If such a criterion of global coherence across an entire corpus of theory were to be uniformly adopted, then 'who would escape whipping?' Although coherence is obviously a major goal of any theoretical endeavour, to demand coherence for a theoretical project as extensive and diverse as Parsonianism is too savage. (Turner, 1986: 183)

Lest I be misunderstood, I am not suggesting that the aforementioned modalities of engagement with social theory have nothing to recommend them. The metaphor of social theory as 'vision' is a useful one, and one which I shall develop throughout this book. Similarly, uncovering logical structures and testing their coherence is also a crucial dimension of theoretical engagement. However, both of these approaches miss something that is so obvious that it is easily overlooked: the fact that social theory is a language-borne practice. As such, it is ontologically more than just a logical structure; it also has a dynamic and a specificity that cannot be reduced to its social or historical origin. Ironically, the difficulty of 'seeing' this is not connected with an obstacle that obscures our sociological vision; rather, it arises from the denial of the opacity of language itself. The language of social theory is predominantly 'seen' as transparent, consequently not 'seen' at all. Thus our 'not seeing' is the product of our mistaken belief that we 'see' all too well. As a result, the resistance that writing and language oppose to our theoretical and explanatory endeavours is, one might say, out of sight and out of mind.

This study is not an introductory text to social theory in the customary sense briefly sketched out above. Moreover it does not claim to be a text about 'doing social theory' generally, though it certainly is a contribution to such an enterprise. It is an attempt to show what happens when we begin to take the language-borne nature of social theory seriously. That is to say, what happens when we refuse the reassuring 'illusion of control' over theoretical language which is implicit in much contemporary theorizing, specifically with respect to the concept of social structure. I do this by looking at the discursive and narrative strategies that are presupposed by attempts to formulate concepts of social structure in the writings of five major theorists – Emile Durkheim, Talcott Parsons, Max Weber, Karl Marx and Louis Althusser. As such, I hope that it is understood as a contribution towards expanding contemporary debates about social structure, but also as an attempt to clarify some of the practical aspects involved in theorizing.

In what remains of this introductory chapter, I am first going to develop an argument that deals with why debates over and about social structure need to be expanded to include the language-borne nature of theoretical practice[1] and why I have chosen the five aforementioned theorists to do so. I will then show how one of the avenues for engaging with the language-borne nature of social theory is through the study of how metaphorical strategies are deployed in theoretical discourse.

DEBATING OVER AND ABOUT SOCIAL STRUCTURE

The concept of social structure is both a core concern of sociological theory, and a term whose definition is highly contested. Curiously, however, although there is no consensus regarding the term itself, there is an implicit contemporary consensus regarding how sociologists, and other social theorists, should argue over it: the debate over, and about, social structure is seemingly always a 'structure and agency' debate. Structure and agency are seen as mutually implicated with one another, both logically and substantively, and the tension between the two is seen as providing one of the crucial nodal points around which sociological theory develops, and has developed in the past. For instance Archer (1995) claims that the concept of social structure provides an 'acid test' for any sociological theory.

Ironically, however, from the very beginning it is recognized that the tension between the two terms is insurmountable:

> The problem of the relation between the individual and society, or between action and social structure lies at the heart of social theory and the philosophy of the social sciences. In the writings of most major theorists . . . this problem is raised and allegedly resolved in one way or another. Such resolutions generally amount to the accentuation of one term at the expense of the other . . . the problem is not so much resolved as dissolved. (Thompson, 1989: 56)[2]

Moreover, if one examines the debate more closely it is hard to miss the fact that the structure–agency problem is frequently a proxy for a long-standing philosophical and theological debate regarding the relationship between freedom and determination. Thus, the concept of agency in its myriad embodiments is used in order to capture the element of 'indeterminacy' or 'contingency' in social life, the 'processual moment' wherein the potential for 'transformation', and not merely 'reproduction', lies.[3] Now, I do not want to suggest that the philosophical problem of the relationship between freedom and determination is inconsequential. However, I do think that it is important to recognize that the questions one can usefully pose regarding the concept of social structure are not exhausted by this philosophical problematic.

Holmwood and Stewart (1991) have quite persuasively argued that one of the consequences of opposing structure to agency in terms of determination and freedom is that it allows explanatory and conceptual inadequacy to be reproduced. Whenever the behaviour of agents deviates from what we would 'structurally' expect them to do, this can be explained away by the freedom to choose otherwise connoted by the concept of agency – alternatively, it is also possible to invoke 'false consciousness'. In both cases, the predictive adequacy of the structural accounts of theories do not need to be revised: error becomes a virtue! Said differently, '... assertions of agency have the negative function of denying structural determination' (Barnes, 2000: 27); the status of structure *vis-à-vis* agency remains theoretically, conceptually and causally unresolved, or dissolved.

It would seem that if debates over social structure are to advance, then it is necessary to attempt to open up new theoretical spaces where different types of questions can be posed.[4] For instance, we can begin by recognizing that social theory as a language-borne practice (Foucault, 1992; Woodiwiss, 1990, 2001) has historically grounded discursive conditions of possibility (more on this below). Thus, instead of subsuming all past attempts to develop a concept of social structure into the structure–agency problematic, we can begin to explore the specificity of the different conceptual networks and the narrative and metaphorical strategies in which they are embedded.[5]

As will be shown in the subsequent chapters, if one carefully examines the development of notions of social structure in classical sociology, it is clear that the concept of structure was not primarily organized around the opposition between freedom and determination. Frequently, conceptions of 'natural organization' were metaphorically deployed in an attempt to identify and conceptually formulate the distinctiveness of social organization, or to use the Durkheimian term the 'sui generis' quality of social life. In the chapters that follow, I want to highlight the conceptual gains that can be made from not approaching the concept of social structure merely in terms of the structure–agency debate. I am going to argue that due to the language-borne nature of social theory, any attempt to formulate or enunciate concepts of social structure is going to contain limitations and opportunities which are discursive in nature; and that these need to be put at the very centre of our debates over social structure.

The commitment to this type of theoretical enterprise has dictated the choice of the authors whose concept of social structure will be scrutinized in subsequent chapters. On the one hand my analysis of the narrative strategies, which underpin the work of Durkheim, Weber and Marx, will seek to demonstrate that their various attempts to develop a concept of social structure were not primarily organized around the structure–agency problematic. Parsons and Althusser have been chosen because of the position that they occupy in the structure–agency debate. Their work is often seen exclusively as hingeing on an unacceptable emphasis on structural determination at the expense of agency. However, I will show that if one examines the narrative strategies and metaphors that each of these authors invokes, it is clear that their work cannot be so easily dismissed in terms of their alleged structural determination. However, before moving on to the substantive chapters it is necessary to investigate the relationship between language and social theory further.

LANGUAGE AND SOCIAL THEORY

It is by no means the case that sociology has understood its use of concepts, or the language-borne nature of theory, in a naive way; 'classical sociology' was very much aware of some of the difficulties involved in constructing representations of social life through the mediation of theoretical language (e.g. Alexander, 1982a; Durkheim, 1982a; Parsons, 1949; Weber, 1949).[6] Nonetheless, it is also true that the 'linguistic turn' (e.g. Rorty, 1979; Sapir, 1949; Winch, 1970; Wittgenstein, 1967) and post-structuralism (Derrida, 1976, 1978; Foucault, 1992) have raised issues that have problematized the transparency of concepts and theoretical discourse, like never before.

The implications of this, have, unfortunately, led some to celebrate the so-called phenomena of 'the floating signifier' – the apparent incapacity to fix 'signifiers' (words) to 'signifieds' (meanings). However, the recognition of the fluidity of meaning and the potential polyvalence of concepts need not undermine the need for rigorous conceptual development, or serve to 'deconstruct' the very possibility of social theory (these are points which I hope to illustrate performatively through out this book). As Culler argues,

> While it [deconstruction] does enjoin skepticism about possibilities of arresting meaning, of discovering a meaning that lies outside of and governs the play of signs in the text, it does not propose indeterminacy of meaning in the usual sense: the impossibility or unjustifiability of choosing one meaning over another. On the contrary, it is only because there may be excellent reasons for choosing one meaning rather than another that there is any point in insisting that the meaning chosen is itself also a signifier that can be interpreted in turn. (1986: 189)

From a different perspective, Foucault claimed that although the number of possible enunciations within a discursive formation could be great, they nonetheless remain limited. This is due to the fact that discourses, and the meanings which they make possible, are not fixed at the level of the general structure of language (*langue*) but in institutionalized 'fields of discursive events' (Foucault, 1992: 27). Thus, one of the reasons why theoretical terms (signifiers) cannot be entirely free-floating is because they are embedded in both institutional and discursive networks of practice that limit the range of meanings (signifieds) to which they can be attached, as well as the uses to which these meanings can be put (Bourdieu, 1991; Foucault, 1992; Woodiwiss, 1990, 2001).

Surprisingly, though, for a discipline allegedly in the throes of the linguistic turn, analyses that focus on the specificity of the conceptual networks in which concepts are embedded, and the conceptual and explanatory gains that they make possible, are much rarer than those that examine the institutional embeddedness of concepts and theoretical discourses in terms of power relations. This is perhaps nowhere clearer than in the current fashion for reducing the analysis of concept formation to sociologism (i.e. the extra-theoretical and extra-conceptual determinations of concepts and meanings). In this case, the explanatory scope, the potentialities inherent in determinate configurations of concepts and meanings are subordinated to the identification of their social and cultural origins. Every concept is irremediably tarnished by the trace of its origin. This type of analysis, as Woodiwiss (2001: 22–5) points out, can be seen in the exchange between Bob Connell (1997) and Randall Collins (1997) in the *American Journal of Sociology* regarding the status of classical sociology. The debate on the status of classical sociology is reduced to a discussion of whether classical sociology arose from the imperial gaze or not. Consequently what is being discussed in evaluative terms is whether classical sociology is good for us as human beings (Woodiwiss, 2001: 25).

This type of analysis leaves no room for an examination of the explanatory adequacy of concepts and theories. For instance, in discussing Durkheim, I am going to be examining the processes through which biological metaphors make it possible to articulate new notions of structure and social complexity. In doing this, I am not arguing that the importation of such metaphors can be disassociated from among other things, 'the status accorded to medical discourse by political practice' (Foucault, 1992: 69). However, I want to highlight two important points.

First, the inner organization of social theories should make us wary of arguments that posit a reflection in sociological theory of political positions or other interests. Discursive practices, such as social theory, have rules of formation, structures or fields, etc. – they are not amorphous or neutral spaces. Political or other interests need to be filtered through or translated by these rules before they can be proper objects of discursive practices. It is indubitable that non-discursive and discursive practices are mutually intertwined, but the manner of this weaving is highly complex. The second point is that even if we are dealing with issues at the level of discursive influences, as in the case of the importation of metaphors from one discursive field of inquiry to another, the generation of new concepts, and the strategies that this presupposes, have to be understood in part as arising from the organization both within and across discursive spaces.

It is not sufficient to argue for the relative autonomy of theoretical practice and language; it is not enough to merely argue against sociologism. It is, also, necessary to begin to look for, position, and develop investigative techniques that will allow us to create a space in which the relative autonomy of theoretical and conceptual development can be explored. In the next section, I am going to argue that Foucault's much neglected *Archaeology* provides a promising point of departure for such an enterprise.[7]

LOCATING CONCEPTS IN SOCIAL THEORY

Foucault (1992) used the archaeological approach to criticize traditional accounts of the history of ideas. He argued that these accounts erred in portraying the development of knowledge as continuous, linear and progressive. He wanted to draw attention to the fact that the history of knowledge contained significant discontinuities and ruptures.[8] Foucault, not unlike Althusser, maintained that a linear conception of history was derivative from the erroneous premise that history could be understood in terms of conscious human activity: 'Making historical analysis the discourse of the continuous and making human consciousness the original subject of all historical development and all action are the two sides of the same system of thought' (Foucault, 1992: 12). Consequently, Foucault's investigation aims at uncovering 'the principles and consequences' of the 'autochthonous transformations' that take place 'in the field of historical knowledge' (Foucault, 1992: 15) by decentring the subject. In other words, he does not assume that changes in the history of knowledge are reducible to the conscious volition of subjects.

In rejecting the notion of the 'sovereign subject' as the source of the discourses of the human sciences, Foucault is confronted with a problem. How does one account for the relative unity of discourses? Foucault suggests four possible answers that he argues are inadequate. The first possibility is that all the statements found in a particular discourse will be concerned with the same object. The second is that a discourse can be identified in terms of the types of statements that it deploys. The third is that the unity of a discourse can be identified in terms of the existence of 'a system of permanent and coherent concepts', and finally the last possibility is that the unity of a discourse could be understood in terms of a general theme, or theoretical strategy (Foucault, 1992: 21–37).

As a result of the inadequacy of each of these possibilities, Foucault argues that we should understand the 'unity' in terms of what he calls a 'discursive formation'. A discursive formation contains rules for combining all four of the possibilities listed above (objects, types of statements, concepts and themes or theoretical viewpoints), which is why neither of them, alone, can account for the unity of a discourse. Any discursive formation will contain the possibility of a number of configurations of objects, concepts, theoretical strategies and types of statement. In the case of sociology, for instance, neither of the individual elements, alone, could account for its status as a unitary discipline. There is no agreement on what its object are (e.g. Structures? Culture? People?), or how one should go about practising sociology (e.g. Quantitative analysis? Qualitative analysis? Hermeneutics?). A system of permanent and coherent concepts does not persist, nor is there a general theme or theoretical framework to be found (e.g. Modernization? Exploitation? Identity? Structural differentiation?). Counter-intuitively, then, the unity of a discursive formation is in fact a 'system of dispersion':

> Whenever one can describe, between a number of statements, such a system of dispersion, whenever, between objects, types of statement, concepts, or thematic choices, one can define a regularity (an order, correlations, positions and functioning, transformations), we will say, for the sake of convenience, that we are dealing with a discursive formation. (Foucault, 1992: 38)

Foucault goes on to specify the rules of discursive formations (Foucault, 1992: 40–71; Gutting, 1989: 231–9). However, we need not pursue them further here.[9]

What we do need to consider further, however, is the scope of analysis that Foucault is attempting to open up with his archaeological method. This is perhaps easier to do if we examine the metaphor that underpins Foucault's archaeological approach. Given Foucault's interest in discourses, and their 'rules of transformation', it might seem that Foucault is following Saussure in thinking about the organization of discourses along the analogy of '*langue*'. However, Foucault quite explicitly states that an analysis of language (*langue*) will only be able to identify a certain set of rules capable of producing an infinite number of meanings.

Foucault maintains that archaeology is not concerned with investigating the structure of language itself; its aim is to uncover the 'rules' responsible for the production of a 'discursive event'; that is to say why it is the case that one discursive event occurred and not any other (Foucault, 1992: 26–7). For Foucault a 'statement is always an event that neither language (langue) nor meaning can quite exhaust' (Foucault, 1992: 28). Put differently, the determinants of the rules of discursive formations 'are social in the general sense – that is, in Foucault's terms they are "non-discursive" as well as discursive' (Woodiwiss, 1990: 63).[10]

Moreover, it is important to also keep in mind that when Foucault is talking about statements, he is not talking about particular sentences, propositions or signs. He defines statements as dynamic processes, as 'enunciative functions' (Foucault, 1992: 106). Thus a particular statement is a relationship between the rules of formation of objects, types of statements, concepts and theoretical strategies. Statements are the crystallization of the relationship between all four types of elements in a discursive formation.

Therefore, 'rules' are not conscious rules of construction like those which can be identified in logic or grammar; they also do not possess a transcendental status (Gutting, 1989: 242). For Foucault, they are the actual systems of relations among the elements of a discursive formation: 'The fact of its belonging to a discursive formation and the laws that govern it are one and the same thing' (Foucault, 1992: 116).

Above, I suggested that the metaphor underpinning Foucault's archaeology is not that of linguistic structure. Major-Poetzl (1983) has convincingly argued that Foucault conceives of the social space in which discourses are located along the line of post-Newtonian field physics. Foucault's archaeological writing is delivered in the language of spatial–temporal categories. In field physics objects are not primary or *a priori*; they are the result of the intersection of a number of different forces. Ontologically, they are relational. Moreover, the emergence of certain objects need not be understood in terms of general forces in the field, they can also arise from local configurations.[11]

Similarly, Foucault presents discursive events as concrete crystallizations of a number of social forces, some general, others local. This is no doubt why Foucault emphasizes that different types of statements are located in a diversity of 'surfaces of emergence' (hospitals, asylums, etc.), and are legitimated by different 'authorities of delimitation' (professionals, officials, etc.). This is also why Foucault insists on the non-discursive dimension of discursive formations. Thus, in *The Archaeology of Knowledge*, Foucault presents a framework for approaching knowledge production practices as arising from the simultaneous and complex articulation of both discursive and non-discursive elements. It is beyond the scope of this study to attempt to produce an *archaeology* of sociology.[12] Instead, I will be developing an analysis of concept formation that is compatible with a Foucauldian archaeological focus. I will do this by focusing on the enunciation of the concept of social structure.

Foucault, following Bachelard and Canguilhem, is quite clear that concepts have to be approached by examining the networks of meanings in which they are located, in other words relationally. A concept is not a theory, nor can its meaning be derived from a theory's logical architecture.[13] Concepts do not precede the discursive networks in which they are embedded. Thus Foucault writes: 'Rather than wishing to replace concepts in a virtual deductive edifice, one would have to describe the organization of the field of statements where they appeared and circulated' (1992: 56).

What is far from clear in Foucault's work is how we should conceptualize the notion of the 'circulation' of concepts. In other words, he does not explore in sufficient detail, or in practical terms, the specific discursive mechanisms that allow 'concepts' to move from one discursive and phenomenological domain to another. In the remaining sections of this chapter, I am going to argue that metaphorical operations are one of the fundamental mechanisms through which meanings circulate within and across discursive formations. Therefore an understanding of how this process works can help clarify some of the features of the language-borne dimension of theorizing and concept formation.[14]

METAPHORS AND SCIENTIFIC EXPLANATION

Ironically, even though the social sciences are often seen as being closer to the humanities than the natural sciences, the analysis of the role of metaphors in concept formation and theorizing is more firmly established in the natural sciences. There is not, as far as I know, a similar body of work in the social sciences. For instance, writers in the realist tradition of the philosophy of science have drawn attention to the importance of models and metaphors[15] for scientific explanation.[16] Most realists, regardless of their many substantive disagreements, would broadly agree on the existence of mechanisms that are ontologically independent of our conceptions of them, and that laws in science do not refer to constant conjunctions of events, but to trends or tendencies that may or may not manifest themselves empirically in open systems (López and Potter, 2001: Introduction). Thus, it is not surprising that realists should emphasize the need to explore how those mechanisms, which are not readily empirically apprehended in constant conjunctions, can be conceptualized or visualized. But what is it precisely about metaphors that make them such important tools in scientific explanation?

In an article dealing with the role of metaphors in scientific practice, the critical realist Lewis argues that

Scientific metaphors are not merely linguistic ornaments that can be discarded in favour of literal description. On the contrary, metaphors are essential to the conception, development, and maintenance of scientific theories in a variety of ways: they provide the linguistic context in which the models that constitute the basis for scientific explanation are suggested and described; they supply new terms for the theoretical vocabulary, especially where there is a gap in the lexicon; and they direct scientists towards new avenues of inquiry, in particular by suggesting new hypothetical entities and mechanisms. Through metaphor scientists draw upon antecedently existing cognitive resources to provide both the model and the vocabulary in terms of which the unknown mechanisms . . .

governing observable behaviour can be conceived and so investigated. Metaphor thereby performs an indispensable cognitive role in scientific theorising
(1996: 504–5).

Thus, if I say that an eye is a camera, I am using my knowledge of how a camera
works in order to discover the mechanisms that might be at work in the eye.
My metaphor is not restricted to a descriptive function, it is also generative in as
much as it provides me with a vocabulary to enquire about the functioning of the
eye which would not be possible without the metaphor. As Lewis writes, the
important thing to bear in mind is that when I say that the eye is a camera, I am
not speaking about both the eye and the camera, rather the metaphor '. . . allows us
to speak of one thing in terms which are suggestive of another' (Lewis, 1996: 496).
In other words it uses 'the known to express the unknown' (Lewis, 1996: 498).

Lewis, drawing on the classical distinction made by Richards (1936), looks at
the metaphor in terms of its 'vehicle' and its 'tenor'. In my example above, the
tenor would be the working of the eye, while the 'vehicle' would be the camera.
My knowledge of cameras provides me with resources to speculate on the working
of the eye, resources that I would lack if I did not draw on my knowledge of the
working of the camera. Of course, the success of my enquiry of the eye in terms of
my knowledge of the camera relies on the adequacy of my knowledge of the working of the camera. But also, and more importantly, it is not just a question of the
adequacy of my knowledge of the vehicle; it is also a question of the compatibility
of the vehicle and the tenor. My knowledge of the workings of a car might be very
good, but it will not allow me to ask meaningful questions about the structure of
the eye. Not all vehicles will take you where you want to go!

However, it is by no means the case that only realists have been concerned with
the role of metaphors in scientific practice. Maasen, usefully, lists three broad theoretical clusters: Semantic, Pragmatic and Constructivist theories of metaphors
(1994: 14–21). The Semantic tradition (Hesse, 1966; Black, 1962) basically overlaps
with the realist philosophical tradition that I have highlighted above. Pragmatic
theories of metaphors can be found in the work of Davidson (1981), Gerhart and
Russell (1984) and Levin (1981), whereas constructivist renditions are found in the
work of Rorty (1979), Knorr-Cetina (1980), Latour (1990) and Lenoir (1988).
Though all three theoretical frameworks tend to stress the role that metaphors
play in scientific innovation, they nonetheless accentuate different aspects of this
process (Maasen, 1994: 22).

Semantic theories, as is the case with realist theories, tend to stress the utility of
metaphorical or analogical reasoning in the generation of new concepts for the purpose of addressing specific problems. They highlight the interactive dimension
between the tenor and the vehicle, as the site for the generation of new concepts.
Pragmatic theories, on the other hand, emphasize the ways in which metaphors are

processed, or normalized, by the existing disciplinary tools (Maasen, 1994: 22). Rather than just emphasizing the interaction between the host and metaphorical domain, they highlight how metaphors can serve to re-organize the tools already available within the host domain. Finally, constructivist accounts see the recourse to metaphors arising when problems within a discipline are not susceptible to solution within the context of existing disciplinary tools. Consequently, metaphors are seen as solutions to problems in other disciplines which are believed to be successful solutions to the existing problems in the host discipline (Maasen, 1994). The most radical form of constructionism sees a full-fledged metaphorical appropriation as producing an entirely new, and incommensurable, language game (e.g. Rorty).

METAPHORS, THEORETICAL LANGUAGE AND DISCURSIVE EXIGENCIES

Debates among these different approaches are too numerous to detail here.[17] However, there are elements, from each of the aforementioned perspectives, which will inform the analysis that I will be developing. From the semantic perspective, I take on board the emphasis on the opportunity for the generation of new conceptual networks that make it possible to enunciate new meanings via new concepts and the relations among them. From the constructivist perspective, I incorporate the necessity of the discursive mediation of all knowledge production, as well as its embeddedness in wider networks of practices (this emphasis is not absent in realist accounts, though it is, often, not sufficiently thematized). Finally, from the pragmatic perspective, I incorporate the internal theoretical re-alignment which metaphorical operations necessitate.

Notwithstanding these and many more important insights contained in all three theoretical perspectives, I want to highlight the ways in which they are deficient for the analysis that I am going to develop in this study. First, all three approaches, at least implicitly, work with a notion of discipline as a relatively coherent and easily demarcated entity. I believe it is more fruitful to examine the relations between the disciplines at the level of the discursive and non-discursive connections that cross-cut disciplinary boundaries. This opens up an analytical space where it is possible to examine the circulation of meanings and theoretical strategies across discursive fields. It also allows us to locate concepts and conceptual strategies in these spaces (e.g. the space shared by biology, sociology and psychology).

This is not to say that disciplines have no reality. Instead, it is an attempt to examine the relationships between disciplines at an *archaeological* level, viz. in terms of the network of statements which they might share: thus the possibility that portions of the same discursive networks will be able to produce enunciative events in distinct disciplines. For instance, evolutionary theory in biology and evolutionary theory in sociology are both interrelated at the archaeological level, but they produce distinct discursive events. Thus it is necessary to see exchange and transfer between disciplines as taking place across semi-permeable boundaries and not as unfolding between well-defined and closed conceptual networks. The inter-penetration of disciplines can then be understood, in part, in terms of the complex weaving together of mutually shared and related systems of statements that consti-tute different disciplinary knowledges, ideologies, popular knowledges, etc.

Second, with the possible exception of the constructivist approach, the afore-mentioned strategies for dealing with metaphors focus on the level of concrete and conscious decisions made by subjects. I want to argue for the utility of examining metaphorical processes as they are embedded in larger conceptual networks, because on many occasions metaphorical strategies are being discursively deployed without the subject being aware of it. Thus, in a Durkheimian sense, these wider conceptual networks are of a *sui generis* variety; their existence is presupposed by theoretical practice. The existence of unacknowledged metaphorical processes are not unique to social theory; they are, as Lakoff and Johnson (1980) have argued, embedded in everyday communication and thinking. Yet precisely because of this, it is crucial to explore the specificity of the metaphorical processes found in the discursive spaces where the practice of social theory unfolds.

As a result of the two preceding points, I also want to argue that metaphorical functions are not only determined by the problems perceived by subjects in the host domain, but also by the organization of statements within the host domain that make some metaphorical strategies possible but not others. That is to say, I want to accentuate the extent to which the possible number, and the nature, of metapho-rical strategies are intimately connected with the organization of discursive spaces, and the networks of concepts which they make possible.[18]

In summary, if one begins to see disciplines as being traversed, and constituted by connections with other domains, it becomes obvious that as social theorists we are drawing on already existing conceptual networks; social theory is always inter-textual and interdisciplinary. These networks, however, should not be seen as rigidly determining what can and cannot be said. They should not be seen as con-taining the concepts themselves; they should be understood as providing the basis for the production of concepts, theoretical effects as well as the circulation and exchange of meanings. The networks, as universes of possibilities, certainly contain rules of exclusion, but they also contain myriad potentialities for the development of concepts and theoretical strategies. From an archaeological perspective, these networks, or systems of meaning exchange, should not be seen as somehow stand-ing outside of, or hovering around, social reality. Inasmuch as disciplines are con-stituted by both discursive and non-discursive practices, the conceptual networks which make social theory possible are part of the reality that social theory attempts to represent.

It is their *sui generis* nature, the fact that they are a pre-condition for theoretical practice, that makes it possible to examine conceptual development as a relatively autonomous process. Now, if we take metaphorical operations as an important instance of theoretical practice, then it is clear that not only the selection of different metaphors, but also the process through which metaphors are 'processed', are dependent on constraints and potentialities which are in part discursive in nature. Some metaphors are not possible, others though possible will be failed metaphors: metaphorical linkages contain 'discursive exigencies'. They introduce a variety of tensions, incompatibilities and desiderata. Some are conceptual, others are methodological and yet others are logical.

These tensions require the active practice of subjects. Sociologists and social theorists deploy a number of discursive processes, some conscious but others not, in order to overcome these exigencies. However, the exigencies themselves may be such that they are entirely insurmountable. Thus the failure to overcome the discursive exigencies associated with metaphorical functions can be ascribed to (1) specific subjects, (2) extra-theoretical factors, (3) the systems of statements and conceptual networks which the metaphor produces, or (4) all three. In this book I am going to be mainly concerned with the third case.

Finally, I find that all three theoretical approaches to metaphors tend to put too much emphasis on the 'problem solving' aspect of metaphorical operations. By introducing the notion of discursive exigency, I want to accentuate the ways in which problems are also constituted by metaphorical functions. Thus metaphors are not only possible solutions to determinable problems; they also help frame the very nature of some of the problems within scientific discourse (Knorr-Cetina, 1980).

METAPHORS AS MEDIA OF EXCHANGE

Thus far, I have been concerned with sketching out the wider context in which the language-borne nature of social theory can be critically appraised. I have argued that metaphorical operations provide an important avenue for the investigation of some of the discursive strategies which are implicit in theoretical practice. In this section, I want to develop in more detail the conception of metaphor which I will be using in my five case studies by distinguishing between two types of metaphorical operations.

Following Maasen (1994), it is possible to distinguish between two types of metaphorical linkage: *transformation* and *transfer*. A *transformation* takes place when a metaphor sets up a relationship between a host domain and another phenomenological domain where the latter is used to generate new domain specific concepts in the host domain. A well-known example of this type of operation is the

enunciation of the notion of the 'circulation' of wealth in terms of Harvey's conception of the circulation of blood (Foucault, 1994: 179); an example of this type of
operation in everyday life is the idea that life is a journey.[19] This metaphorical
operation can be conceptualized as a 'catalyst' because in the process of producing
new concepts, meanings and theoretical strategies, the initial connections with the
domain from which the metaphor was drawn are severed. In the case that I have just
mentioned, the signifier 'circulation' is attached to signifieds and theoretical strategies in the discourse of Political Economy and not biology or physiology. I will
refer to this type of process as a *Modality A* metaphorical operation.

A *transfer* also sets up a relationship between a host domain and another phenomenological domain; however, what distinguishes it from a *transformation* is that it fails
to produce new domain-specific concepts, meanings and theoretical strategies in the
host domain. A classic example of this would be Durkheim's organismic metaphor
where social scientific analogues for 'organs', 'physiology', etc. are not developed.[20]
I will refer to this process as a *Modality B* metaphorical operation. In a certain sense, in
a *Modality A* operation the metaphorical roots are superseded. This, however, is not
the case with the *Modality B* variety; the epistemic content of the new concepts, and
theoretical strategies, remain dependent on the semantic ties established between
both domains. Consequently, networks of concepts will not be adequately integrated producing 'gaps' leading to both conceptual and theoretical instability.[21]

It is important to keep in mind that the distinction between *Modality B* (transfer) and *Modality A* (transformation) metaphors is one of degree. All metaphorical
operations begin their careers as a *Modality B* variety with the potential of achieving
the status of *Modality A*. The extent to which this is possible depends, in the first
place, on the inherent opportunities contained in the metaphorical operation itself.
Some *Modality B* metaphorical operations will be explanatory dead ends from the
very beginning. For instance, as we saw above, while there is some potential in
thinking about an eye in terms of a photographic camera, the same does not
apply to thinking about the eye in terms of a car. But equally important, it depends
on the extent to which active creative theoretical work manages to attach terms
(signifiers) to new meanings (signifieds). This theoretical work, as Derrida (1976)
has argued, does not take place in a decontextualized thinking-space through a
logical language which is transparent and which unproblematically represents
pure thought. It involves the effort of writing; that is to say, intervening in semantic spaces in order to produce determinate effects of logic and coherence. This, of
course, is also a matter of degree, for as post-structuralists are surely right to point
out, polysemy is an inescapable feature of all meaning systems.

This last point, however, can be developed further by sketching the more general social and conceptual context in which the semantic links created by metaphors
are established. Maasen (1994: 28) has argued that earlier accounts of the meaning-
creating role of metaphors often understood the process as a discrete *transfer* or

transmission of packets of meaning across bounded disciplines (e.g. from biology to sociology). This, however, linked the deployment of metaphorical strategies too narrowly to the instrumental and intentional strategies of atomistic actors, and failed to capture the complex social and cultural arrangements which were presupposed by these types of strategies. Maasen suggests that it is more fruitful to develop

> ... a non-linear model of the transfer of metaphors. According to this notion, the continuous transfer of particular metaphors or systems of metaphors, generates what Foucault has called a 'dispositif': a network of social, political, and scientific discourses, which – in Mitman's words – generate a 'general field of meaning'. (1994: 28)

By locating the use of metaphors in this broader social context, it becomes possible to see them

> ... as *sites and media of exchange* both in the intrascientific and extrascientific domains. Such exchanges, which 'trade on' the capacity of metaphoric language to shift meaning, 'create an "ecological" network driven by the tension-fraught need or desire *both* to "fix" meanings and to disrupt, generate and transform them'. (Maasen, 1994: 29; italics in the original)

Thus, the success of a particular metaphor, or its very possibility, is in part dependent on this wider context.[22]

Maasen's critique of the 'discrete transfer/transformation model' and her development of the idea of metaphors as 'media of exchange' parallels my critique, in the previous section, of the different metaphorical perspectives and my attempt to locate theoretical practice in wider social and conceptual networks. Thus, when considering the two types of metaphorical operations, it is worth keeping in mind that both exist in a broader field of meaning or discursive space. If one takes seriously the need to investigate the opportunities and limitations contained in specific metaphorical operations one has to do more than merely locate them in the general field of meaning. It is important to investigate the extent to which the presence of a particular discourse in a field of meaning generates new domain-specific concepts and theoretical strategies with increased explanatory purchase.

I believe that the distinction, developed above, provides a crucial stepping-stone for a more measured appraisal of the conceptual and explanatory fertility of *Modality A* metaphorical operations in theoretical discourse. In the remaining chapters of this book, I will use these distinctions in order to examine some of the metaphors underpinning the conceptual networks from which five theorists – Durkheim, Parsons, Weber, Marx and Althusser – attempted to formulate concepts of social organization or social structure.

I think that this task is important because, as Maasen (1994) has argued, metaphors have often been seen, and continue to be seen, with some suspicion in sociological theory (Maasen, 1994). For instance, Nisbet (1969) produced a powerful critique of metaphors of growth and evolution in social theory; however, in doing so he marginalized the constitutive role of metaphorical operations in the development of new concepts and theoretical strategies. Alternatively, the recognition of the centrality of metaphors in theoretical discourse is frequently, uncritically, celebrated and used as a plank in an iconoclastic attack on the very possibility of sociological explanation. In the analyses that follow, I hope to show that it is possible to steer a course fruitfully between these two alternatives.

SUMMARY

In this chapter I have argued for the need to take seriously the language-borne nature of social theory. I have suggested that, among other things, this means that we have some understanding of the basis for the relative autonomy both of theoretical language and concept formation. I have maintained that this aspect of theoretical practice is too frequently ignored: the refusal to engage with theoretical language is evident both in introductory social theory texts, but also in contemporary debates on social structure. Thus this book is, in part, an attempt to begin to remedy this situation.

I have posited, as a possible starting point for this type of analysis, the Foucauldian attempt to visualize knowledge production practices in wider discursive and non-discursive spaces in terms of his notion of *archaeology*. I have also argued that within this general model of theoretical practice, an understanding of the functioning of metaphors provides us with a way of thinking about how different conceptual networks establish semantic connections and exchange meanings. Metaphorical operations also play a fundamental role in conceptual and theoretical innovation, thus an understanding of their functioning should also help us to begin to ask novel, and, it is hoped, more fruitful, questions in contemporary debates about social structure.

Underpinning my discussion is a conception of social theorizing as a discursively creative practice which relies on the way in which metaphors make possible the development of new concepts. This amounts to recognizing that concepts are not originary, they are effects of determinate language practices. Still, this creativity is not to be understood as being entirely open-ended. There are limits to the types of metaphor than can be deployed, and this is largely determined by the ways in which conceptual networks coalesce in discursive fields. But there are also constraints on the processing of metaphors and their integration in the wider logical and conceptual architecture of different theories. Thus, it becomes crucial to develop an understanding of their functioning, because they will continue 'functioning' even if we attempt to ignore them.

In the next five chapters I will be using the arguments developed in this introduction in order to show that if one takes seriously the language-borne nature of social theory, then it becomes possible to ask a range of questions about the concept of social structure that rarely register in contemporary discussions about and over social structure. The concluding chapter will take stock of the implications of the analyses presented in each of the individual chapters for our understanding of reading and writing social theory, as well as contemporary debates over and about social structure. In doing this, I hope to be offering an unorthodox introduction to some of the more neglected facets of 'doing social theory'.

Before turning to my first case study – Durkheim – I need to make an important qualification. The type of analysis that I am advocating necessitates that I focus on the work of specific theorists. Durkheim and Althusser wrote in French, Weber and Marx wrote in German. Although I have a reading knowledge of French, unfortunately I cannot say the same about German. Thus, I have been forced to restrict my analysis to English translations of these authors' texts. It may very well be the case that some of my substantive points might not hold in the original language texts.

If it is the case that an argument could be made for a distinction between say a German Marx and a translated English Marx, and I believe that this would need to be argued and not merely asserted, then my arguments would hold only for the English Marx. My concern is not so much to get at the true meanings that these terms held for their authors. My approach is much more practically oriented; within the contexts of the conceptual networks, in the case of this study these are English networks, I am trying to highlight the discursive exigencies which are faced when metaphorical functions are deployed to enunciate the concept of structure as a certain form of social organization. Thus I do not rule out that a German or a French discursive space could have different discursive exigencies. However, if this were shown to be the case, it would not undermine what I am attempting to do here; instead it would suggest new avenues for research. Finally, given the fact that the sociological tradition is multilingual, it is surprising that so little work has been done, in sociological theory, not in terms of the problems of the translation of specific concepts or fragments, but regarding the 'translatability' of the wider conceptual fields in which concepts, theoretical logics and sentences are located.[23]

CHAPTER 1

Durkheim's Structures:
Writing the Emergence of the Social

INTRODUCTION

Any attempt to map the length and breadth of sociological theory must contend with the fact that it faces a historical, social and discursive terrain which is vast, heterogeneous, contradictory and multi-layered. To speak about social theory in the singular is to find a way of reducing its complexity by introducing some type of economy in the way in which we read, think and write about social theory. It is, whether acknowledged or not, to mark distinctions; it is to make decisions about what is to be included and what is to be excluded, what is to be valued and what is not. Hence the metaphor of economizing. However, economizing in the field of social theory is not only restricted to the ways in which we construct our 'preferences' (prioritize our choices) in the market of concepts, theoretical strategies, etc., it is also about how we use these products in our own theoretical productions. In other words, it is also about the development or the production of strategies that will provide us with the greatest possible returns.

In the marketplace of debates concerned with the development of the concept of social structure there is in operation a particular economic strategy, an 'economy of scale' that from one perspective, at least, seems to provide a good return. An economy of scale in production as is well known means that a lower cost can be achieved by organizing production at a larger scale. *In the context of debates of social structure the 'economy of scale' can be achieved by producing as many readings as possible of the different conceptions of social structure in terms of the structure–agency framework.* The premise is that all accounts of social structure are first and foremost attempts to solve the structure–agency problem. Thus, all that is needed is to locate different conceptions of social structure on a continuum that is flanked on the one side by the ideal type of structural determination and on the other by unrestrained agency or action. After this initial theoretico-productive process has been worked out, and put to work, it can be used to produce countless readings of different theorists at a relatively low cost.

Within this economy of scale there is no doubt about how to produce a reading of Durkheim. He is the theorist of structure and structural determination. His fundamental (onto)logical error is that he privileges structure over agency. This may be so, but, as I argued in the Introduction, the returns of the structure–agency debate are also relatively meagre. This is, in part, due to the fact that too much economy is introduced into the reading of theoretical texts when the transparency of theoretical language is taken for granted. As Culler argues, 'The threat of non-transparency is the danger that, instead of permitting direct contemplation of thought, linguistic signs might arrest the gaze and, by interposing their material form, affect or effect the thought' (1986: 91). In other words, once it is accepted that social theory is not just the crystallization of an original and 'pure thought' process we have no choice but to examine the types of language practices that make it possible. It becomes important to reverse the hierarchy which privileges 'social theorizing' over 'writing'. Social theory is produced inside and not outside of writing.

What I am proposing to do in this chapter, and throughout this book, is to attempt to disrupt the economy of scale described above; to arrest our theoretical gaze by focusing on the materiality and the productivity of the linguistic sign and the rhetorical strategies in which it is embedded. Rather than thinking about concepts of structure as arising from fundamental commitments that can be positioned in the structure–agency continuum, I want to explore the way concepts of structure can be understood as arising from textual and rhetorical effects. Concretely in this chapter, I am going to argue that the concepts of structure that exist in Durkheim's writing are not primary or originary. Their specificity and their form are, in part, the effects of the metaphorical and discursive strategies that Durkheim unfolds, perhaps unwittingly, in order to think about and to 'visualize' the social world as a 'sui generis' domain. It is in the field of the discursive exigencies that these strategies produce that we must locate part of our analysis of the failure and success of Durkheim's concepts of social structure.

POSITIONING DURKHEIM

In his introduction to *The Elementary Forms of the Religious Life* Durkheim writes:

> Society is a reality *sui generis*; it has its own peculiar characteristics, which are not found elsewhere and which are not met with again in the same form in all the rest of the universe. The representations which express it have a wholly different content from pure individual ones and we may rest assured in advance that the first add something to the second. (1968: 16)

This, and variations of this formulation, point to the semantic space from which Durkheim speaks about the existence of the 'thing' which he calls society. An entity which is something more than the arithmetic sum of its component parts, whose component parts are not even individuals. In making this theme – society is a reality *sui generis* – his theoretical signature, Durkheim's sociology produces two distinct but related effects. First, it delimits the field of objects with which he believes the discipline should be concerned, that is to say that class of objects which he calls 'social facts'. Second, it sets up the context from which his methodological protocols will be developed. Durkheim reasons that if sociology is distinguished from other disciplines in terms of the specificity of its subject mater – *a sui generis* social reality – then this must have autochthonous methodological implications. The most important of which is expressed in his fundamental injunction that social facts should be explained in terms of social facts, and not in terms of facts derived from other levels of reality (i.e. biological, psychological).

These two effects depend on the functioning, and viability, of a mechanism of exclusion designed to distinguish social phenomena from others which might appear to be social while in reality belonging to a different domain of inquiry. In *The Rules of Sociological Method* he writes:

> Each individual drinks, sleeps, eats, reasons; and it is to society's interest that these functions be exercised in an orderly manner. If then, all of these facts are counted as 'social facts', sociology would have no subject matter exclusively its own, and its domain would be confused with that of biology and psychology (1982a: 50).

At the end of the first chapter in *The Rules*, Durkheim defines a social fact as

> ... any way of acting, whether fixed or not, capable of exerting on the individual an external constraint;

or:

> which is general over the whole of a given society whilst having an existence of its own, independent of its individual manifestations. (1982a: 59, italics from original removed)

Thus the distinctive feature which defines the class of objects which he calls social facts is its *sui generis* nature. An index of their autonomy is to be found in both their externality and generality. In order to illustrate what he means by this he introduces a number of examples such as the duties associated with being a brother or a husband, the need to use French money and the French language in France, the penalties and social sanctions associated with transgressing moral rules or customs, the need to adapt oneself to the latest productive techniques if one is to avoid financial ruin, the ways in which individuals are distributed in social space, the modes of communication that connect them, etc. Durkheim stresses that it is crucial to grasp the externality of social facts, otherwise

> ... we are the victims of an illusion which leads us to believe we have ourselves produced what has been imposed upon us externally. But if the willingness with which we let ourselves be carried along disguises the pressure we have undergone, it does not eradicate it. (1982a: 53)

Therefore, for Durkheim, the most unassailable proof that the social exists as a *sui generis* entity which is both external to, and exercises an influence over, individuals, is found in the fact that we cannot merely wish it away. There are 'ways of acting' that exist independently of our volition. For Durkheim, however, this is not something which is germane only on the individual level; that is to say it is not just as individuals that we are subject to an 'external' reality. If the social pertains to a *sui generis* realm, it also exerts itself at the level of the historical development of societies: changes at this level cannot be understood exclusively in terms of randomly generated events.

In fact, particular events, like specific individual actions, do not exhaust the object of study in history, nor in sociology. In a debate with the historian Seignobos, Durkheim asks: 'But what would be said about a biologist who considered science as merely a story about the events of the human body, without studying the functions of that organism?' (1982b: 213). Just as biology does not restrict itself to narrating the 'bodily history' of individuals, history and sociology cannot be restricted to making haphazard connections between events and extraordinary individuals, which in any case only serves to fuel idiosyncratic chronologies. Beneath the surface appearance of events, tensions and forces not reducible to individuals are shaping the course of historical events:[1]

> So far as events are concerned, we are presented with an indefinite mountain of facts, in whose midst the mind can only introduce with difficulty some scientific order. I admire the historians who can live comfortably amid the pile of disordered events. But beyond the events, there are the functions, the institutions, the ways, fixed and organised, of thinking and acting. (Durkheim, 1982b: 224)

If this is the case, if 'functions', 'institutions' and 'the ways of thinking and acting' are fixed, then some concept of determination has to become an integral part of the human sciences. In *The Elementary Forms of the Religious Life*, Durkheim argues that in the absence of such a conception, 'It follows that veritable miracles are believed to be possible . . . It is admitted, for example, that a legislator can create an institution out of nothing by mere injunction of its will, or transform one social system into another . . .' (1968: 27).

Connected with the foregoing there is an intimation of the centrality of grasping the importance of social time for social theorizing. Not in the sense that the concept of time is constituted as a social category through collective representations which Durkheim deals with in *The Elementary Forms of the Religious Life*, but that the historical movement of social types is not reducible to the neat logic of the linear chronological unfolding of events which characterizes our everyday horizons. In *The Rules of Sociological Method*, he writes: 'Thus historical development loses the ideal but simplistic unity attributed to it. It becomes fragmented, so to speak, into a myriad of sections, which, because each differs specifically from the rest, cannot be pieced together in a continuous fashion' (1982a: 109).

This comment is suggestive of, for instance, Braudel's distinctions of the 'Long Durée', 'Generational Events' and 'Events', where different temporalities correspond to the unfolding of different types of processes, whose 'life histories' transcend the lives and events of individuals, even social formations:

> ... all of us naturally tend to think of the world around us only in the context of our own brief existence, and to see its history as a speeded-up film in which everything happens pell-mell ... however, the life of human beings involves many other phenomena which cannot figure in this film of events: the space they inhabit, the social structures that confine them and determine their existence, the ethical rules they consciously or unconsciously convey, their religious and philosophical beliefs, and the civilisations to which they belong. These phenomena are much longer-lived than we are; and in our lifetime we are unlikely to see them totally transformed. (Braudel, 1993: xxxvi)[2]

In an essay entitled 'Sociology and the Social Sciences' Durkheim writes, 'In a word, history plays a role in the order of social realities analogous to that of the microscope in the order of physical realities ...'. He goes on to argue that '... it alone allows us to create explanations ... to account for the various elements which served in its formation ... to show their ... raisons d'être' (1978: 84). Historical development, for Durkheim, traverses and is traversed by a dense social tissue, a complex organization, or association, of social elements. It is precisely this tangled skein which needs to be made visible by a 'scientific' and sociological visuality; for Durkheim this organizational web is the very foundation of social life. The theme of complexity or organization is so central to his strategy for understanding social life that he deploys it to mark the distinction between the social and everything else: '... social phenomena are distinguishable from the other phenomena by virtue of their complexity' (Durkheim, 1982a: 148).

If one reads through *The Rules of Sociological Method* with the aforementioned in mind it becomes apparent that Durkheim is speaking about social facts in two distinct registers. On the one hand there is the register of the well-known illustrative examples such as language, social roles, moral rules, customs, etc. In a sense these are very close to our quotidian conceptions of the social. It is what people have in mind when they say things such as 'society makes people do things'. On the other hand, there is another which is much harder to grasp, as it requires us to break with the horizons in which our everyday conceptions of the social are located. This is the register that tries to reveal, through a sociological visuality, the distinctiveness and specificity of the complexity which makes social life possible. Thus, as Schmaus has quite cogently argued, for Durkheim the constraints associated with language, social roles, etc. are but 'various outward expressions' of a more fundamental social force (1994: 47).

Moreover it is precisely in this register where Durkheim's most powerful metaphors are located and it is their effects which form the basis for Durkheim's most distinctive contribution to a novel theoretical visuality. Symptomatically it is also at the level of this register that Durkheim is accused of putting forward 'metaphysical' or 'mystical' entities such as the 'social mind' or 'collective representation'. In the next section, I am going to begin to analyse the elements that make this type of theoretical visuality possible by exploring the discursive networks from which they arise.

DURKHEIM'S 'GENEALOGY OF SOCIOLOGY'

As is well known, in *The Elementary Forms of the Religious Life*, Durkheim would suggest that the conceptual grids used in scientific explanation were not of a different nature from those found in 'primitive' religions. Nonetheless, it is important to keep in mind that Durkheim was always sensitive to the fact that the viability of scientific thought, as a collective social practice, was dependent on wider social conditions.[3] The ability to speak about society as a *sui generis* reality was located by Durkheim himself in the historical development of wider networks of statements. It was not a product of spontaneous generation.

For instance, sociology shared, and to some extent was dependent on, the concept of society developed in the tradition of moral philosophy (which could be traced back to Plato and Aristotle). However, to Durkheim's mind, it did not, or should not, share its ungrounded theorizing of society in terms of some putative timeless moral good. Sociology was to be concerned with trying to understand the actual organization of society as opposed to how it ought to be organized (1978: 71).[4] Secondly, sociology shared with the field of economics the idea that societies were systemic in nature thus revealing law-like regularities (Durkheim, 1978: 73). Third, Durkheim argued that there were fundamental points of contact and continuity between sociology and the natural sciences. He believed that notions of natural determination and natural laws which were central to the

natural sciences had to be adapted to the sociological explanatory enterprise (Durkheim, 1978: 78).

Finally, Durkheim also distinguished a scientific sociology from philosophically
inspired individualist and idealist variants. In 'Individual and Collective Representations', he once again draws on the theme of complexity and writes

> In fact individualistic sociology is only applying the old principles of materialist
> metaphysics to social life. It claims, that is, to explain the complex by the simple,
> the superior by the inferior, and the whole by the part, which is a contradiction
> in terms. The contrary principle does not seem to us to be any less questionable.
> One cannot, following idealist and theological metaphysics, derive the part
> from the whole, since the whole is nothing without the parts which form it
> and cannot draw its vital necessities from the void. We must, then, explain phe-
> nomena that are the product of the whole by the characteristic properties of the
> whole, the complex by the complex, social facts by society, vital and mental facts
> by the *sui generis* combinations from which they result. This is the only path that a
> science can follow. (1974: 29)

In discussing the conditions of possibility of the emergence of sociology, Durkheim also identified the obstacles that sociology had to contend with. For
instance, he identified two wider social processes that contributed to the emergence
of sociology in France and blocked it elsewhere: the weakening of traditionalism
and 'the survival of a specific form of rationalism' (Gane, 1988: 38). However, the
most fundamental obstacle that sociology faced was the very complexity of social
phenomena: 'In effect, since they are far more complex, the order which inheres in
social phenomena is far more difficult to perceive, and consequently one is led to
believe that they occur in a contingent and more or less disordered way' (Durkheim, 1978: 72). Thus although the recognition of social complexity is what
makes sociology possible as a distinctive explanatory enterprise, the selfsame complexity also acts as sociology's most important epistemological obstacle!

This notion of complexity produces a number of interesting discursive effects in
Durkheim's writing. As just noted, it is simultaneously a condition of possibility
and a possible obstacle for sociology. Seen from a different perspective, it is what
distinguishes the phenomena of sociology from other phenomena and as such
gives sociology its own field of study with its own concepts, theories and methods.
However, this demarcation is only made possible by the introduction of concepts
and theoretical strategies from other disciplines and phenomenological domains –
biology and physiology and organisms and life respectively – into the very core of
his theoretical visuality. Significantly it is also these domains which are missing
from Durkheim's genealogy of the emergence of sociology. Thus the very act
that utters the autonomy of sociology as a discipline paradoxically undermines

said autonomy by opening it up to concepts and theoretical strategies taken from another domain of study.

Durkheim's enunciation of social complexity, and the strategies that he deploys to make this an operable concept, are dependent on the metaphorical relationships that he establishes with the fields of biology and physiology. The *sui generis* character of society, and the untenability of its reduction to individual consciousness or psychology, is arrived at through an organismic analogy:[5]

> Though a cell contains nothing but mineral elements, these reveal, by being combined in a certain way, properties which they do not have when they are not thus combined and which are characteristic of life (properties of sustenance and of reproduction); they thus form, through their synthesis, a reality of an entirely new sort, which is living reality and individual consciousness, by associating themselves in a stable way, they reveal, through their interrelationships, a new life very different from that which would have developed had they remained uncombined; this is social life. (Durkheim, 1978: 76)

Durkheim's use of the organismic analogy is so pervasive,[6] so intricately woven into the conceptual networks from which he speaks, that it is easy to overlook the extent to which it is constitutive of the notion of complexity and organization that is at the very core of his understanding of sociology.

THE ORGANISMIC METAPHOR AS A SUPPLEMENT

The above is, of course, easy to miss if one concentrates on the general features that Durkheim uses to identify social facts, as described in the first chapter of *The Rules of Sociological Method* (i.e. externality, generality and coercive power). It is also easy to miss because when Durkheim explicitly draws on these metaphors he presents them as mere illustrative analogies. For instance at the beginning of the essay entitled 'Individual and Collective Representations' he writes: 'If analogy is not a method of demonstration in the true sense of the word, it is nevertheless a method of illustration and of secondary verification which may be of some use' (1974: 1). As such they appear to be nothing more than useful but expendable supplements. However, as the work of Derrida and others has suggested, a supplement is never exactly what it appears to be. In the words of Culler, 'The supplement is an inessential extra, added to something complete in itself, but the supplement is added in order to complete, to compensate for a lack in what was supposed to be complete in itself' (1986: 103). Seen from this perspective, Durkheim's conceptualization of social complexity is simultaneously both independent (complete) and dependent (incomplete). In other words, his notion of social complexity exists only as an effect of a supplement in the form of an organismic metaphor: a metaphor that discursively binds sociology to the life sciences in Durkheim's writing.[7] It is the functioning of this discursive space which must be explored if we are to develop an understanding of the potentials and limitations associated with the effects of structure that Durkheim's writings produce.

In the Introduction, I presented a distinction between two types of metaphorical operations that can be used for this type of analysis: *Modality A* and *Modality B*. They represent two different ways in which a host domain can maintain a metaphorical relationship with another disciplinary or phenomenological domain. In a *Modality A* operation the initial connection is to a large extent superseded because the metaphor has led to the development of new concepts, meanings and theoretical strategies that are specific to the host domain. A transformation has taken place. The initial metaphor has provided a ladder that can subsequently be abandoned.

A *Modality B* operation, however, never really moves beyond the initial transfer of meanings, concepts and theoretical strategies. The signifiers (terms) remain attached to the signifieds (meanings) in the domain with which the metaphorical relationship was established. The meanings that are produced depend on the semantic ties that exist with a foreign domain. They are incomplete and always need to point outside of their domain in order to be meaningful. This is in contrast to the *Modality A* types which are capable of achieving a certain degree of semantic closure; they manage to create meaning as an effect of how they are embedded in their own field and not a field outside of itself. An important dimension of creative theoretical practice is precisely to attempt to modify *Modality B* into *Modality A* relationships.

The metaphorical modality that one is dealing with can be determined by examining the stability of the signifiers in the text. To the extent that a signifier remains floating – it is attached to a multitude of meanings – then we know that we are dealing with a *Modality B* relationship. For instance, as is well known, Durkheim, within the framework of the organismic metaphor, likened individuals to cells: 'What does one human being the less matter to society? Or one cell fewer in, the organism?' (Durkheim, 1984: 33). However, as Lehmann quite persuasively argues, Durkheim is remarkably inconsistent and contradictory with respect to his conceptualization of the individual. Sometimes he sees individuals as entirely socially constituted; at other times individuals are reduced to dangerous and insatiable biological organisms; yet other times, he makes a distinction between an individual consciousness and a social consciousness. Still other times, individuals seem to be mechanistically determined by social forces; while at others some individuals escape said social determination (1993: 78–103).

Similarly, the term 'organs' in the social body sometimes refers to institutions such as morality, the state and the economy (the heart, brain and viscera of society), while at other times it refers to specialized occupations (Lehmann, 1993: 17). Closely connected to this, by organization or differentiation he sometimes refers to the degree of 'coalescence' that inheres in the elementary social segments (Durkheim, 1982a: 115), while at other times he is making reference to the interdependence of occupational groups via specialization (Durkheim, 1984: 272),[8] or social class (Durkheim, 1984: 243). Again, normally Durkheim superimposes the opposition between social morphology and physiology over that of structure and function (more on this below); however at times he surprisingly superimposes it over anatomical morphology and occupation. For instance, in *The Division of Labour in Society*, he writes: 'Many facts go to show that men performing different social functions are distinguished less from one another than once they were, by body shape, features or build. Pride is even taken in not having the appearance of one's occupation' (Durkheim, 1984: 273). Similarly, but more distressingly, he draws on women's alleged morphological features in order to explain the sexual differentiation of social functions (Durkheim, 1984: 20–1). These are, of course, just a handful of the 'floating signifiers' to be found in Durkheim's work. As they have been systematically identified by Lehmann (1993), I want to turn my attention to a different yet related matter.

The presence and number of the 'floating signifiers' identified above strongly suggests the prevalence of *Modality B* metaphorical relationships. However, the information provided by this general diagnosis is limited. It is necessary to move further into the processes that produce these effects. When a metaphorical relationship is established it introduces a number of logical, conceptual and theoretical tensions or demands. Sometimes these can be overcome, sometimes not. We need to explore to what extent the language-borne effects which metaphors produce can be made to fit in with existing theoretical and logical commitments; or to what extent it is possible to remould these commitments so that they can be aligned with the conceptual and semantic possibilities introduced by the metaphor. To take a brief example outside of the realm of social theory: 'the highway of life' metaphor. If this is going to allow us to develop a new understanding of 'life', it needs to be embedded with compatible conceptions of what it means to live and other types of statements that refer to living. For instance, we need to have some conception of life as a movement from one point to another, as a process over time, as something which sometimes moves too quickly and causes us to make the wrong choices and take the wrong exits. We need to be able to think of ourselves as vehicles that can run out of petrol, or break down, get rusty, etc. The point is that unless we are able to make these adjustments, 'think of ourselves as vehicles', for instance, the metaphor just will not work. It will not provide us with the conceptual tools to go beyond our present understanding. It is precisely this type of re-arranging and re-alignment that must be produced if the tensions and demands of metaphorical operations are to be met.

In the next two sections I will develop this type of analysis by examining Durkheim's concept(s) of structure. Lehmann argues, rightly I believe, that the 'organicist metaphor qua social theory is crucial to Durkheim's vision of social "structure". In fact, in a sense, this is his vision of "social structure"' (1993: 16). As a general statement this is true; however, in order to understand the way in which Durkheim's writing produces the effect of social structure we must distinguish between two different metaphors. On the one hand there is a conception of structure that derives from the brain–mind or body–life opposition and focuses on the emergence of psychic or vital phenomena. This conception is aimed at trying to think how a 'higher', relatively autonomous order of reality can emerge from the organization of components from a 'lower' level. He frames this sociologically in terms of the opposition between social morphology (social structure) and social physiology (social life). On the other, there is the society as body metaphor, in which different social institutions are seen as being functionally interdependent 'organs' and society as organ(ized).

I want to proceed to show how in both cases the strategies embedded in Durkheim's attempt to produce the concept of social structure through his writing are *Modality* B metaphorical relationships. As a consequence, it should become clear that the tenability of Durkheim's concept of structure relies, in a substantial way, on the supplements provided from the outside. His key signifiers are attached to signifieds outside of the phenomenological domain which Durkheim wants to set aside for sociology. But also and equally important, I want to show how the construction of a concept of social structure is not even Durkheim's main concern.

WANTED: SIGNIFIEDS FOR SOCIAL MORPHOLOGY AND PHYSIOLOGY

In *The Rules of Sociological Method*, Durkheim constructs his *sui generis* claim by arguing that social reality can be characterized in terms of its relationship of externality *vis-à-vis* individuals, and its generality. Both of these features, to Durkheim's mind, corroborate the fact that social reality is something distinct from the numerical sum of the individuals that compose it. The basis of social life is thus not to be sought in the properties of individuals but in the properties of societies themselves. Consequently sociology has no other choice than to explain social phenomena in terms of social facts. Durkheim, however, never equates social facts narrowly with social structure. The latter is included in the former, which is significantly broader. Within Durkheim's paradigm, society is something more than just social structure. How then does Durkheim distinguish between structure and other social facts? One of the ways in which he does this is by using an organismic metaphor to create an opposition between structure as 'social morphology' and social life as 'social physiology'.[9]

As we saw above, Durkheim defined social facts as 'ways of acting' that were both capable of exerting an external constraint on individuals and that had a general existence in society independently of individual manifestations. However, Durkheim worries that this definition might be understood as referring only to social activities, its 'ways of functioning', to the exclusion of society's more crystallized or sedimented features:

> However, one may well ask whether this definition is complete. Indeed the facts which have provided us with this basis are all *ways of functioning*: they are physiological in nature. But there are also collective *ways of being*, namely, social facts of an 'anatomical' or morphological nature. Sociology cannot dissociate itself from what concerns the substratum of collective life. Yet the number and nature of the elementary parts which constitute society, the way in which they are articulated, the degree of coalescence they have attained, the distribution of population over the earth's surface, the extent and nature of the network of communications, the design of dwellings, etc., do not at first sight seem relatable to ways of acting, feeling and thinking. (1982a: 57; italics in the original)

Durkheim goes on to show how these morphological features can in fact be legitimately seen as social facts that are on the one hand capable of constraining the way individuals act, feel and think, and on the other have an existence independently of individual manifestations (1982a: 57–8). What seems to distinguish morphological or anatomical from physiological social facts is their degree of 'crystallization' or their material sedimentation. However, Durkheim is also at pains to make it clear that they do not represent two different types of reality; they are of the 'same nature':

> Thus there exists a whole range of gradations which, without any break in continuity, join the most clearly delineated structural facts to those free currents of social life which are not yet caught in any definitive mould. This therefore signifies that the differences between them concern only the degree to which they have become consolidated. Both are forms of life at varying stages of crystallisation. It would undoubtedly be advantageous to reserve the term 'morphological' for those social facts which related to the social substratum, but only on condition that one is aware that they are of the same nature as the others. (Durkheim, 1982a: 58)

Despite the fact that social structure or social morphology is seen as just a more crystallized form of collective 'life', in the explanatory project set out in *The Rules of Sociological Method*, or precisely because of this it plays a crucial role. Because it is a more crystallized form of social life it is easier to detect, and as such forms the basis for the classification of different social types.

Durkheim argues that it is neither necessary nor possible to survey all known societies in order to develop a classification of social types.[10] Instead, drawing on classificatory schemes from the life sciences, he suggests that it is enough to isolate the essential components of any society and to examine the different ways in which they can be organized:

> We know that societies are made up of a number of parts added on to each other. Since the nature of a composite necessarily depends upon the way in which these are combined, these characteristics are plainly those which we must take as our basis. It will be seen later that it is on them that the general facts of social life depend. Moreover, as they are of a morphological order, one might term that part of sociology whose task is to constitute and classify social types social morphology. (Durkheim, 1982a: 111)

Durkheim deepens and further enmeshes the notion of social morphology in the organismic metaphor by likening the 'inner environment' of a society to the inner environment of an organism:

> If the determining condition for social phenomena consists . . . in the very association, the phenomena must vary with the forms of that association, i.e. according to how the constituent elements in a society are grouped. Furthermore, since the distinct entity formed by the union of elements of all kinds which enter into the composition of a society constitutes its inner environment, in the same way as the totality of anatomical elements, together with the manner in which they are arranged in space, constitutes the inner environment of organisms, we may state: *The primary origin of social processes of any importance must be sought in the constitution of the inner social environment.* (Durkheim, 1982a: 135; italics in the original)

Drawing on the analysis that he developed in *The Division of Labour in Society*, Durkheim identifies two important aspects of the social inner environment: '. . . firstly, the number of social units or, as we have also termed it, the "volume" of the society; and secondly, the degree of concentration of the mass of people, or what we have called the "dynamic density"' (1982a: 136). However, Durkheim is careful to point out that 'dynamic density' should not be seen as just the physical concentration of people, '. . . but the moral concentration of which physical concentration is only the auxiliary element, and almost invariably the consequence' (1982a: 136).

If we take stock of the theoretical effects that Durkheim's writing of the opposition between social morphology and physiology has achieved thus far, it becomes clear that he is able to create a connotative resonance between organismic and social life. The importance of this resonance is that it opens up a conceptual and semantic field where Durkheim is able to work on signs that try to capture some of the fundamental features of social life. Just as in organisms, in the social organism it is possible to distinguish between anatomy (form) and physiology (function). Similarly social organisms can be classified in terms of the complexity of organization revealed at the morphological level and the implications that this has for how they (should?) function at the physiological level. Therefore it is also possible to distinguish between normal and pathological states. However, what this metaphor of society as social organism does not allow him to do is to provide a clear signified for the concept of social morphology.

This can be seen in two effects that the metaphor produces. In the first place, Durkheim's definition of social morphology, as he himself recognizes, is not exhaustive. Moreover, the major criterion which he provides for distinguishing between social morphology and physiology is the ambiguous one of 'crystallization', itself a metaphor. Secondly, the relationship between morphology and physiology is never made clear. In many of the passages quoted above, it seems that Durkheim is arguing that morphology is causally responsible for physiology. That is to say that the general form of society, the organization of its substratum (the number of people, their concentration, the organization of kinship groups, the way they are distributed in social space, etc.) determines its mode of functioning (its ways of acting, feeling and thinking), its collective representations.

This, however, cannot be so because as we also saw above 'dynamic density' already contains moral facts, which following Durkheim's distinction should be located in the domain of social physiology. Thus within the space opened up through this organismic metaphor, morphology cannot be the material cause of physiology because physiology is already implicit in the materiality of morphology. Social organization cannot be the cause of social life, because social life is always already contained and a cause itself of social organization:

> Morphology can give rise to different physiological processes because its forms are organisations and associations of parts which are already imbued with life. Physiological phenomena are already present in the morphological order. Morphology and physiology are interchangeable because physiological phenomena are presumed in the morphological order from the start. (Hirst, 1975: 167)

Thus inasmuch as the social morphology–physiology metaphor has an effect on Durkheim's visualization of social structure, it does so only by providing a general typology of simple and complex societies with reference to general features of their organization. The opposition itself and the networks of statements in which it is embedded do not produce a discrete concept of social structure. Moreover, it is

only by drawing on the signifieds (meanings) from the domain of biology and physiology that the indeterminacy of meaning associated with social morphology is
sutured. Consequently, the distinction between social morphology and physiology
is not drawn internally within the field of sociology but externally from fields in
which the concept of the organism exists. The sign 'social structure' is a product of
a *Modality B* metaphorical relationship.

It has been suggested that Durkheim's earlier emphasis on social morphology as
an important causal force is abandoned as he shifts his attention to 'collective representations' or social physiology.[11] Indeed, even in *The Rules of Sociological Method*
'collective representations' have a centrality that was basically lacking in *The Division of Labour in Society*. Thus in the preface to the second edition of *The Rules of Sociological Method*, Durkheim defends himself against the accusation that his method
presupposes the positing of some mystical 'social mind' by writing:

> Social facts differ not only in quality from psychical facts; *they have a different sub-
> stratum*, they do not evolve in the same environment or depend on the same
> conditions. This does not mean that they are not in some sense psychical, since
> they all consist of ways of thinking and acting. But the states of the collective
> consciousness are of a different nature from the states of individual conscious-
> ness; they are representations of a different kind. The mentality of groups is not
> that of individuals: it has its own laws. (1982a: 40)

Notwithstanding this, most scholars associate Durkheim's writing on social morphology with a materialist phase in which Durkheim is taken to be arguing
that social life can be explained in terms of the organization of its material substratum (for instance, Alexander, 1982b; Davy, 1919; Lukes, 1992; Parsons, 1949;
Pickering, 1992).

However, to approach Durkheim's work in this way is to assert the primacy of
the structure–action debate as an interpretive schema for organizing his contribution to social theory. Furthermore, I think that this obscures the extent to which
Durkheim was not so much concerned with developing a concept of social structure as with providing sociology with a new theoretical visuality. To my mind, the
social morphology–physiology metaphor does not really provide a vehicle for writing the concept of social structure as the material cause of a society's collective
ideational system; it provides a vehicle for enunciating the specificity of social life
as a complexly organized *sui generis* phenomenon. Durkheim tried to produce a
series of theoretical signs that would represent social life as a phenomenon that
was rooted in the organization or combination of elements without being reducible
to these elements. And it was precisely this effect of emergence that Durkheim tried
to write through the metaphor of social morphology. This is clear in another
instance of his attempt to define social morphology:

Social life rests upon a substratum determinate in both size and form. It is made up of the mass of individuals who constitute society, the manner in which they have settled upon the earth, the nature and configuration of those things of all kinds which affect collective relationships. The social substratum will differ according to whether the population is of greater or lesser size and density, whether it is concentrated in towns or scattered over rural areas, according to the way in which towns and houses are constructed, whether the space occupied by a society is more or less extensive according to the nature of the frontiers which enclose it and the avenues of communication which cross it. *On the other hand, the constitution of this substratum directly or indirectly affects all social phenomena just as all psychological phenomena are linked either obliquely or immediately to the condition of the brain.* Thus here is a whole range of problems plainly of interest to sociology which must derive from the same science, since they all refer to one and the same object. It is this science which we propose to call 'social morphology'. (Durkheim, 1982c: 241; italics added)

This definition in many ways resembles previous ones; however, what is distinctive about this one is that it draws a parallel between the emergence of social life and the emergence of psychic phenomena. It distinguishes the morphology of the brain, its distinctive form of organization, from psychic phenomena. Although the former is necessary for the latter to emerge, this does not mean that psychic phenomena can be reduced to the biochemical elements, brain tissue, etc. Psychic phenomena are qualitatively different. This is an argument that he reiterates repeatedly in 'Individual and Collective Representations':

> To say that the mental condition does not derive directly from cells is to say that it is not included in it, that it forms itself in part outside of it and is to that extent exterior to it. If it was directly derived it would be within it, since its reality would derive from no other source. (Durkheim, 1974: 24)

In this case the effect that social morphology (or social organization) produces is that of engendering a series of signs that can signify the relative autonomy of a qualitatively different level of reality. It produces the effect of a stratified reality. Each stratum may depend on elements from other strata (e.g. psychic life depends on the organization of the brain tissue, functioning of cells) without for this reason being reduced to them. We must not lose sight of the fact that Durkheim's major aim in his early writing is to establish the *sui generis* nature of social reality in order to guard against the reduction of social phenomena to the actions and thoughts of individuals. Thus, Durkheim is arguing, through the metaphor of emergence, that despite the fact that the substratum of society is formed by individuals and the way they are organized (distributed in social space, etc.) this very organization produces a more complex and higher order of reality. And it is precisely for this reason that Durkheim claimed that the complex had to be explained in terms of the complex. It is also why Durkheim claimed that '... there is between psychology and sociology the same break in continuity as there is between biology and the physical and chemical sciences' (Durkheim, 1982a: 129).

That Durkheim's writing is concerned with the process of emergence and not a variant of material determination *per se* is evident in the fact that he is able to develop a variation of this argument where it is the individual psyches that provide the substratum from which collective representations and life arise without in this way undermining the structure of the emergence metaphor:

> The representations which form the network of social life arise from the relations between the individuals thus combined or the secondary groups that are between the individuals and the total society. If there is nothing extraordinary in the fact that individual representations, produced by the action and reaction between neural elements, are not inherent in these elements, there is nothing surprising in the fact that collective representations, produced by the action and reaction between individual minds that form society, do not derive directly from the latter and consequently surpass them. (Durkheim, 1974: 24–5)

A little later on, he adds: 'In such a combination, with the mutual alterations involved, they become something else. A chemical synthesis results which concentrates and unifies the synthesised elements and by that transforms them' (Durkheim, 1974: 26). In *Suicide*, he invokes the same metaphorical relationship in order to once again discursively produce the emergence effect. He claims that the denial of social life as a qualitatively distinct level is comparable to saying that

> ... there is nothing more in animate nature than organic matter, since the cell is made exclusively of inanimate atoms. To be sure, it is likewise true that society has not other active forces than individuals; but individuals by combining form a psychical existence of a new species, which consequently has its own manner of thinking and feeling. (Durkheim, 1966: 310)

The most important conclusion that can be drawn from the foregoing is that the concept of structure is not primary in Durkheim's sociology. Significantly, it is not even the key nodal point around which his other concepts are organized; it is many senses peripheral and marginal. Thus the term 'social structure' is the effect of his central theoretical strategy which is principally concerned with establishing social life as an emergent and complexly organized *sui generis* level. This theoretical strategy, as we have seen, has its semantic and conceptual roots in the different variants of the organismic metaphors that he deploys.

One of the consequences of this marginality is that the term social structure has no clear signifieds in the realm of social theory. However, this marginality is not without its corrosive effects. Although the metaphor allows Durkheim to think about the social as a relatively autonomous level that is independent of the elements which constitute it, the metaphor also introduces an important discursive exigency which Durkheim is unable to meet. The metaphor demands that a distinction be drawn between the elements and the phenomenon that emerges. However, as we have seen above, Durkheim does not manage this. In the form–function (anatomy–life) metaphor, the elements of social morphology already contain the phenomena of social physiology. This remains true even when Durkheim realigns the metaphor in terms of the brain–mind opposition. The cells, neurons and brain tissue (i.e. associated individuals) that are the basis for social life already contain that life, otherwise their association would not be possible. Consequently the organismic metaphor is undermined by the effect of a peripheral component, the term structure. Inasmuch as the signifieds that crystallize the meaning of structure are taken from domains outside of sociology the discursive exigencies of the metaphorical relationship are not overcome and it remains a *Modality B* process.

The failure of the metaphor also derives from theoretical tensions associated with the very concept of life which Durkheim is importing into his discourse. These tensions were organized around materialist and vitalist conceptions of life. The former reduces life to its most basic material units, whereas the latter holds on to an almost spiritualist or mystical conception.[12] The symptoms of this tension are also clear in Durkheim's social life metaphor as he vacillates between one and the other.

Significantly, one of the most interesting ideas contained in this vacillation is the intimation that organization and life are inextricably tied together. This is clear in Durkheim's critique of Simmel's attempt to distinguish form from content: 'In reality "what contains" and "what is contained" here do not exist, but are two aspects of social life, the one more general, the other more specific' (Durkheim, 1982d: 192). This is an insight that is at the core of contemporary thinking about life and social organization.[13] However, within the context of the models of life that Durkheim was invoking through his organismic metaphor this understanding of life was not possible. Thus the failure of Durkheim's metaphor does not arise only from his failure to work properly on the signs of his social theory, it also arose through the lack of resources within the domains with which he was establishing metaphorical relationships.

SIGNIFIER (SOCIAL ORGANS) SEEKING COMPATIBLE SIGNIFIED FOR MEANINGFUL RELATIONSHIP

In the next section, I will deal with the extent to which a concept of structure associated with collective representations emerges in Durkheim's analysis of religious life. However, before doing so, I want to look briefly at another way in which Durkheim textually produces the effect of structure in *The Division of Labour in Society*. Although there are some points of contact with the notions of structure as social morphology that I have examined above, in many ways it is distinct from it and the reasons for the difference are worth noting. In *The Division of Labour in Society*, he writes:

> Societies where organic solidarity is preponderant are entirely different . . . These are constituted, not by the replication of similar homogeneous elements, but by a system of different organs, each one of which has a special role and which themselves are formed from differentiated parts. The elements of society are . . . neither placed together end-on, as are the rings of an annelid worm, nor embedded in one another, but co-ordinated and subordinated to another around the same central organ, which exerts over the rest of the organism a moderating effect. This organ itself is no longer of the same character as outlined above, for, if the others depend upon it, in turn, it depends on them. Undoubtedly it still enjoys a special place, and one can say, a privileged one. But this is due to the nature of the role that it fulfils and not to some cause external to its functions or some force imparted to it from outside. (1984: 132)

Equating society to a body, composed of organs, as is well known, is not an idiosyncratic feature of this particular excerpt. Throughout Durkheim's writing we find the terms society and body (organism) used interchangeably (Lehmann, 1993: 19–22). Their interchangeability is further strengthened by the fact that Durkheim argues that the basis for societal evolution is the same as that of the evolution of organisms (Durkheim, 1984: 2–3 and 140–1).

There is a temptation to think that the 'social organism' that Durkheim is invoking here is the same as the one we have discussed above. Yet this is not so; they have different metaphorical roots and consequently produce different discursive and conceptual effects. Similarly, one could be enticed into thinking that 'organ' is interchangeable with structure as 'social morphology'. However, in this metaphor 'structure' is just the general 'shape of the body' (Durkheim, 1984: 126, 131 and 272–3). It is constituted in a different conceptual field and is a much simpler idea. Strictly speaking there are two forms of structure. One corresponds to 'primitive' societies that evidence low levels of differentiation and are essentially characterized by homogeneity and mechanical solidarity. The other corresponds to differentiated, heterogeneous and complexly organ(ized) industrial societies. The first is in reality structure-less, the social protoplasm or primitive protozoan, and the second that associated with an organ(ized) or differentiated society. In both cases, the term structure relates to two distinct structuring principles, the first that of homogeneity, the second of differentiation – segmental *v*. organ(ized) (Durkheim, 1984: 242–3).

Although in this metaphorical relationship the substratum is composed of cells, there is no real attempt to work out the sign sociologically; the important thing is the opposition between a simple (homogeneous, segmental) body and a (heterogeneous, functionally interdependent, differentiated, organ(ized)) body. Moreover, as mentioned above, the signifier (term) 'social organ' is attached to a plurality of signifieds (institutions, occupational groups, individuals, and sometimes class). This corroborates the fact that Durkheim is incapable of fitting this signifier with an appropriate sociological signified.

It is crucial to notice that the social morphology metaphor produces the effect of emergence, whereas the social organs metaphor produces the effect of functional co-ordination. In this sense it is not really possible to equate the social morphology–physiology to the social organ–social body opposition. The first discursive opposition, and its conception of structure, is used to enunciate the emergence of a *sui generis* social life with components from another level (individuals and their forms of association), whereas the second is used to distinguish between two differing structuring principles.

Thus in 'Individual and Collective Representations', a textual site where Durkheim is concerned with demonstrating the specificity of collective representations as a distinct level of reality, he introduces the possibility of the society as organ metaphor only to immediately abandon it in favour of society as an emergent psychic life (Durkheim 1974: 1–2). In *The Division of Labour in Society*, on the other hand, which is seen as Durkheim's more 'materialist text', because of the lack of emphasis on collective representations, the society as body metaphor preponderates. Of course, in *The Division of Labour in Society* we find the 'conscience collective'! However, if it is true that Durkheim speaks about the 'conscience collective' it is in its capacity of a regulatory organ, rather than as an emerged social phenomenon: that is, the conscience rather than a consciousness. Consequently, the distinction between an earlier materialist and a later idealistic stage (Lukes, 1992; Alexander, 1982b; and Parsons, 1949) would be more productively replaced by a differential understanding of the discursive and conceptual effects attached to both his 'social emergence' and 'social body' metaphors. The different metaphors give rise to theoretical strategies that do not map easily on to a materialist–idealist or a determinist–voluntaristic dichotomy.

A STRUCTURE FOR COLLECTIVE REPRESENTATIONS?

In *The Elementary Forms of the Religious Life* Durkheim investigates the social origins of religion and the extent to which religion provides the basis for the very categories required for thought, which are ultimately the midwives of scientific reason (Durkheim, 1968: 427–9). In this way he seeks to show that knowledge is also a social fact (Durkheim, 1968: 429). The crux of his argument is that all societies make distinctions between the sacred and the profane. The sacred is characterized by something for which there is a special feeling of reverence, of awe. It is something that is both greater than individuals and commands their respect. This something, religion, is nothing other than a signifier for the social in the form of a collective representation.

Not only that, religion also sets out the conditions through which society thinks itself, and in this sense the link with scientific thought is made:

> Religion sets itself to translate these realities into an intelligible language which does not differ in nature from that employed by science; the attempt is made by both to connect things with each other, to establish internal relations between them, to classify them and to systematize them. (Durkheim, 1968: 429)

Durkheim argues that thought is possible on the condition that we have concepts which allow us to relate things beyond our immediate environment: at the very least we must possess the possibility of making generalizations. Durkheim insists that it would be impossible for individuals to create notions of generality simply via sense perceptions or their individual representations. Individuals are always located and finite, receiving a limited diet of perceptual data. What is more, their 'sensual representations are in a perpetual flux' (Durkheim, 1968: 433). The concept, on the other hand is

> . . . as it were, outside of time and change; it is in the depths below all of this agitation; it might be said that it is in a different portion of the mind, which is serener and calmer. It does not move of itself, by an internal and spontaneous evolution, but, on the contrary, it resists change. It is a manner of thinking that, at every moment of time, is fixed and crystallized. (Durkheim, 1968: 433)

The Elementary Forms of the Religious Life contains a wealth of insights and problems (see especially Lukes (1992: 450–85) and Schmaus (1994: Chap. 8)). However, I want to focus on two points that in some sense are marginal to the main purpose of the text: first, the extent to which the *sui generis* quality of collective representations continues to be an effect of the metaphor of emergence and second the extent to which Durkheim produces a new concept of structure in the realm of collective representations.

There can be no doubt that *The Elementary Forms of the Religious Life* contains Durkheim's most sustained attempt to develop his theory of collective representations. However, it would be a serious mistake to believe that because of this he has broken with the emergence metaphor which allowed him to posit the specificity of the social as a *sui generis* reality in *The Rules of Sociological Method*.[14] The conceptual space in which *The Elementary Forms of the Religious Life* unfolds continues to rely on the effects derived from the emergence metaphor. The extent to which this is so is revealed in the following excerpt:

> In showing that religion is something essentially social, we do not mean to say that it confines itself to translating into another language the material forms of society and its immediate vital necessities. It is true that we take it as evident that the social just as the mental life of an individual depends upon his nervous system and in fact his whole organism. But collective consciousness is something more than a mere epiphenomenon of its morphological basis, just as individual consciousness is something more than the efflorescence of the nervous system. In order that the former may appear, a synthesis *sui generis* of particular consciousness is required. Now this synthesis has the effect of disengaging a whole world of sentiments, ideas and images, which once born, obey laws all their own. They attract each other, repel each other, unite, divide themselves, and multiply, though these combinations are not commanded and necessitated by the condition of the underlying reality. (Durkheim, 1968: 423)

With respect to the second point, is it possible that Durkheim's more sustained work on the sign 'collective representations'[15] produces a new concept of structure whose domain of effectivity is located in the realm of collective representations themselves? In other words, does Durkheim develop a conceptual language that explains how the different components within the domain of collective representations interact among and produce effects among themselves? At the end of the text he presents an analysis of the social conditions of the possibility of language in what can be taken as the harbinger of Saussurean structural linguistics (Durkheim, 1968: 433).

However, if we examine the language he uses to produce the effect of the autonomous functioning of the field of collective representations we find a very basic metaphorical relationship with mechanical physics. Durkheim claims that once collective representations are 'born' they 'obey laws all of their own'. They have the capacity to 'attract', 'repel', 'unite', 'divide' and 'multiply' (Durkheim, 1968: 423). This 1912 formulation is essentially the same as his 1901 formulation in the preface to the second edition to *The Rules of Sociological Method* (Durkheim, 1982a: 41) and the earlier 1898 formulation in his article 'Individual and Collective Representations' (Durkheim, 1974: 30–1). In fact, as Rossi has pointed out: 'One notices throughout his [Durkheim's] work an insistence on the "methodical" study of social facts as "things" and a neglect of the "logical order" of "objectified ideas"' (Rossi, 1983: 99). The effect of writing a metaphorical relationship with physics is merely to assert once again the existence of *sui generis* laws within the field of collective representations comparable to those found in physics. It does not produce a proto-structural-linguistic synthesis. It merely provides the intimation of its possibility. Moreover, this relatively undeveloped physicalist metaphor of complexity for the field of collective representations is not developed in opposition to the earlier emergence metaphors. It sits comfortably within them.

CONCLUSION

The enunciation of the concept of social structure in Durkheim's work is in no sense primary. It is discursively and textually subordinated to the task of enunciating the *sui generis* nature of social life as an autonomous form of organized complexity. This is true whether complexity is signified in terms of social physiology, the social organism, social life or collective representations. However, the marginality of the term structure is not without its textual, hence theoretical effects. The fact that it is marginalized while having no clear signifieds (meanings) within the domain of social theory allows Durkheim's writing to continue producing the effect of emergence. Simultaneously, it signals the fact that Durkheim has not been able to overcome the discursive exigencies associated with the organismic metaphor. His social theoretical signs continue to obtain their signifieds from the domains of biology and physiology and reveal the truth of their origin in a *Modality B* metaphorical operation.

To attempt to periodize Durkheim in terms of an early materialist and late idealist stage or to see Durkheim fluctuating between social determinism and voluntarism fails to capture the centrality of the effects of his writing for his 'thought'. Throughout this chapter I have argued that it is more fruitful to focus on the textual and metaphorical strategies through which Durkheim attempts to enunciate a notion of complexity appropriate to the social world as an emerged phenomenon.

Through these metaphorical relationships, Durkheim is able to enunciate a conception of the social world which is not reducible to individuals, a social world which to a certain extent is not anthropomorphic. This produces yet another desirable effect in Durkheim's writing. Although the metaphors are based on the mind and the body, the individual functions through them rather than consciously creating them. And yet, social morphology (social structure), social physiology, social organs, social life are ultimately incapable of being fixed with signifieds within the realm of social complexity. These signifiers either very promiscuously share a number of signifieds, or they stick to those signifieds in the phenomenological domain of biology, neuro-physiology or psychology. The most fundamental lesson that can be learnt from Durkheim's sociology is that the concept of structure has profound metaphorical debts. In a certain sense, as Foucault pointed out in *The Order of Things* and in *The Archaeology of Knowledge*, the connection between biology and sociology is not accidental but constitutive. It is the source of one of the most pervasive metaphors of complexity for the human sciences.

CHAPTER 2

Marx: Labouring for Structure

INTRODUCTION

Contemporary social theory has a tendency of pairing Marx's writing with the concept of social structure as if this were an unambiguous sign around which his entire theoretical project unfolds. Thus it is difficult not to experience a sense of paradox when for instance one discovers that the term appears infrequently in *Capital*, which after all is the classical Marxist work on economic structure *par excellence*. Moreover if one scans *The Economic and Philosophical Manuscripts of 1844*, *The German Ideology* and the *Grundrisse*, the term's usage suggests that it is being employed in a very general sense as a synonym for 'form' or 'organization'.

Given the foregoing, it is hard to believe that the term structure is the key with which it is possible to unlock Marx's work. Nonetheless, Marx's writing, evidently has the intention of producing textual and discursive, hence theoretical, effects through which society is enunciated as some type of 'structured' totality, some form of organized *sui generis* social complexity. Moreover, as would later be the case for Durkheim, Marx represents the basis of this *sui generis* form of social organization as a relational effect of how individuals are associated. Thus in the *Grundrisse* he claims that 'Society does not consist of individuals, but expresses the sum of interrelations, the relations within which these individuals stand (1978c: 247). Similarly, in his *Sixth Thesis on Feuerbach*, he writes, 'But the human essence is no abstraction inherent in each single individual. In its reality it is the ensemble of social relations' (1978b: 145). And famously in his 1859 Preface to *A Contribution of the Critique of Political Economy*, Marx wrote that 'In the social production of their life, men enter into definite relations that are indispensable and independent of their will . . .' (1978a: 4). More generally, Marx's continued insistence on the need to distinguish between surface effects and the internal relations that produce them indicates the extent to which he is committed to writing of the nature of social reality in terms of some form of autonomous social organization: indeed as a form of organization that is not apparent at the level of our everyday knowledges or even in the codification of the economic knowledges of his time (i.e. Political Economy).

Consequently, notwithstanding the infrequency of the 'empirical' appearance of the signifier (term) 'social structure', Marx's writing still suggests that it is possible to investigate the discursive and metaphorical processes by which the effect of structure is written or produced. In this chapter, I am going to argue that the effect of social structure, in Marx's writing, can be located in at least three relatively distinct discursive strategies. The first is a rather vague and unstable conception of organization that arises in the context of Marx's early attempt to provide the signs 'labour' and 'production' with social theoretical signifieds. The second is the now infamous base–superstructure metaphor. The irony of the base–superstructure metaphor is that it simultaneously provides the most defensible and indefensible conception of social structure. It is defensible because it is explicitly identifiable as a conception of social structure: it is named as such. Within the economy of scale associated with the structure–action problematic this degree of explicitness is extremely valuable. It obviates the need to understand the concept (uneconomically?) as the effect of writing. However, what makes the concept of structure produced by the base–superstructure metaphor indefensible is that the signifier 'structure' exists and persists only as the textual product of a *Modality B* metaphorical operation, which is ultimately unsustainable.

The third notion of structure emerges in a textual and conceptual space which is produced, in part, as a result of Marx's rewriting of the concept of 'labour' in terms of an 'energeticist' metaphor. The site for this third conception of 'structure' is *Capital*. However, in *Capital*, it is not named as such. Thus as with Durkheim, we find ourselves in a situation where the alleged central concept, social structure, is rarely tackled head-on. Instead we find that it is a derivative effect of more general metaphorical strategies. Moreover its lack of visibility makes it virtually indefensible as its presence is rarely recognized or acknowledged. As a result, this possible enunciation of social organization is frequently subsumed under the oppressive weight of the conception of structure produced by the base–superstructure metaphor.

In focusing on the three discursive strategies and the semantic networks in which they are embedded, I want to continue to highlight the importance of reversing the hierarchy between social theorizing as an activity which allegedly takes place in a realm of pure thought, and writing which is taken as its unproblematic and transparent embodiment. It is important to recognize the extent to which it is thought that embodies the effect of writing and not the other way around. This, as Marsden points out is, at times, particularly visible in Marx's theorizing:

> Marx, however, formulated his problem and discovered its putative explanation using pen and page to fashion words; by writing, editing and revising, probing, searching out, using the line of words like a fibre optic, illuminating the path just before its fragile tip. (1999: 17)

Many of the debates regarding Marx's concept of structure have, for the most part, unfolded within the context of the space opened up by the structure–agency problematic. What has been at stake has been the attempt to elucidate the relative importance of structure *vis-à-vis* agency, in other words, where Marx's conception of structure should be located on the structure–agency continuum. As such, these debates have been concerned with exploring Marx's ontological conception of social life. Ontology is the theory of being, or of what exists. Social ontology is specifically concerned with the modality of existence particular to elements that make social life possible.

However, general ontological statements of the existence of 'society' are not in themselves sufficient to generate concepts of social organization. I hope that I made this point sufficiently clear in my analysis of the concepts of social organization produced by Durkheim's writing. An ontological statement – 'society is something more than the sum of the people who make it up' – is not an axiom from which theoretical strategies and concepts can be elegantly deduced. Ontological commitments are not pure thought; they are not separable from the language-mediated processes that produce them. Consequently, the opportunities for the development of concepts within the semantic and logical spaces opened up by specific ontological statements will also be language-based. For instance, if the *sui generis* nature of society is enunciated via an organismic metaphor then the structure of the metaphor itself is going to determine the possibilities for concept development. We will look for the social equivalents of organism, interdependence, morphology, physiology, etc., and ways in which they can be conceptually and logically linked. However, if it is enunciated through the base–superstructure metaphor the discursive exigencies, the logical and semantic demands, associated with concept development, will be entirely different. Social life will be conceptualized in terms of two distinct yet interdependent spheres, one of which is 'determined', 'conditioned', etc. by the other.

Consequently, if in reading social theory we are to take seriously the fact that theorizing, and concept development, is a language-borne practice we will need to interrogate the types of writing practices found in social theorizing and the theoretical effects which they can produce. Thus in this chapter I will also argue that the problems associated with Marx's earlier formulations of social organization are in part explainable in terms of the metaphors through which his writing produces theoretical effects. Some metaphorical operations introduce a series of discursive exigencies – logical and conceptual demands – that cannot be resolved, or at least Marx does not manage to overcome them. A sure indicator of this failure is the extent to which certain regions of his writing remain trapped in *Modality B* metaphorical processes. However, I also want to argue that the possibility of thinking about structure within a Marxist framework is not limited to the effects produced by the base–superstructure metaphor. A later 'energiticist' metaphor provides Marx with a series of conceptual and semantic tools that allow him to displace many of the crippling limitations associated with his early attempts. Through the 'energiticist' conception of labour, Marx's writing inaugurates a powerful theoretical visuality that is capable of articulating a theoretical representation of the specificity of social organization as a *sui generis* phenomenon. As such it provides a more powerful basis from which to read Marx's concept of social structure. However, before doing so I will first deal with Marx's earlier attempts.

THE METAPHORS OF POLITICAL ECONOMY

Interestingly, Marx's reading of Political Economy in *The Economic and Philosophical Manuscripts* can be seen as a critique of a metaphorical conception of human beings and the labour that they realize in and through society. For instance, when Marx objects to the way in which workers are represented as if they were no more than animals, he is surely highlighting what he saw as the 'brutalization' of individuals.[1] But there is also a wider point being made. Political Economy '. . . does not consider him . . .when he is not working as a human being; but leaves such consideration to criminal law, to doctors, to religion, to the statistical tables, to politics and to the poor-house overseer' (Marx, 1977: 24). In other words the writing of Political Economy has the effect of placing a number of important human attributes and activities outside of its field of representation. The signifier 'human being' in as much as it appears in the discourse of Political Economy only captures the human being as an abstract worker.

Marx links this inability to capture the true nature of human beings to the limitations inherent in conceptualizing them 'unrealistically' in terms of abstract labour. For instance, as Marx repeatedly insists throughout *The Economic and Philosophical Manuscripts*, one of the effects of considering human activity exclusively through the lens of abstract labour is that it allows Political Economy to deploy the metaphor of the machine and its functional requirements to capture the essence of human activity. For Marx, one of the devastating effects of this metaphor is that questions regarding the appropriate level of wages are written as questions about the 'maintenance' or the 'servicing' of productive instruments (Marx, 1977: 76).

According to Marx, Political Economy is unable to capture the reality of the experience of work in capitalist societies. 'Concrete human labour' has no signified in Political Economy, it cannot be thought, or what is the same it cannot be written. One of the consequences of the inability to grasp the true nature of human beings is that the discourse of Political Economy is haunted by the spectre of a presence that it cannot acknowledge. On the margins of Political Economy's vision we find traces of human figures who can only exist in the domain of Political Economy as ghosts: '. . . these are figures who do not exist for political economy but only for other eyes, those of the doctor, judge, the grave-digger, and bum bailiff, etc.; such figures are spectres outside its domain' (Marx, 1977: 76). Among other things, this leads Political Economy to attempt to rationalize its exclusions by labelling those things that are internal and necessary as external and accidental (Marx, 1977: 62). Moreover, inasmuch as Political Economy tries to fix the meaning of labour through a connotative resonance with the concept of commodity, it introduces logical incoherence into its conceptual system. For instance, labour within the schema is both a commodity and not a commodity. It violates the very definition of commodity as enunciated in Political Economy: '. . . even by the principles of political economy it is no commodity, for it is the "free result of free transaction"' (Marx, 1977: 30).

To the abstraction of conceiving labour in terms of a commodity, Marx opposes the concreteness of labour as a productive and creative activity. However, it is not the case that once Marx's early critique of Political Economy is finished and the schema judged inadequate the true nature of labour and individuals emerges in some pristine unmediated form. Marx criticizes the way in which the language of Political Economy fails to capture what is essential to the experience of the worker in capitalist society and sets himself the task of rectifying this situation. However, this process takes place through the introduction of a new set of metaphorical co-ordinates, i.e. through writing. It is to these co-ordinates that I am turning my attention in the next section.

LABOURING FOR STRUCTURE

As is well known, the argument that Marx advances in the *Economic and Philosophical Manuscripts* takes the form of a philosophical anthropology. Marx needs to ground his argument in some type of trans-historical human attribute so that he can both explain the historical specificity of private property, and create the discursive and theoretical grounds for its critique. The trans-historical attribute, or essence, that Marx identifies is the ability that individuals have to project, plan and produce free from natural determination. Individuals are not determined exclusively through physical need (Marx, 1977: 68–9). According to Marx, it is precisely this capacity, or potentiality, that Political Economy is incapable of seeing. Political Economy sees labour only as an abstraction; it cannot grasp that concrete productive labour is simultaneously an affirmation of the individual and the species being (Marx, 1977: 69).

For Marx it is the existence of alienation and private property that prevents individuals from living according to the creative potential that is inscribed at the very core of their humanity as a species being. Inasmuch as the resources required for labour are in the hands of the capitalist class, as private property, workers are caught in a form of social organization, a division of labour, which compels them to engage in a type of work that is neither free nor creative. In this context, private property is seen as unnatural in the sense that it goes against an individual's 'natural' propensities. It serves to deform how they live as a species being. The existence of private property '. . . expresses the fact that the manifestation of his life is the alienation of his life, that his realisation is his loss of reality . . .' (Marx, 1977: 93–4). This loss of reality, moreover, is reflected in the 'unnatural' and abstract mode of representation in which individuals exist in the language of Political Economy – as instruments of production or commodities.

Inscribed in the way in which Marx writes his critique of private property and its representation in the language of Political Economy is an overwhelming yearning for a return to some type of totality. This desire is crystallized on the one hand by the way he opposes capitalist to a possible post-capitalist society and on the other by the contrast between the abstract way in which Political Economy represents individuals and Marx's own attempt to grasp what is most essential about them. Thus both the discourse of Political Economy and the reality of capitalism connote absence, abstraction, incompleteness, fragmentation and alienation. Post-capitalist society and Marx's notion of the species being connote presence, concreteness, totality, naturalness, and organic communal nature.

In this sense Marx's discourse is, in part, the product of the wider pessimism that characterized German social thought's encounter with modernity. Moreover, as Habermas (1987: Chapter 3), Love (1986: 21) and McLellan (1973: 121) have argued the emphasis on productive labour also invokes the romantic idealization of aesthetically creative labour in the context of a traditional community. Marx's conceptualization of the division of labour as a loss of connection, as an instance of alienation from the intrinsic nature of a species, powerfully evokes images of the undermining of an organic communal nature. It is akin to Tönnies' later characterization of *Gemeinschaft* in opposition to *Gesellschaft*, Simmel's ambiguity about the exchange-mentality of the Metropolis and Weber's characterization of modern society as being dominated by rationalization.[2]

Marx's enunciation of modernity remains, at this stage, strongly embedded in the Hegelian formulation, and the system of statements from which it arises. Thus his ethical solution to the dilemma of modernity parallels Hegel's: 'It is precisely because Hegel's vision of the contradictory and self-destructive character of modern society was so keen that he tried so hard to resuscitate and adapt to modern conditions certain aspects of the "organic" feudal order . . .' (Cummings, 1998: 50).[3]

Now, whatever merit this conceptualization of human freedom and creative productive activity may have for an ethical critique of capitalism (modernity?),[4] the semantic and narrative strategies from which the notion of labour is enunciated are not able to produce a workable concept of social structure. The reasons why this is so are to be found in the metaphors through which Marx unfolds his critique of Political Economy.

As I argued above, Marx's critique of Political Economy, in *The Economic and Philosophical Manuscripts*, rests largely on his rejection of the concept of abstract labour and the way it disfigures the essence of human beings as a species being. Thus it is not surprising that one of the rhetorical strategies through which this rejection is produced is through the metaphor of presence, immediacy and plenitude: in other words through the opposition of the unmediated reality of work and its representation as an abstract activity in the language of Political Economy. In drawing on this metaphor, Marx is activating a trope – a metaphysics of presence – that has been central to the development of Western thought:

> ... the enterprise of returning 'strategically', in idealization, to an origin or to a 'priority' seen as simple, intact, normal, pure, standard, self-identical, in order *then* to conceive of [pour penser *ensuite*] derivation, complication, deterioration, accident, etc. All metaphysicians have proceeded thus ... This is not just *one* metaphysical gesture among others; it is the metaphysical exigency, the most constant, profound and potent procedure. (Derrida, in Culler, 1986: 93; emphasis in the original)

This strategy is explicitly embodied in Marx's injunction that we begin our analysis and critique of capitalist society, and Political Economy, by looking at labour in its ideal and unspoilt form (i.e. free and creative self-expression).

One of the effects of such an idealization is that it provides a particularly powerful grounding for normative critique. All the deviations from the ideal (free creative work), all deteriorations are 'unnatural' (alienation). However, invoking the idealization of an origin or a 'priority' through the metaphor of presence also produces a second and perhaps more important theoretical effect. It creates the illusion that reality and thought can be understood as being co-present. In other words it contains the possibility that language can be the transparent embodiment of reality. This effect is created almost mechanically in the first manuscript of *The Economic and Philosophical Manuscripts* through the juxtaposition between the writing of Political Economy and Marx's own writing.

Anyone who picks up *The Economic and Philosophical Manuscripts* for the first time and thumbs through the first manuscript will be surprised by the number and the length of the citations reproduced from the writing of various Political Economists. The excerpts are punctuated by Marx's staccato comments. These comments link the different citations in an expository order, but they also serve to illustrate sarcastically the logical contradictions (i.e. labour is a commodity yet violates the definition of a commodity) and the outrageous and grotesque conclusions that the writing of Political Economy produces (i.e. human beings are akin to machines, or base instinctive beasts). In doing so Marx incessantly draws our attention to the way Political Economy abstracts from the reality, concreteness and plenitude of the actual experience of work. Consequently, it ignores the real misery associated with capitalist production and fails to grasp the creative potential implicit in concrete labour.

The opposition between the abstract language contained in the lengthy excerpts of writing reproduced from the work of Political Economists, and Marx's briefer appeals to the concrete and real acts of labour – 'the actual economic fact' – creates the illusion that the problem is with writing itself. If one can move beyond the mediation of writing and its abstractions to the real essence of things then the truth of capitalist society can be revealed. Marx's comments tear into the space where Political Economy exists as writing, and introduces reality and not abstractions. In this way, Marx tries to erase the trace of his own writing. By the time Marx gets to the section on estranged labour he is no longer abstracting (writing) he is making reality and thought co-present.[5]

However, as Derrida notes: '. . . Immediacy is derived . . . all begins through the intermediary' (Derrida, 1976: 157). The immediacy of the thing in itself (labour) and its 'originary perception' (as an actual economic fact) is the effect of the metaphor of presence, a rhetorical strategy which paradoxically seeks to escape language. However, not only does Marx not manage to break out of writing: the illusion of escaping writing is in fact connected to a second metaphor through which Marx's writing attaches signifieds to the signifier labour. This is the metaphor of labour as artistic creation and self-expression:

> Marx assimilated labor to creative production by the artist, who in his works externalizes his own essential powers and appropriates the product once again in rapt contemplation. Herder and Humboldt had sketched out the ideal of the all-round self-realizing individual; Schiller and the Romantics, Schelling and Hegel had then grounded this expressivist idea of self-formation in an aesthetics of production. Inasmuch as Marx now transfers aesthetic productivity to the 'species life,' he can conceive social labour as the collective self-realization of the producers. (Habermas, 1987: 64)

The problem with writing labour in this way is that it is only capable of grasping the 'structure' of capitalist social formations negatively. Capitalist social relations are those relations that undermine traditional communities and reproduce the intrinsic powers of the species in an alienated way. Thus, as Habermas has pointed out from a different theoretical perspective, Marx 'is unable to distinguish in this repressive uprooting of traditional forms of life between the aspect of reification and that of structural differentiation of the lifeworld . . .' (1989: 341).[6] What is lacking in the discursive spaces opened up by the metaphors of labour as presence and as the artistic self-expression of the species are the semantic and conceptual resources which would make it possible to write, or think, about capitalism as a *sui generis* form of social organization and its role in the structural differentiation of modern societies. It is not possible to elucidate the basis for the systematicity of capitalism as a social system. On the one hand, the metaphor of presence disciplines any attempt to abstract from the plenitude of the 'concrete' action of production that might be the basis for thinking, or writing, about capitalism as some type of social totality. On the other hand, the only legitimate totality is that of the species being such that it is ultimately '. . . nature itself that reproduces itself through the reproduction of the subject-writ-large, society, and of the subjects active within it' (Habermas, 1987: 342). The structure of capitalist society is only conceptualized as an obstacle to this romantic totality. Rather tellingly, in *The Economic and Philosophical Manuscripts* the source of profit is deceit and the ownership of private property is presented in terms of coercion. Both are represented as unnatural forms of communion between members of the same species being and not as emerging out of systemic wide processes.

Not surprisingly, by the time Marx is writing *Capital*, a text where he does manage to represent capitalism in terms of a number of systemic effects, he has abandoned both the metaphor of presence as well as the metaphor of labour as artistic self-expression. This, however, does not mean that Marx's writing does not show traces of metaphors or other language-borne rhetorical strategies; nor does it mean that Marx abandons the signifier labour. As I shall argue below, it is precisely a new metaphor, an energiticist metaphor, which in part allows him to attach new signifieds (meanings) to the signifier (term) labour and in this way prepare the semantic and conceptual ground for a penetrating analysis of the systemic nature of the capitalist social formation. However, before turning to this, I will first explore Marx's best-known attempt to produce the concept of structure through the base–superstructure metaphor.

STRUCTURE AS THE EFFECT OF THE BASE–SUPERSTRUCTURE METAPHOR

The 1859 Preface to *A Contribution to the Critique of Political Economy*, is, as is well known, the site where the classical formulation of the base–superstructure model is located. It is also one of the few places where it is possible to find the presence of the actual term structure:

> The sum total of these relations of production constitutes the economic structure of society, the real foundation, on which rises a legal and political superstructure and to which correspond definite forms of social consciousness. (Marx, 1978a: 4)

Society is likened to a building. Its superstructure arises from its economic structure, its foundation. The base, in the case of a building, is embedded in the ground;
in society it is embedded trans-historically in the real material conditions of production. To deploy a strategy where the economic structure is enunciated as the foundation of social life is to produce a discursive effect where its centrality and primacy
vis-à-vis the superstructure is on a certain level secured metaphorically.

However, this alone tells us little about the theoretical and analytical potential of
writing, or thinking, social structure through this discursive effect. To take seriously the role that metaphors play in theoretical production means something
more than merely looking for metaphors. All social-theoretical productions are
happy hunting grounds for the avid metaphor hunter. What is required is an analysis of the potential of the metaphorical links themselves, as well as the ways in
which they might be used to open up or transform existing conceptual systems.
Thus, in order to move on to a more productive level of analysis it is necessary to
determine whether we are dealing with a *Modality A* or *B* metaphorical operation.
In other words, is it the case that the semantic conduits that the metaphor makes
possible are used in order to generate new domain-specific concepts? Is it theoretically and analytically meaningful to speak about a social base and its superstructure?
Can the idea of an above and a below connoted by the base–superstructure metaphor be used to link different spheres of social life? If the answers to these questions
are affirmative then we are dealing with *Modality A* metaphorical operation. However, if the answers are negative then we are dealing with a *Modality B* variety whose
plausibility is contingent on not breaking the initial semantic connections. In other
words, base and superstructure will only be meaningful inasmuch as they continue
to rely on the meanings associated with the base and superstructure of an actual or
imagined building.

In the next section I am going to argue that the theoretical effect of social structure
produced by the base–superstructure opposition is unsatisfactory. The attempt
to organize a conception of social structure around the notion of a base and superstructure presupposes the ability to separate social life into two relatively distinct
spheres such that one can be seen as 'arising from' or 'resting upon' the other. However, this effect is not achieved. The discursive exigencies associated with this
requirement are not overcome. Thus the metaphor retains its *Modality B* status.
Second, I will argue that the failure to achieve this effect should perhaps not be
located in Marx's lack of ability but in the semantic and conceptual limitations of
the metaphor itself. The brief presentation of the base–superstructure metaphor
found in the Preface does not, of course, contain an analytical account of the components of the economic base and the analytical relationships that it establishes with
the superstructure. However, such concepts are enunciated in the earlier co-
authored work with Engels, *The German Ideology*. Thus, I shall focus on this text in
the next section.

'MAKING' AND 'PRODUCING' SUPERSTRUCTURES AND CONSCIOUSNESS

The polemical aim of *The German Ideology* is made obvious from the very beginning. In contrast to the 'illusions of consciousness' associated with German idealism, Marx and Engels begin with real individuals and their real material activities (Marx and Engels, 1978: 149). Real physical activities are, in a manner that closely parallels the position that Marx developed in *The Economic and Philosophical Manuscripts*, both the premises and empirically verifiable outcomes of the activities of individuals. It is these activities and the property relations that organize them which are the foundation of consciousness, and not vice versa (Marx and Engels, 1978: 150).

In this context, it has frequently been asserted that Marx and Engels' overstatement of the determinative power of the material or productive sphere of social life has to be understood as a tactical intervention against the Young Hegelians and their rampant idealism. Thus, if one reads the crucial texts carefully, one finds that it is the word 'conditions' that is often employed, instead of 'determines'. Consequently, it is argued that the base–superstructure metaphor should not be seen as licensing a simplistic variety of economic determinism.[7] Notwithstanding this, the question that we must address is whether Marx and Engels are capable of developing the metaphor in such a way that it is possible to write and think the specifity of the base and the superstructure as well as their mode of interrelationship. The answer to this question lies in the work they do on and through the metaphor.

Any reader of *The German Ideology*, sympathetic or not, will probably notice that there is a fast-moving pace in the rhetorical texture of the text. The key terms in the text are 'making' and 'producing'. These terms, and the network of conceptual resonances which they invoke, create a sense of movement and activity; producing subsistence products seamlessly flows into the making of history: 'The first historical act is thus the production of the means to satisfy these needs, the production of material life itself' (Marx and Engels, 1978: 155–6). Making and producing is the paradigmatic form of meaningful historical action; it '... remains constantly on the real ground of history; it does not explain practice from the idea but explains the formation of ideas from material practice' (Marx and Engels, 1978: 164). It is this material practice that the authors oppose to the abstractions found in German idealism. It is the trans-historical point zero of human history (Marx and Engels, 1978: 156).

In arguing in this way, Marx and Engels demonstrate their reliance on the discursive effect of the metaphysics of presence trope that structured the writing of *The Economic and Philosophical Manuscripts*. Priority is given to the originary moment of productive labour as the trans-historical source of all human relations. However, rather than opposing the primacy of concrete labour to the abstractions of Political Economy, it is opposed to the ideological abstractions of German idealism.

Consequently, ideas and the symbolic artefacts through which they are crystallized (e.g. religion, morality, metaphysics, law, ethics) are made derivative. This
opposition is also rhetorically reinforced in *The German Ideology* through continued
reference to the equivalence between organic material and social material productive processes:

> We set out from real, active men, and on the basis of their real life-process we
> demonstrate the development of the ideological reflexes and echoes of this life-
> process. The phantoms formed in the human brain are also, necessarily, subli-
> mates of their material life-process, which is empirically verifiable and bound to
> material premises. (Marx and Engels, 1978: 154)[8]

One of the discursive and theoretical effects of the deployment of the metaphor
of presence is that ideas and consciousness are rather unconvincingly made derivative from a pristine moment of originary material practice. This is, of course, in
direct opposition to the explicit theoretical commitments that Marx makes for an
understanding of consciousness, not as being causally determined by the external
material world, but as emerging within the context of practice itself. (Marx,
1978b: 144)

Whatever the difficulties involved in maintaining a hierarchy and an opposition
where the alleged immediacy of 'real life-processes' are privileged over consciousness and ideas in the phenomenological domain of everyday human interaction, in
The German Ideology a new order of discursive exigencies is superimposed. This is
because the superstructure is also enunciated as a form of social consciousness, as 'a
superstructure of distinct and peculiarly formed sentiments, illusions, modes of
thought and views of life', or as 'an idealistic superstructure' (Larrain, 1979: 50).
One of the consequences of this is that there is no form of analytically distinguishing between the potentially, and likely, differing logics of the reality of an individual's lived experience, and that of the reality of the social and cultural processes
that exist at the level of the social system or the 'idealistic superstructure'.

Thus, in *The German Ideology*, two analytically distinct levels of analysis are conflated. The reason for this is that the effect of social structure, as the interaction
between two discrete social spheres, requires the interaction of two tropes in
order to be written: the metaphysics of presence that asserts the primacy of concrete
productive activity and the base–superstructure metaphor proper. The latter metaphor is deployed in the attempt to represent social life as some type of organized
whole in a semantic context where it is possible to assert that a particular sphere can
be seen as the foundation for the other. As such it introduces a principle of semantic
hence theoretical visuality by which the dynamics of a complexly organized social
system might be grasped as the relationship between two discrete spheres.

This principle, however, is semantically grounded in a series of physicalist connotations; it is based on the logic of 'an above' and 'a below'. Thus the metaphor

creates the conceptual necessity of writing the two spheres as being mutually exclusive chunks of social reality. This is necessary if one is to be written as resting on top
of the other. In the physical variant of the model, it is the actual physical position of
the base – below the superstructure – that gives the model some degree of commonsense plausibility.[9] However, this physical logic of an above and a below is not
conceptually meaningful at the level of the social formation. The relationship
between the base and superstructure cannot be a physical and positional one. Moreover, inasmuch as it is seen as a physical and positional relationship then the metaphor is only functioning in a *Modality* B state.

Consequently, in the discursive process by which the transfer of meaning from
the physical to the social model takes place, the priority that the base has in terms
of its physical position *vis-à-vis* the superstructure has to be re-conceptualized. And
it is precisely at this point that the base–superstructure metaphor interfaces with
the discursive effect of the metaphysics of presence. The relationship is rewritten as
a causal and historical priority. If making the conditions of daily individual existence is the premise and origin of all history, then the organization of material
life also serves to oppose the economic structure to the superstructure, both historically and causally. The semantic and conceptual microcosm contained in the discursive effect of the metaphysics of presence – that of the logical priority of productive work over thought and consciousness – is projected at a systemic level
where it takes the form of a logical, causal and historical priority of the base over
the superstructure.

However, the problem with transferring the materia–consciousness opposition,
produced by the metaphysics of presence trope, on to the base–superstructure
opposition is that the superstructure is cleansed of any material connotations.
This, as Raymond Williams has argued, leads to a conceptual and theoretical
logic where the cultural aspects of production and the material and relational
aspects of politics and ideology cannot be written (Williams, 1977: 95–100).[10]
If they are then the opposition between the base and the superstructure cannot but
fracture on what should have been its principal axis. This is because the priority of
the base over the superstructure is not based on its actual physical position in space
(literally below the superstructure) as it is in the commonsense physical model but
in the priority of materiality over consciousness. If it is acknowledged that both
social spheres (base and superstructure) contain materiality and consciousness,
then although it may still be possible to keep them distinct, the priority of the
base over the superstructure is no longer tenable. However, this is precisely what
the base–superstructure metaphor is deployed to assert.

Thus, there is a discursive and theoretical instability written into the very structure of the transfer of the base–superstructure model from the physical to the social
domain that undermines its logical integrity. The extent to which this instability
remains contained depends on the continued existence of semantic links with the

physical model. In other words, it only remains plausible as a *Modality B* metapho-rical operation; it depends on our willingness to theoretically 'see' the social base and superstructure in a physicalist mode as if the social base were actually and lit-erally below the superstructure.

The enunciation of social life via the base–superstructure metaphor, however, is not limited to the translation of a physical and positional priority into a historical and causal one. For instance, it also opens up a productive conceptual and semantic space where it is possible to produce a series of concepts whose role is to attempt to write the distinction between the base and superstructure as two mutually exclusive spheres. Thus the base is conceptualized systemically in terms of property relations, the organization of production and the social classes that the aforementioned pre-suppose. This is done through a historical narrative that details the emergence of private property and conceptualizes history as the consequence of how successive generations 'exploit the materials, the capital funds, the productive forces handed down to it by preceding generations . . .' (Marx and Engels, 1978: 172).

However, because in *The German Ideology* this is the only historical narrative then the development of different forms of social consciousness and institutions – the idealistic superstructure – has no history at all. They are a mere reflection of the material base. Thus at a systemic level the superstructure is defined negatively in terms of all those forms of social existence that fall outside of the sphere of material base. The potentially differing logics between ethics, religion, law, political ideol-ogies, etc. are conflated and left unanalysed. Moreover, the actual agencies that produce the superstructure are not explored. There are no concepts available to write the ways in which the relationships between the base and superstructure are mediated. This is nowhere clearer than when Marx and Engels claim that 'The ideas of the ruling class are in every epoch the ruling ideas: i.e., the class which is the ruling material force of society, is at the same time its ruling intellectual force' (1978: 172). The logic of the base is without mediation translated into the logic of the superstructure.

The semantic potential that the base–superstructure metaphor contains is that of generating a theoretical visuality that might be capable of representing the social formation as some type of complexly organized totality, and it is here where its greatest appeal rests. Moreover, it also very suggestively connotes the idea that societies should be visualized as having different levels or spheres of organization. In other words it introduces a visuality where in principle it would be possible to distinguish the logic or principles of organization of different spheres (i.e. the econ-omy, politics, culture, etc.) as well as how they are interrelated. Thus it produces the effect of a heterogeneous and complexly layered social formation: a social formation with ontological depth whose structure is not entirely visible in the patterns of every-day interaction. Nonetheless, the problem with the base–superstructure metaphor is that it is semantically tied too strongly to the commonsense notion that the vertical relationship between two chunks of reality can be explained in terms of an above and below. When translated into the sphere of the social world and combined with the effect of the metaphysics of presence it can only exist as logical and historical priority. Consequently, it does not open up a conceptual space where it is possible to specify the actual interactions between the diverse elements of the base and superstructure or the specificity of each. The physicalist connotations of the metaphor produce an analytical opaqueness which cannot be overcome within the conceptual parameters of the metaphor. This produces a paradoxical discursive and theoretical effect. The very rhetorical gesture that introduces the possibility of writing the social formation as a *sui generis* form of organization – the deployment of the base–superstructure metaphor – acts as a block to its further development.

However, it would be wrong to think that all of Marx's attempts to produce the effect of social structure remained ensnared in this untenable physicalist visuality. It is not true that if one accepts that the concept of social structure produced by the base–superstructure metaphor must be abandoned that there are no other discursive resources through which to write or think the effect of social structure. A particularly powerful strategy for producing an alternative conception of social organization is contained in the metaphor of energized labour, and it is this metaphor which I now turn my attention to in the next section.

ENERGIZING NINETEENTH-CENTURY SOCIETY

There can be no doubt that the term 'labour' is one that consistently appears in Marx's work. However, the empirical appearance of a term (signifier) should not be mistaken as evidence of continuity at the level of meaning (signified). With this in mind, it is important to note that implicit in *Capital* is a conception of labour, though often unnoticed, which is formulated in a semantic field that is significantly different from that which grounds Marx's earlier works:

> In *Capital* Marx also refers to labor as 'a process by which man through his own actions, mediates, regulates and controls the metabolism between himself and nature,' but this can be read as a metaphor for a process that is now understood entirely in energeticist terms. (Rabinbach, 1992: 77)

Rabinbach (1992: 321) argues that the shift in meaning of the term 'labour' has not gone entirely unnoticed. For instance, Heller (1981) identified a displacement from a 'paradigm of work' to a 'paradigm of production'. Similarly, Althusser pointed out that Marx abandoned the anthropological conception of work in his later writings (Althusser and Balibar, 1970: 171).

Rabinbach, however, suggests that the shift in meaning is, perhaps, better understood in the context of the energeticist framework that coalesced trans-nationally around the 'new science' of energy, or thermodynamics, associated with, among others, the work of Hermann Helmholtz, Sardi Carnot, James Prescott Joule and Julius Robert Mayer.[11] The significance of this development lies in the fact that it produced a crucial social, political, cultural and scientific site where fatigue, productivity and the conservation of energy were constituted discursively as scientific, moral and political objects of study (Rabinbach, 1992: Chapter 3).

As Kuhn (1959), Prigogine and Stengers (1985) and Smith (1998), for instance, have shown, the process through which the paradigm of thermodynamics became hegemonic in nineteenth-century science, and society (Rabinbach 1992), is a complex and highly nuanced one. Nonetheless, at the level of the scientific community:

> Physicists learned about the relationship between heat and work and found the two to be interchangeable. They also realised that all forms of energy, from mechanical to thermal, are convertible to each other. These realisations led to an understanding which was fundamentally different from the idealised world of the clockwork universe and mechanically organised systems of transformations ... It involved both a shift from time-symmetry to a distinction between past and future, and a move from idealisations to descriptions of nature. (Adam, 1990: 61)

Moreover, this novel way of conceptualizing nature as a reservoir of a fundamental and convertible energy not only operated across scientific disciplines (e.g. Helmholtz was also a physiologist), but also provided new ways of relating 'society' to 'nature' and of conceptualizing labour and society itself. Thus,

> The discovery of energy as the quintessential element of all experience both organic and inorganic, made society and nature virtually indistinguishable. Society was assimilated to an image of nature powered by protean energy, perpetually renewed, indestructible and infinitely malleable. (Rabinbach, 1992: 46)

This in turn created some of the conditions of possibility through which ideas of productivism, efficiency, fatigue and the science(s) of work were developed around the metaphor of 'the human motor' (Rabinbach, 1992: Chapter 1). Thus, '... the nation that most efficiently used and conserved the existing supply of the world's energy – including both labor power and technology – would also win the race for industrial supremacy' (Rabinbach, 1992: 70).

ENERGIZED LABOUR AND MARX'S CAPITAL

Some of the social and political concerns around fatigue, productivism and wasted labour (energy) are clear in Marx's work by the 1860s as he moves away from a conception of 'emancipation *through* labor, to emancipation *from* productive labor by an even greater productivity' (Rabinbach, 1992: 73, italics in original).[12] As Rabinbach points out, the conversion to an energeticist conception of labour is not clearly signposted by Marx but a careful reading of Marx's *Capital* reveals the extent of the debt (Rabinbach, 1992: 76–81).[13]

The most important potentiality contained in the energeticist metaphor is that it provides a semantic context where it is possible to break with the representation of labour exclusively in terms of the discrete concrete actions of individuals; labour is refigured as 'a natural force among others united by the universal equivalence of *Kraft*'. Thus, 'Labor is no longer a creative or singularly human act; it is one kind of work aimed at the production of use values' (Rabinbach, 1992: 77). The semantic resonance inaugurated by this metaphorical interface makes possible the rewriting of labour as a bivalent concept which makes it feasible to introduce a crucial distinction between individual concrete acts of labour and labour as a general and abstract expenditure of social 'energy': abstract labour.

Concrete labour denotes the fact that some type of physical and mental activity is necessary in all societies in order to produce the historically specific means of human and social subsistence. However, the recognition of this dimension of labour does not lead Marx in *Capital*, as it did in his earlier writings, to invoke the notion of concrete labour as a trans-historical activity, which in all societies shapes the organization of social life. It does not produce the discursive and theoretical effect of a base that determines the superstructure. In the writings of the mature Marx on the specificity of capitalist organization, the signifier labour is simultaneously attached to two signifieds that grasp both its concrete and abstract dimension (Marx, Vol. 1; 48–9).[14] However, it is the latter, abstract labour, which makes it possible to represent discursively what Marx believes is the distinctiveness of the form of social organization inherent in capitalism: the production and exchange of commodities.

What distinguishes capitalist society as a form of social organization from other societies is precisely the existence of abstract labour and the way in which it functions to 'mediate a new form of social interdependence' (Postone, 1997: 59). The basis of this form of interdependence is the fact that the products of labour are produced and exchanged as commodities. As a result, a structural precondition of this form of organization is that the commodity 'must not be produced as the immediate means of subsistence of the producer itself' (Vol. 1: 166). Consequently, '. . . no one consumes what they produce . . . nevertheless, one's own labor or labor products function as the necessary means of obtaining the products of others' (Postone, 1997: 59).

In order to understand the distinctiveness of the theoretical visuality produced by the idea of abstract labour power it is necessary to explore its relationship to the concept of the commodity in more detail. Marx, as is well known, begins Volume

One of *Capital* with a discussion of the 'strange' and 'queer' thing called a commodity. He does this by introducing a distinction between use-value and exchange-value (Vol. 1: 44). The use-value of a commodity is its utility, its ability to satisfy human wants and as such is related to the type of thing it is (e.g. food satisfies hunger, a house satisfies a need for shelter). Use-values are qualitatively diverse and thus remain incommensurable. For instance, the use-value of a car is difficult to equate with the use-value of a book. However, it is not only commodities that have use-values; all human products must have a use-value if anyone is going to bother to produce them in the first place. Thus what makes a product a commodity is not its use-value, but its exchange-value.

Exchange-value, however, is not inherent in the actual bodily or material form of the commodity as is the case for use-value. The commodity as we saw above is not something which the direct producer consumes immediately; it is a socially mediated deferral of consumption. It represents the potential of being exchanged for something else. However, if exchange is to be possible then all commodities must have something in common in order to be exchangeable. According to Marx, what they all share is the fact that they contain an expenditure of human labour, of productive activity. Thus the value (exchange-value) of a commodity is given by the amount of labour it embodies. Importantly though, this is not the same productive labour of Marx's earlier writings. He is not here referring to concrete acts of labour; instead he is referring to a homogeneous mass of human labour-power (social energy):

> The total labour-power of society, which is embodied in the sum total of the values of all commodities produced by that society, counts here as one homogeneous mass of human labour-power, composed though it be of innumerable individual units. (Vol. 1: 46)

Hence, though a commodity would not have an exchange-value were it not for the concrete labour that it embodies, the value of the commodity is the result of a plurality of social acts which exists as a *sui generis* social reality: '. . . their social existence can be expressed by the totality of their social relations alone' (Vol. 1: 71).

It is the socially determined labour time, an effect of the capitalist social organization, which makes exchange possible at all. It allows a certain quantity of commodity A to become an equivalent for a certain quantity of commodity B (Vol. 1: 62). The extent to which commodity exchange presupposes a different social and spatial organization is revealed though a comparison with direct barter. In the latter, the actual transaction takes place as a discrete negotiation between specific individuals who necessarily have to be temporally and spatially co-present. In contrast, though commodity exchange presupposes the existence of both a buyer and a seller there is no need for them to be temporally and spatially co-present (Vol. 1: 114).

What is more, the systemic features of exchange cannot be represented in terms of discrete concrete acts. The condition of existence of concrete exchange acts depends on the operation of a general and abstract social mechanism that makes commodities convertible into one another. This abstracting and socially mediating function, Marx argues, is performed by abstract labour which he conceptualizes as labour-power (*Arbeitskraft*), a term first coined by Helmholtz:

> We say labour, i.e. the expenditure of his vital force by the spinner, and not spinning labour, because the special work of spinning counts here, only so far as it is the expenditure of labour-power in general, and not in so far as it is the specific work of the spinner. (Vol. 1: 184)

The similarity with Helmholtz's formulation is particularly clear:

> ... the work of the smith requires a far greater and more intense exertion of the muscles than that of the violin player ... These differences, which correspond to the different degree of exertion of the muscles in human labour, are alone what we have to think of when we speak of the amount of work of a machine. We have nothing to do here with the manifold character of the actions and arrangements which the machines produce; we are only concerned with an expenditure of force. (Helmholtz, 1995: 99)

In this context, however, it would be wrong to read this as a *Modality B* metaphor as does Carver when he objects that

> While human labour (as a form of energy) can be expended on material things over time to produce changes in their properties, a theory that labour is 'materialised' in the 'material bodies' of commodities in some way (or that it *is* one of their properties, or that the material properties of commodities *are* accumulated labour) seems to me to confuse energy with matter or with its properties. (Carver, 1998: 79; emphasis in original)

Marx is not asserting that the value of a commodity represents the accumulation of physical energy. This much is clear when he writes

> Not an atom of matter enters into the object-ness of commodities as values: in this it is the direct opposite of the coarsely sensuous object-ness of commodities as physical objects ... However, let us remember that commodities possess value object-ness only in so far as they are all expressions of the same social unity, human labour; their object-ness as a value is purely social. (Marx, cited in Postone, 1996: 145)

Implicit in the discursive strategy that Marx is deploying is a connotative resonance between the notion of a universal *Kraft* in the natural world, and the notion
of abstract labour in the capitalist social formation. The conceptual architecture
associated with the former makes it possible to posit a commonality among all
the different forms of energy in such a way that they become commensurable and
convertible from one to the other. Similarly, the notion of abstract labour and its
embodiment as value in the commodity makes it possible to abstract from the par-
ticularity of the different concrete labours that produced the commodity. This
abstraction provides the social ground for the convertibility of one commodity to
another thus making commodity exchange possible as the principle mode of organization for the capitalist system.

However, the signifier labour-power in Marx's writing does not draw its signified from the theoretical domain of thermodynamics though it is a metaphorical
relationship with this domain that makes the notion of labour-power enunciable
in the first place. Marx's writing semantically and theoretically crystallizes the
fact that in the capitalist social system the heterogeneity of different and unique
concrete acts of production can and do exist in an abstract and socially objective
form as commodities. Labour-power does not refer to some special species-specific
pseudo-naturalistic energy which can be embodied in commodities. It refers to the
fact that in a capitalist system the social 'object-ness' of a commodity, its social
energy, is determined by socially necessary labour time. Thus,

> Although value is constituted by the production of particular commodities, the
> magnitude of value of a particular commodity is ... a function of a constituted
> general social norm. The value of a commodity, in other words, is an individu-
> ated moment of a general social mediation; its magnitude is a function not of the
> labor time actually required to produce that particular commodity but of the
> general social mediation expressed by the category of socially necessary labor
> time. (Postone, 1996: 191–2)

Moreover it is the fact that all commodities have a social existence through their
embodiment of abstract labour that allows them to circulate in the capitalist social
system. It is the mechanism without which the production and exchange of commodities could not exist as a general form of social organization.

ENUNCIATING SIMULTANEITY

Not only does the energeticist discursive field produce the theoretical concept of
abstract labour or labour-power, it also provides the basis for thinking about how a
single act exists simultaneously in different social spheres. This can be observed

when Marx deals with the origin and genesis of surplus value and its concealment in the wage form. He argues that the capitalist pays for labour-power, the ability to work for a determinate period of time, and does not actually pay for the labour embodied in the commodities produced. The value of labour-power is the value necessary to reproduce a worker's capacity to work. For example, if half of the value created through a labourer's productive action serves to reproduce her own labour power, the other half goes to the owner of the means of production as surplus value: thus a concrete act of labour can be simultaneously conceptualized as both reproducing labour power and making capitalist accumulation possible. This is impossible to represent within a theoretical visuality that privileges the concrete as a logical and historical priority which determines social life. Not only can abstract labour be stored in social objects in the form of value (exchange-value), it can simultaneously exist in distinct spheres of social life. To take another example:

> If in consequence of a new invention, machinery of a particular kind can be produced by a diminished expenditure of labour, the old machinery becomes depreciated more or less, and consequently transfers so much less value to the product. (Vol. 1: 203)

The causality implicit in this citation is not susceptible to being explained in the temporal and spatial contexts of the interaction from which it (the invention of the machine) arose. The relationships of different values, in virtue of the socially necessary labour which they embody, can only be understood within the logic of a system where elements of labour can be represented as travelling social 'circuits', far removed from the particular instances in which they were initiated.

It demands a representation far removed from our everyday thinking about social life and its conditions of possibility. However, there is no need to stop here. The enunciative possibilities are much richer: labour could also be seen as setting off what we could call action-pathways leading to other concrete and systemic 'events'. It implies systematic connections with the technical organization of skills and the use of space. It connects with regimes of discipline, and articulates with natural structures (depletion of resources, pollution, etc.). In other words, inasmuch as labour, is conceptualized as an abstract social mediation by Marx, and becomes a nodal point around which it is possible to make connections with different systems of actions (the different spheres and circuits of capitalism), it has repercussions for those social systems related to law, the state, consumption, education, scientific research, health, the environment, etc. [15]

It is important to stress that we are not dealing here with the perennial unintended consequences of action. Rather, given the configuration of property relationships, socially necessary labour times, the relationship between certain commodities to socially determined consumption criteria, the relationships of the values contained in different means of production and the relationship with different modalities of labour organization to productivity, the systemic causal links that are set off are not truly enunciable within the unintended consequences of the individual action schema.

Thus, the unintended consequence of cheapening the production of shirts, is possibly the increasing of the general rate of profit. However, the fact that this social action sets off the series of causal links leading to this consequence cannot be understood in the context of an individual actor (Vol. 1: 299–300). It is the connection between production and consumption (in this case the socially specified bundles required for the reproduction of labour power), articulated through a series of systemic mechanisms, that makes this outcome both possible and describable in social scientific terms. This travelling of social 'forces', this flow of social 'energy' (the causal sequence through which the cheapening of shirts translates into the reduction of the value of labour-power) can only be grasped within the context of a conceptual language that can abstract from the concrete interactions of individual actors. It is premised on a systemic *sui generis* co-ordination, or alignment, of action systems (productive, circulative and reproductive in this case) that allows for the same action to have causal efficacy in three different spheres simultaneously. Similarly, it only makes sense to speak of labour-power in the context of the ways in which it connects with wider social circuits, its potentiality for creating surplus value, for reproducing its own value and transferring value from the means of production to the newly produced commodities. In turn, this is contingent on adequate conditions of production, on adequate circuits of circulation, on the turnover periods for reproduction within the production circuit in which it is embedded, etc.

In this and previous sections dealing with Marx's *Capital*, I have not been so much concerned with giving an account of, or defending, Marx's substantive explanations.[16] Instead, I have been attempting to draw attention to the different order of spatiality, temporality and causality implicit in his unfolding of the concept of abstract labour into a series of concepts and theoretical strategies whose aim is to represent the capitalist social system as a form of organization that is steered by the social objectification of abstract labour as value. This is, also, evident when Marx describes the relationships between the different circuits of capital (productive, commodity and money capital):

> In a constantly revolving circle every point is simultaneously a point of departure and a point of return. If we interrupt the rotation, not every point of departure is a point of return. Thus we have seen that not only does every individual circuit presuppose (implicate) the others, but also that the repetition of the circuit in one form comprises the performance of the circuit in other forms. The entire difference thus appears to be a merely formal one, or as a

merely subjective distinction existing solely for the observer . . . Since every one
of these circuits is considered a special form of the movement in which various
industrial capitalists are engaged, this difference always exists only as an individual one. But in reality every individual industrial capitalist is present simultaneously in all three circuits. (Vol. 2: 104)[17]

More examples could be presented, but I think that the ones given suffice to
highlight the extent to which the conceptual architecture to be found in *Capital*
emerges from a semantic context qualitatively different from those in which the
earlier writings were written. Consequently, the conception of structure, implicit
in *Capital*, is not formulated merely as a simple arithmetic aggregate of a plurality of
concrete actions. Instead, social organization, or structure, is conceptualized as an
articulation of systemic attributes which make production, exchange and distribution possible in a social system mediated by abstract labour. Key concepts (labour,
value, production, circulation, capital, profit, etc.) do not denote concrete substan-
tialist, visible entities or events; instead, they presuppose a new form of scientific
'visuality'. They denote a *sui generis* co-ordination of a plurality of different events,
and processes. Structure, as social organization, is not enunciated as mechanistically
determining concrete events, rather it is seen as constituting a spatial,[18] temporal
and social field that provides the very basis for the existence of these events.

However, the very possibility of this theoretical architecture is not contained in
general ontological statements of the existence of an independent social sphere, or
in the mere commitment to some species of material primacy. The possibility of this
theoretical system is predicated on discursive networks, and strategies, that make it
possible to enunciate simultaneity, interdependence, complex causal processes, and
sui generis social mechanisms. As such, the embeddedness of *Capital* in an energeticist metaphor, of the *Modality A* variety, is not peripheral, but constitutive of the
effect of social complexity and organization produced through the text.

CONCLUSION

Underpinning the argument presented in this chapter, as is the case throughout
this book, is the need to take the language-borne nature of social theory and sociological concepts seriously. This presupposes that we do not take writing to be the
transparent embodiment of thought. It is writing that produces determinate ways
of theoretically visualizing the social world; it provides us with the principles of
organization that align our scientific 'visuality'. Consequently, an understanding
of their functioning is a crucial prerequisite for understanding the practice of
social theorizing.

For instance, the debate regarding the base–superstructure model has most frequently been approached in terms of the tenability of the 'economic determinist' thesis. This, however, has served to hide another order of conceptual problems with the model that I have highlighted in this chapter. The base–superstructure model is formulated within a conceptual system that connotes a 'visuality' of 'material physicality'. This means that questions are posed in terms of 'an above' and 'a below'. The notion of ontological depth exists in purely physicalist terms. Thus, it blocks an understanding of the ontological depth of social structure as being a 'virtual', and simultaneous, complexity.

I have argued here that, to a certain extent, Marx manages to escape the physicalist connotations of the base–superstructure model by deploying an energeticist metaphor. At this point, I am not going to repeat the argument already made. Rather, I would briefly like to suggest some of the potentialities contained in the later concept of structure, as well as some of its limitations. I think that the implicit discursive and theoretical architecture that allows Marx to speak of the distinction between concrete productive action, and systemic processes, can be fruitfully applied as a principle of theoretical 'visuality' to other dimensions of social life. In a certain sense, this potential is implicit in *Capital*. However, having said this, there is no analogue in the realm of ideology, political practice, law, science, culture, etc. to that of labour power. There are no explicit discursive and conceptual tools with which to understand their systematic basis as is the case with production, circulation and exchange. Nonetheless, it can be argued that Marx's formulation of the systemic basis of the capitalist social system could in turn be taken as the metaphorical conceptualization of analogous mechanisms in these other domains.[19]

Moreover, this suggests an important, yet often ignored, dimension of attempts to formulate concepts of social structure; that is to say an examination of the semantic potentialities and limitations of the conceptual systems that we deploy. Thus what is at stake is not only whether structures determine agents absolutely or not, but the adequacy with which our concepts and theoretical strategies can represent a social complexity with *sui generis* agencies not describable, or 'seeable', in the frame of reference of individual agents. These debates could be made richer by an awareness of the creative and explanatory potentials of metaphorical operations in our sociological discourses.

CHAPTER 3

Weber's Structures: Deferral, Rationality and the Heroes of History

INTRODUCTION

Weber never concerned himself with trying to define social structure in any rigorous sense. In many ways his unwillingness to do this can be understood as arising from his principled refusal of the concept of society itself. Thus in *Economy and Society*, although Weber writes about societal tendencies to action or sociation, he does not write about society as a totality or a *sui generis* entity. Indeed to the extent that the effect of society emerges in Weber's work, and it is present throughout, it is written as the effect of the particular complex historical 'configurations' or 'constellations' of individuals' meaningful actions. As is well known, Weber claimed that if he took on the mantle of the sociologist at all, it was precisely '. . . to put an end to the use of collective concepts, a use which still haunts us' (cited in Frisby and Sayer, 1986: 68).

This of course does not mean that Weber understood social life as being devoid of principles of organization or regularity. He did not, could not, accept that social life and the historical unfolding of different forms of sociation were incalculable or impervious to causal explanation. Inasmuch as this was so his writing presupposes a number of different conceptions of social structure. This however is often obscured by Weber's explicit and programmatic methodological individualism and by the absence of a formal and consistent definition of structure.

That the effect, if not the concept, of social structure is a central discursive strategy that organizes Weber's texts is clear in his substantive and historical writings; so much so that they can almost be read as being concerned with the structural level alone (Kalberg, 1994). As a result, it is frequently asserted that there exists a radical disjunction between Weber's methodological prescriptions, where we find a concern with the individual and his or her meaningful actions as the ultimate reality of social life, and his actual explanatory practice. Although I think that there is some merit in pointing out the disjunction and the conceptual, theoretical and discursive

tensions that it presupposes,[1] I want to argue that it is not correct to maintain that
his methodological writings are devoid of the effect of social structure altogether.
In fact, and paradoxically, Weber's methodological writings simultaneously contain both the possibility and impossibility of producing a conception of social
structure. The discursive space in which this (im)possibility is present is articulated
in such a way that the promise of a concept of social structure exists only in the
context of a continuous and infinite deferral of the very possibility that it introduces. It is a space of seduction that nurtures a theoretical and conceptual desire
that is radically and fundamentally transitive.

Said differently, the reason why Weber's methodological writings do not
produce a formal concept of social structure is because the mode of existence of the
notion of social structure is inseparable, as we shall see in the next section, from the
idea of its radical historicity. For Weber, social structures are not so much things in
themselves, but the conceptualizations of successions of complexly organized and
amorphous historical flows of actions that can never be fully grasped by general or
'generalizing' scientific concepts.[2] In fact, the notion of social structure points
beyond itself by connoting a certain excess that always escapes scientific conceptualizations; it exists as the singularity of particular historical configurations or constellations. However, inasmuch as the potential events of history are infinite *vis-à-
vis* the finite minds of women and men, the meanings of social structure are always
subject to revision and always inherently incomplete. Thus, on a certain discursive
level, the idea of social structure 'haunts' Weber's writing; it exists as a deferral that
never reveals itself in its full positivity. The 'charm' of an explicit methodological
individualism is not enough to exorcise it from his writings. It lingers as a trace in
the complex multilevelled–pluricausal connections of the unfolding of history, or
perhaps more accurately, of the crystallization of historical events or processes.

This notion of reality that denotes both a complexity[3] and a historical heterogeneity[4] that always escapes generalizing concepts such as social structure is also
traversed by a second discursive vector that introduces a possible rule of theoretical
visuality: a rule that has the potential of producing the effect of social structure as a
principle of regularity and organization in the context of the chaos and meaninglessness of the world. This is a theoretical visuality that is entrenched in the notion
of rationality, a notion that is absolutely integral to Weber's *Weltanschauung* (worldview) as well as that of his contemporaries (Albrow, 1990: 29–45).

In harnessing the semantic and discursive potential contained in the notion of
rationality as a principle of regularity and calculability, Weber's writing does not,
however, collapse the social world into a seamless and homogeneous rational totality. Meaning is not inherent in the world.[5] Instead, Weber maintains, in Kantian
fashion, that certain aspects of the world can be conceptualized as being underpinned by some type of order and meaning which is ultimately grounded in the

effect of human rationality. This rationality provides the basis for regular action, calculability and mutual orientation among social actors, and between the long gone 'heroes' of history and present-day historians or cultural scientists.

Because rationality is conceived as a principle of order around which different types of social behaviour are clustered, the invocation of the Kantian premise of universal rationality functions in Weber's writing as a metaphor that is discursively capable of producing the effect of social organization or social structure in scientific thought. Nonetheless, as I will show below, due to the manner in which it is developed in Weber's writing, it remains a *Modality B* metaphor. This is due to the fact that the metaphor of rationality can only produce the effect of patterned social configurations insofar as it excludes irrationality as a sign capable of signifying social order. However, it turns out that irrationality itself continuously erupts into Weber's writing as a mode of patterned social behaviour and organization (Holmwood and Stewart, 1991: Chapter 5; Sica, 1988). This makes the effect of social structure produced through the metaphor of rationality semantically, conceptually and theoretically unstable.

In both cases, the effects of social structure and the potentialities and limitations that they possess cannot be addressed merely at the level of an opposition between structure and agency; if only because we are not so much dealing with a concept as with a discursive and semantic effect of structure. I would argue that it is more fruitful to try to understand the creative theoretical work that is done not outside of but through language in the attempt to develop a theoretical visuality, with which the complex organization of social life might be represented. In this chapter, I will first continue to explore the discursive strategies through which the continual deferral of Weber's concept of social structure is produced as the effect of its radical historicity. This will be followed by a discussion of the metaphor of rationality and the semantically and theoretically unstable effects of structure that it produces. Finally, I will examine the ways in which these two elements become fused together in a heroic narrative that privileges historical emergence over social reproduction. I will argue that this modality of heroic emplotment sets important semantic and conceptual restraints on the general effect of social structure that can be produced from within Weber's theoretical visuality.

In doing so, I hope to sidestep the now taken for granted opposition between a methodological individualist and structuralist Weber. In this context, I want to continue arguing for the viability of an approach to the concept of social structure that does not remain ensnared in the 'economy of scale' associated with the opposition between structure and agency, determination and freedom. I want to continue exploring the possibilities and limitations contained in the metaphorical and narrative strategies through which theoretical effects are written and as a result are thought.

SOCIAL STRUCTURES AS HISTORICAL TRACES

As it is well known, Weber maintained that there was a radical disjunction between the reality of the world and the concepts that are deployed in order to, however tenuously, produce knowledge of its structure (Woodiwiss, 2001: 40–7). For Weber, this knowledge only exists in the form of conceptual representations, or mental pictures (Weber, 1949: 90–4). These, however, are never fully capable of representing reality in all its dense plenitude: 'the infinity and absolute irrationality of the multiplicity [of elements] of which everything concrete consists provides an epistemologically really cogent *demonstration* that it is an absolutely senseless thought to attempt a "copy" of reality through any kind of science' (Weber, cited in Burger, 1976: 66; italics in the original).

In the context of this discursive space, it is hardly surprising that he did not provide an exhaustive and rigorous definition of social structure. The effect of social structure in Weber's writing is inseparable from the actual historical unfolding of social life. Consequently, it is as unique and heterogeneous as the possible series of historical events or processes one might attempt to represent. One could for heuristic reasons, and as we shall see below the logic of scientific explanation requires it, construct ideal types in order to make comparisons between different cases. But ultimately ideal types as general and generalizing concepts are abstractions that are incommensurable with the opaque and dense crystallizations of particular instances of social life and human history. Thus actual 'social structures' are precisely those social configurations that always remain outside of scientific representation.

It is important to realize that the notion of abstraction in Weber's work, following Rickert,[6] has two distinct meanings which are in turn aligned with two modalities of knowledge production or logics of explanation: one associated with the natural or 'generalizing' sciences, the other with the cultural, historical, social or 'concrete' sciences. In the first case, abstraction refers to the process through which concrete reality is emptied of qualitative content in an attempt to define generic relations that are potentially both quantifiable and universal in scope (i.e. applicable everywhere despite qualitative differences):

In consequence, the results of these [generalizing] sciences become increasingly remote from the properties of empirical reality. Empirical reality is invariably *perceptual* and accessible to our experience only in its concretely and individually qualitative peculiarities. In the last analysis, the product of these sciences is a set of absolutely nonqualitative – and therefore absolutely imaginary – conceptual entities which undergo changes that can only be described quantitatively, changes the laws of which can be formulated in equations that express causal relations. The definitive logical *instrument* of these disciplines is the use of concepts of an increasingly universal *extension*. For just this reason, these concepts become increasingly empty in *content*. The definitive logical products of these disciplines are abstract *relations* of *general validity* (laws). Their domain is that set of problems in which the essential features of phenomena – the properties of phenomena which are worth knowing – are identical with *generic features*. (Weber, 1975: 56–7; italics in the original)

The sciences of concrete reality (historical, cultural and social sciences) on the other hand are no less dependent on abstraction, but in this case, abstraction refers to the process by which those qualitative elements that are judged as contributing to the individual peculiarity of an event or process are selected for the purpose of creating a causal account. Thus,

The sciences of concrete reality, on the other hand, attempt to establish a kind of knowledge which is necessarily unattainable if we accept the perspective of the nomological sciences: knowledge of *concrete reality*, knowledge of its invariably qualitative properties, those properties responsible for its peculiarities and its uniqueness. Because of the logical impossibility of an *exhaustive* reproduction of even a limited aspect of reality – due to the (at least intensively) infinite number of qualitative differentiations that can be made – this must mean the following: knowledge of those aspects of reality which we regard as essential because of their individual *peculiarities*. (Weber, 1975: 57; italics in the original)

In writing this opposition between the two logics of explanation it is worth keeping in mind that Weber did not believe that these two explanatory approaches corresponded with a difference of ontology between the natural and the social world. In fact, his intervention in the *Methodenstreit* was aimed at demonstrating precisely the opposite point (Weber, 1949; 1975).[7] Both logics of explanation could be applied in either domain. However, Weber did maintain that our interest in the area of the social, cultural and historical sciences could not be satisfied through abstract generalizations because what drove knowledge in this sphere was precisely an understanding of the particularities of specific events or processes. He argued that a generalizing logic of explanation would deprive us precisely of the type of knowledge that fuelled our historical interest:

The logical idea of such a science [natural science] would be a system of *formulae* of absolutely general validity. This system would constitute an abstract representation of the features common to all historical events. It is obvious that historical reality, including those 'world-historical' events and cultural phenomena which we find so significant could never be deduced from these formulae. Causal 'explanation' would simply amount to the formation of increasingly general relational concepts which would have the purpose of reducing, insofar as possible, all cultural phenomena to purely quantitative categories of some sort. (Weber, 1975: 64; italics in the original)

Similarly, Weber argues that it is not the case that the historical causal explanations that are developed in the cultural sciences cannot be applied in the domain of the natural world; they can. But, the interest that drives the knowledge of the natural sciences is not knowledge of the particular but knowledge of general universal laws: 'That we do not attempt this sort of thing [historical causal explanation] in the natural sciences is not a consequence of the objective nature of natural phenomena. It is rather a consequence of the logical peculiarities of the theoretical goals of the natural sciences' (Weber, 1975: 217).[8]

Notwithstanding the fact that Weber drew on the opposition between the two logics of explanation he nonetheless pointed out that a number of sciences could be located on the continuum between these two explanatory ideals (Weber, 1975: 58). A case in point is the fact that Weber located sociology not as a 'historical science', but as a 'natural science' whose goal was the production of generalizing concepts (ideal types) that could conceptualize the regular patterns and configurations that underpinned social life (Burger, 1976: 68).[9] He maintained that the 'generalizing' concepts produced by sociology had an important function in the development of historical causal sequences. However, although their generalizing thrust was a necessary condition for the development of historical causal explanations, it was not in itself sufficient. Historical knowledge was always by definition knowledge of the particular in all its complex and radical uniqueness.

As Burger has argued, at the most general level what made historical explanation possible for Weber was the fact that

> ... historically human individuals held particular values which they attempted more or less successfully to embody in social arrangements. Those historical humans occurring in the description of a particular historical development who (more or less) consciously held values of the same kind as those which from the point of view of the investigator are embodied in the phenomena, i.e., which a historian decided to use as the viewpoint from which a particular historical investigation is undertaken, are at the center of the description of the historical development of these phenomena. (1976: 82–3)

Thus, ideal types[10] in their attempt to model recurring patterns or constellations of conduct arising from the value orientation of actors – or group of actors – could never provide historical knowledge itself. Hence, Weber's often cited insistence that

An ideal type is formed by the one-sided *accentuation* of one or more points of view and by the synthesis of a great many diffuse, discrete, more or less present and occasionally absent *concrete individual* phenomena, which are arranged according to those one-sidely emphasized viewpoints into a unified *analytical* construct ... In its conceptual purity, this mental construct ... cannot be found empirically anywhere in reality. It is *utopia*. (Weber, 1949: 90; italics in the original)

Weber goes on to argue that 'historical research faces the task of determining in each individual case, the extent to which this ideal-construct approximates or diverges from reality' (Weber, 1949: 90). Thus, within Weber's distinctive theoretical visuality, ideal types of patterned conduct cannot be confused with the actual concrete social structures that are always complexly organized constellations of historically unique factors. Within this discursive and theoretical conjuncture, there can be no such thing as definition of social structure in general.

To the extent that actual social structures are located in the multiplicity of historical events, then the effect of social structure can only be produced through its continual deferral. This is because the immensity of the actual historical flow of events is always capable of overflowing any attempt to fix its meaning:

Life with its irrational reality and its store of possible meanings is inexhaustible. The concrete form in which value-relevance occurs remains perpetually in flux, ever subject to change in the dimly seen future of human culture. The light which emanates from those highest evaluative ideas always falls on an ever changing finite segment of the vast chaotic stream of events, which flows away through time. (Weber, 1949: 111)[11]

Thus historical individuals, the concrete crystallizations of specific social configurations or social structures, are always subject to revision, hence exist in a state of continued (im)possibility:

The stream of immeasurable events flows unendingly towards eternity. The cultural problems which move men from themselves anew and in different colors, and the boundaries of that area in the infinite stream of concrete events which acquires meaning and significance for us, i.e., which becomes an 'historical individual', are constantly subject to change. The intellectual contexts from which it is viewed and scientifically analysed shift. The points of departure of the cultural sciences remain changeable throughout the limitless future as long as a Chinese ossification of intellectual life does not render mankind incapable of setting new questions to the eternally inexhaustible flow of life. (Weber, 1949: 84)[12]

Thus there is a sense in which Weber is, as I will argue in a section below, a historian of the event and of the emergence of unique constellations of conduct (the protestant ethic, economic traditionalism, etc.). Since every single event can potentially be construed as a historical individual, the task of history and the elaboration of conceptions of social structure remain fundamentally open, and from the very beginning incomplete.

Put differently, Weber's concept of social structure is only visible as the effect of his entire work. I am not suggesting that one needs to examine all of his substantive work as a prelude towards a process in which Weber's true definition of 'social structure' can be distilled. It is not the case that we need to subject his key concepts (e.g. patrimonialism, economic traditionalism, bureaucracy) to a battery of comparative operations in an attempt to unveil a series of structural elements, or logics, which they all share. On the contrary, what I am arguing is that the general effect of social structure is created through the radical heterogeneity of the concrete historical configurations of his substantive historical work.

Weber does not provide us with a general concept of structure that can be unproblematically and seamlessly applied to a variety of historical contexts. The effect of structure that is discursively produced in the context of the opposition of the two explanatory logics is precisely a paradoxical intimation of the im(possibility) of developing a general and generalizing concept of social structure.

Nonetheless, Weber's writing, like all writing, is not the product of a singular and homogeneous discursive cluster of statements. It unfolds as a complex and uneven discursive space that is constituted by a number of discursive vectors that can reinforce or contradict each other. The effect of social structure produced by the opposition between the two logics of explanation is also given semantic content via a second discursive enterprise which is also capable of producing signifieds (meaning) for the signifier (term) social structure. This second strategy is organized around the metaphor of rationality and it is to this second discursive strategy that I now turn.

SOCIAL STRUCTURE AS THE EFFECT OF (IR)RATIONALITY

As I noted above, Weber did not write the specific challenges that the social sphere posed to the task of explanation and representation as a fundamental ontological distinction between the social and the natural realm. Consequently, he could not be anything but scathing of the German Historical School's attempt to romanticize humanity by characterizing its distinctiveness in terms of the unpredictability and irrationality of actors (Weber, 1975). For Weber, the dignity of individuals as free beings did not lie in their irrationalism or their alleged unpredictability. Quite on the contrary Weber argued that individuals were never freer than when they acted rationally and were calculable both to themselves and to others (Weber, 1949: 124–5; Weber, 1975).

The way in which rationality manifests itself in human behaviour is written by Weber as a mentalistic operation where the actor conceptualizes the conditions of her activity and aligns these with expected results guided by her own values.[13] That is to say, the actor is embodied as a calculating and predictive scientist whose success at producing certain outcomes depends on the level and adequacy of her knowledge of the social situation:

> The acting person weighs, insofar as he acts rationally – we shall assume this here – the 'conditions' of the future development which interests him, which conditions are 'external' to him and are objectively given as far as his knowledge of reality goes. He mentally rearranges into a causal complex the various 'possible modes' of his own conduct and the consequences which these could be expected to have in connection with the 'external conditions'. He does this in order to decide, in accordance with the (mentally) disclosed 'possible' results, in favor of one or another mode of action as the one appropriate to his 'goal'. (Weber, 1949: 165)[14]

As a result of the above, the task of the historian unfolds as the attempt to reproduce retrospectively the mental calculations that 'his "hero" more or less clearly performed or could have performed' (Weber, 1949: 165) for the purpose of judging which actions had a causal impact on a specific event:

> All serious reflection about the ultimate elements of meaningful human conduct is oriented primarily in terms of the categories 'ends' and 'means'. We desire something concretely either 'for its own sake' or as a means of achieving something else which is more highly desired. The question of the appropriateness of the means for achieving a given end is undoubtedly accessible to scientific analysis. Inasmuch as we are able to determine (within the present limits of our knowledge) which means for the achievement of a proposed end are appropriate or inappropriate we can in this way estimate the chances of attaining a certain end by certain means. (Weber, 1949: 52–3)

Consequently, human rationality expressed in terms of the relationship between ends and means allows historical analysis to rewrite the chaos and meaninglessness of the amorphous flows of human history as a formal and intelligible distillation of rational meaning.[15] It provides a conceptual and semantic grid that generates notions of structured empirical 'patterned regularities', 'configurations' or 'constellations' which without naming social structure directly, nonetheless connotes its effect.

This is true notwithstanding the fact that Weber argues that these configurations have no reality outside of the rational processes by which individuals locate themselves in their social environments and rationally adjust their actions within the constraints of their knowledge and access to resources. Although he insists that empirical social configurations or constellations such as states may appear to the historian as separate collective and *sui generis* entities, he maintains that their structure persists only as the '. . . resultants and modes of organization of particular acts of individual persons, since these alone can be treated as agents in a course of subjectively understandable [rational] action' (Weber, 1978: 13).[16]

This explicit nominalism and its refusal to utter that which cannot be said – collective entities – nonetheless produces its meaning as if by a discursive optical illusion. It depends on the metaphorical process through which a connotative resonance, hence also a semantic transition, is produced between the realm of individual thought and the visible empirical patterns of human conduct that structure specific social constellations or configurations. Consequently, this second effect of structure is produced by metaphorically transposing the logical calculability of the individual means-ends schema on to the social system itself. It produces a theoretical visuality in which empirical configurations of actions are written as the complex mediations of the mental calculations of historically situated individuals. Rationality becomes the steering medium through which individuals become calculable, and understandable, not only to each other, but also to the historian that attempts to reconstruct the causal sequences of action that produced concrete events. Thus rationality is the mental space in which rationally aligned means–ends relationships produce the basic rhythm that pulsates through and in so doing organizes society. It is written as the basis of social order both in harmony and disharmony.

The very discursive strategy that produces rationality as the metaphor through which the effect of social order or social structure can be thought, however, also contains the trace of an excluded *other* which signals the im(possibility) of using rationality as a metaphorical vehicle with which to enunciate social structure. The excluded *other* is of course rationality's opposite, irrationality. To be sure, although Weber does not deny the existence of human irrationality, he does attempt to exclude it from the domain of meaningful social behaviour. Whatever this might say about Weber's personal stance on the question of rationality,[17] this attempted exclusion of irrationality is also a consequence of the semantic and structural exigencies of enunciating social structure as the effect of human rationality.

The metaphor as we saw above aligns rationality with predictability, calculability, order and regularity. Rationality is written as the social medium of exchange through which meaning is created and shared, and as such it is the foundation of the regular patterns of behaviour that organize social life. In this context, irrationality represents the corrosion of this semantic space. The mere hint that irrational behaviour may also engender patterned regularities is enough to undermine the effect of social structure produced by the metaphor of rationality. Thus, notwithstanding the fact that Weber names irrationality as a constitutive reality of social life, he takes every opportunity to set it aside:

> In the middle between the absolute (subjective) rationally oriented action and the absolutely incomprehensive psychic data (although actually bound together in fluid transition) lie the rest of the 'psychologically' understandable irrational interrelationships into whose very difficult theoretical differentiation we could not enter here. (Weber, cited in Sica, 1988: 189–90)

He introduces irrationality as a supplement that historical explanation can do without (indeed must do without), but, as I argued in Chapter 1, the logic of the supplement is paradoxical.

The supplement (irrationality) adds an extra something to that which is already complete in itself (action as means–ends rationality), and as such it is inessential. However the very fact that a supplement is added indicates the extent to which the meaning of social action conceived as means–ends rationality is incomplete. Thus the inessential supplement (irrationality) turns out to be absolutely essential. As Sica has argued in reference to the above citation:

> This sentence gives Weber's closest venture toward utter candor about the limitations of his thought, which he knew to be a function of a reliance upon rationality. With the words 'actually bound together in fluid transition,' Weber lets slip sound perception of motivation, and the necessary interrelation of irrationality and action. But with the complementary phrase, 'interrelationships into whose very difficult theoretical differentiation we could not enter here' he admits that he has no intention of pursuing this bond. (1988: 190)

In part, Weber's unwillingness to pursue the bond must be understood as arising from the discursive exigencies associated with the production of the effect of social structure through the metaphor of rationality: hence the continued need to write the irrational as inessential and somehow outside the domain of historical scientific analysis.

As Sica (1988) has shown in great detail, notwithstanding Weber's best efforts *das Irrationalitätsproblem* (the problem of irrationality) continues to emerge again, again and again. It erupts into his writing, tearing into and disrupting the very fibres that discursively weave the effect of structure. In *Economy and Society* this effect is particularly visible as the process through which Weber's concept of rational action is forced to cede increasingly greater terrain to the phenomenological sphere of irrationality. Thus although Weber begins by introducing four types of action, 'affectual [action] (especially emotional), that is determined by the actor's specific affects and feeling states', and 'traditional [action], that is determined by ingrained habituation' (Weber, 1978: 25), he quickly banishes these to the realm of the irrational, the unthought. Thus, 'purely affectual behavior stands on the borderline of what can be considered "meaningfully" oriented, and often it, too, goes over the line' (Weber, 1978: 25). Similarly,

> Strictly traditional behaviour, like the reactive type of imitation discussed above, lies very close to the borderline of what can be justifiably called meaningfully oriented action, and indeed often on the other side. For it is very often a matter of almost automatic reaction to habitual stimuli which guide behavior in a course which has been repeatedly followed. (Weber, 1978: 25)[18]

Moreover, Weber disarmingly concedes that 'The great bulk of all everyday action to which people have become habitually accustomed approaches this type' (Weber, 1978: 25). Thus, a sizable region of social regularity is produced not through the mediation of rational conduct, but through a type of unreflective behaviour which remains outside of the scope of meaningful social action.

Weber differentiates *wertrational* (value-rational) action from affectual action by arguing that the former reveals both a 'self-conscious formulation of the ultimate values governing the action' and 'the consistently planned orientation of its detailed course to these values' (1978: 25). Finally he defines *zweckrational* (instrumentally rational) action arising in a situation where

> ... the end, the means, and the secondary results are all rationally taken into account and weighed. This involves rational consideration of alternative means to the end, of the relations of the end to the secondary consequences, and finally of the relative importance of different possible ends. Determination of action either in affectual or in traditional terms is thus incompatible with this type. (1978: 26)

However, given this definition it is hard to understand why Weber uses the modifier rational in conjunction with value-rational action. If the ends are already determined, the rational component is to be found only in the selection of the means. This produces an impoverished conception of rationality that tends towards the irrational. Weber admits as much by writing that when observed from the perspective of instrumental rationality, 'value rationality is always "irrational"' (1978: 26). Indeed, '... the more the value to which action is oriented is elevated to the status of absolute value, the more "irrational" in this sense the corresponding action is' (Weber, 1978: 26). Thus value-(ir)rational action also falls outside of the domain of rationality.

Out of the four types of action which Weber describes three are irrational and incompatible with the effect of structure produced by the metaphor of rationality.

What is more, Weber explicitly undermines the very notion of structure as the effect of rationality by writing that

> In the great majority of cases actual action goes on in a state of inarticulate half-consciousness or actual unconsciousness of its subjective meaning. The actor is more likely to 'be aware' of it in a vague sense than he is to 'know' what he is doing or be explicitly self-conscious about it. In most cases his action is governed by impulse or habit. (1978: 21)

A similar discursive disruption of the metaphor of rationality which reverses the hierarchy between rationality and irrationality where the latter becomes the source of social regularity is found in Weber's discussion of legitimate orders:

> An order which is adhered to from motives of pure expediency is generally much less stable than one upheld on a purely customary basis through the fact that the corresponding behavior has become habitual. The latter is much the most common type of subjective attitude. (1978: 31)

Thus an order which is adhered to for instrumental rational reasons turns out be less capable of producing patterned configurations than one in which adherence is unreflective, habitual hence irrational.

The persistent reversal of the hierarchy between rationality and irrationality where the latter becomes the source of patterned social regularities points to the limitations of the effect of structure written through the metaphor of rationality. It is a metaphor which never escapes its *Modality B* status. At its most basic and productive form the metaphorical operation makes it possible to assert that

> Many of the especially notable uniformities in the course of social life are not determined by orientation to any sort of norm which is held valid, nor do they rest on custom, but entirely on the fact that the corresponding type of social action is in the nature of the case best adapted to the normal interests of actors as they themselves are aware of them . . . The more strictly rational (zweckrational) their action is, the more will they tend to react similarly to the same situation. In this way there arise similarities, uniformities, and continuities in their attitudes and actions which are often far more stable than they would be if action were oriented to a system of norms and duties which were considered binding on the members of the group. (Weber, 1978: 30)

In so far as it inaugurates this theoretical visuality it generates a semantic and theoretical space which makes it possible to enunciate a wide-ranging series of impressive and penetrating typologies and concepts that provide splendid dividends especially when combined with Weber's awe-inspiring historical erudition and comparative logic.

And yet the very limits of the metaphor, and the extent to which it cannot become a *Modality A* metaphorical operation, are signalled by the continual eruption of irrationality as a source of patterned behaviour. An eruption that semantically and conceptually serves to reverse the hierarchy between rationality and irrationality in such a way as to put into question the essential causal assertion which lies at the very core of the logic of historical practice as Weber understands it. Moreover in doing so it also undermines the semantic scaffolding which makes it possible to write and think social structure as the effect of rationality. Irrationality cannot both connote pattern, order and regularity and simultaneously be opposed to rationality as its meaningless and chaotic *other*. Thus, the effect of structure produced through the metaphor of rationality can only exist as a *Modality B* variety. In other words, it depends on our willingness to attach the signifiers organization, patterned regularities, social constellations, etc. to the signifieds associated with a mentalisticly conceived means–ends rational action.

As we saw above, the fact that actors are the site of meaningful rational action makes them calculable not only to themselves but to historians. However, inasmuch as irrationality manages to colonize discursively and theoretically greater regions of everyday action it turns out that it is irrationality itself that produces order. Weber's writing, notwithstanding his best efforts, discursively and theoretically locates irrationality as the motor of history: 'In the end a fundamental aspect of this thought contained the recognition that it was irrational forces, great utopias and emotions which dominated men and moved history' (Antoni, 1962: 123).[19]

The failure to produce a consistent and workable notion of structure in this context, however, should perhaps not be seen only or primarily as Weber's failure. To a certain extent, the failure is already inscribed as a structural impossibility in the metaphor itself and the ambiguity of the opposition between rationality and irrationality. Moreover there is also the question of the semantic potential of the specific notion of means–ends rationality which Weber drew on. On a certain level it lacks the semantic suppleness and depth to be able to connote a theoretical visuality of highly complex patterns of social behaviour. That is to say, it is perhaps too small or restricted a semantic space to be able to contain or produce the notion of society as the unfolding of infinitely complex figurations.[20] And it is also perhaps for this reason that it is torn asunder by the ravages of that which is unenunciable within its own semantic field of meaning: irrationality and the unthought as the source of social order.

The fragility of the notion of rationality as a discursive theme through which the effect of social order is written, however, is not only evidenced by the persistent and destabilizing effect of (ir)rationality; it also revealed by its incapacity to contain the actual heterogeneity and complexity of Weber's elaboration of concrete historical configurations. Reading Weber's historical analyses, one gets the impression that the notion of rationality is like a theoretical garment which is many sizes too small and woven with a fabric which is insufficiently robust to clothe the different historical dynamics of patterned social behaviour or structure. In the next section, I want to turn my attention to another discursive strategy found in Weber's writing that to some extent attempts to reinforce the weakness of the fabric of rationality as the basis of social order by weaving into it the thread of a heroic narrative.

WEBER'S HEROES OF HISTORY

References to the heroes of history appear frequently thoughout Weber's writing. This however is not fortuitous; there is a sense in which his substantive historical writings seem to be organized around the figure of the hero and the connotative resonances that it produces. This much was of course recognized by Gerth and Mills in their introductory essay to *From Max Weber*:

> In spite of the careful nominalism of his method, Weber's conception of the charismatic leader is a continuation of a 'philosophy of history' which after Carlyle's Heroes and Hero Worship, influenced a great deal of nineteenth-century history writing. In such an emphasis, the monumentalized individual becomes the sovereign of history ... Weber's conception of the charismatic leader is in continuity with the concept of 'genius' as it was applied since the Renaissance to artistic and intellectual leaders. (1995: 53)

Gerth and Mills claim that the charismatic hero emerges as a central organizing theme in Weber's historical writing despite the nominalism of his methodological writings. I would argue that his methodological writings in fact create the discursive conditions for the casting of the charismatic hero on the stage of history. The conception of history as the emergence of concrete and unique events as well as his conception of social structure as the effect of rationality both create the semantic conditions of viability for the rational heroic actor which is characteristic of Weber's substantive historical writings.

No doubt, as Bologh has quite persuasively claimed, the notion of the heroic man of action and the nineteenth-century masculinity that it connotes is to be found in the work of other writers of the same period such as Freud and Nietzsche:

> Weber, like Freud, placed his hope in heroic individuals – in the lone individual who can take decisive action – one who has killed off the father or the desire for a loving father. Weber's description of the charismatic leader corresponds with Freud's description of the hero – the renunciatory hero who imposes

restrictions, restraints and renunciations; the sacrificing hero who risks his life on behalf of his cause ... If I had to encapsulate all these ideas into an image it would be that of the strong, stoic, resolutely independent, self-disciplined individual who holds himself erect with self-control, proud of his capacity to distance himself from his body, from his personal longings, personal possessions and personal relationships, to resist and renounce the temptations of pleasure in order to serve some impersonal cause – a masculine, ascetic image. (Bologh, 1990: 170)

To be sure, the centrality of the heroic man of action in Weber's writing says something important and fundamental about both the gendered nature of his theoretical discourse and of the wider cultural and social resources on which he drew.[21] However, I would also argue that the centrality of the heroic man of action can also be explained, in part, as a result of the role that the figure of the hero fulfils in bringing together at a narrative level both of the effects of structure examined in previous sections. In other words, it can also be seen as a discursive and narrative response to the exigencies associated with the enunciation of social structure as a historically unique concrete constellation of means–ends rational conduct.

In his seminal discussion of the tropes of Western historical narrative, White (1973) describes the notion of the mode of emplotment as follows:

Providing the 'meaning' of a story by identifying the kind of story that has been told is called explanation by emplotment. If, in the course of narrating his story, the historian provides it with the plot structure of a Tragedy, he has 'explained' it in one way; if he has structured it as a Comedy, he has 'explained' it in another way. Emplotment is the way by which a sequence of events fashioned into a story is gradually revealed to be a story of a particular kind. (1973: 7)

In Weber's case, the mode of emplotment that organizes his narrative is what White has called the Romantic Mode of Emplotment, which he characterizes as follows

The Romance is fundamentally a drama of self-identification symbolized by the hero's transcendence of the world of experience, his victory over it, and his final liberation from it – the sort of drama associated with the Grail legend or the story of the resurrection of Christ in Christian mythology. It is a drama of the triumph of good over evil, of virtue over vice, of light over darkness, and of the ultimate transcendence of man over the world in which he was imprisoned by the fall. (1973: 9)

One of the most important effects of any mode of emplotment is that the coherence of the plot structure itself and the narrative momentum which it creates serves to suture the problematic or contradictory relations that may exist among the different discursive elements. The problems and contradictions become momentarily displaced: complexity and contradiction become reduced, contained and organized through the deployment of particular codes. The meaning contained in the plot structure flows into and infiltrates the different discursive, hence also theoretical, elements (e.g. concepts, causal assertions, theoretical strategies) and in so doing creates the effect of coherence and cohesiveness. The story seems credible because we have learnt to read and write the comedy, the tragedy, etc. as plausible stories.

In Weber's historical writing the particular problems which irrationality, poses to rationality are no less poignant than in his methodological writings;[22] however, they are discursively and theoretically much less destabilizing. In part this is due to the connotative resonance produced by the figure of the hero. Thus, the central narrative code which organizes Weber's historical writing is contained in the 'story' of the struggle through which rationality (virtue) transcends irrationality (vice), freedom over unfreedom. For instance, in his analysis of the emergence of some of the factors that influenced the emergence of the Protestant Ethic, Weber highlights the unflinching conviction, the revolutionary vision and the ability to oppose rational action to the irrationality inherent in economic traditionalism:

> It is very easy not to recognize that only an unusually strong character could save an entrepreneur of this new type from the loss of his temperate self-control and from both moral and economic shipwreck. Furthermore, along with clarity of vision and ability to act, it is only by virtue of very definite and highly developed ethical qualities that it has been possible for him to command the absolute indispensable confidence of his customers and workmen. Nothing else could have given him the strength to overcome the innumerable obstacles, above all the infinitely more intensive work which is demanded of the modern entrepreneur. But these are ethical qualities of quite a different sort from those adapted to the traditionalism of the past. (Weber, 1992: 69)[23]

Similarly, in discussing the question of Prussian migrant workers Weber draws our attention to what must be understood as the heroic quality of their action. In their attempt to transcend the irrationalism and unfreedom of their social situation, they courageously sacrifice mundane rewards driven by the moral imperative to live and struggle to be free (rational) men:

> Migration allows him to escape the necessity of seeking work from the neighboring, local ['heimatlichen'] landlords. But just this work in the locality ['Heimat'] is bound mentally and historically to the traditional relationship of authority: it is the obscure urge toward personal freedom that drives the laborers to labor elsewhere. They sacrifice their customary living conditions to the

striving for emancipation from unfreedom: their dull resignation is broken
through. The much lamented 'moving around' of the land workers is at the
same time the beginning of mobilization of the class struggle. (Weber in Mitzman, 1970: 130)

The hero and heroic struggle connote the possibility of transcending the inherent
irrationality of the world; consequently, they provide a discursive matrix that is
capable of narrating history as the outcome of the struggle for and the crystallization of rational conduct, that is to say a conception of social structure as the effect
of rationality.

Weber was too perspicacious an observer of history and social life to ignore the
centrality of power and privilege in the constitution of the social world. Consequently, Weber locates conflict as a central category in his analysis (Weber,
1978: 48–50). Nonetheless, it is particular type of conflict that manifests itself in
his historical narrative; it is the conflict of titans. In *The Religion of China*, it is the
literati with their ethos derived from the doctrine of Confucianism who become
central in producing the effect of social structure (Weber, 1951: 173). The literati
were conceptualized by Weber as the focal point around which ideological, political
and economic conflict was fraught. Their position of ideological, political and economic hegemony was responsible for defusing the Taoist and Buddhist challenge
as well as keeping feudalism at bay. Naturally, the literati were not the only power
actors. Nonetheless, the centrality of their role remained (Weber, 1951: 108). The
same could be said of the role of the Brahmins in *The Religion of India* and the early
entrepreneurs of *The Protestant Ethic and the Spirit of Capitalism*; not to mention the
Judaic Prophets whose religious systematization is at the very centre of the development of the rational ethos specific to Western society:

> Free of magic and esoteric speculations, devoted to the study of law, vigilant in
> the effort to do 'what was right in the eyes of the Lord' in the hope of a better
> future, the prophets established a religion of faith that subjected man's daily life
> to the imperatives of a divinely ordained moral law. In this way ancient Judaism
> helped create the moral rationalism of Western civilizations. (Bendix, 1960: 256)

Thus, Weber's men of action, his heroes of history, were not only politicians and
warriors; they included those men who were capable of articulating and rationally
systematizing worldviews that lead to the dynamic reconfiguration of social action.

And yet it is clear that Weber's historical narrative is not a narrative of proper
nouns; it is one of common nouns. Bendix's influential intellectual biography of
Max Weber sought to show how economic, political and cultural factors coalesced
into 'social structures' in the process of group formation, and as such formed the
basis of collective patterned activity (1960). This collective activity is always

embedded in hierarchies where control over the means of material, cultural and political production becomes the site of conflict.

One of the most striking things about Weber's writings is that although they are underpinned by an emphasis on social difference and distinction, his theoretical and formal writings on stratification are scattered, confused and incomplete.[24] Nonetheless, throughout Weber's writings difference serves to demarcate those groups of individuals who are the constituents of the social; that is to say, those actors who make the social world a calculable and rational space.[25] A fundamental way in which this effect is produced is through the connotative power associated with the hero but also with the heroic group when their sense of social, economic and cultural distinction allows them to struggle for and pursue collectively defined rational goals.[26] That this should be so is not in the least surprising. As we saw above, the greater part of everyday action is written as the effect of habitual, hence irrational action. It cannot be the basis of a calculable rational order.

Thus one of the distinctive features of Weber's historical writings on the sociology of religion is the extent to which they make possible the discursive and theoretical movement from the phenomenological realm of abstract rational thought to the different domains of social life and in this way produce the effect of social order:

> Here in all its boldness is seen Weber's ability to deduce logical transitions, the practical and theoretical consequences through which a religious dogma is passed to a social class, from this to a legal order, to an art form, to an educational ideal, to a logical system, to a sexual ethic, to an industry and so forth. Here cultures assume the character of isolated and almost impenetrable geometrical forms constructed in crystalline coherence and rationality according to different formulae. In fact at one point Weber calls these studies 'contributions to a sociology of rationalism'. (Antoni, 1959: 161)

And it is precisely Weber's heroes of history, and heroic groups, which are both the bearers of this rationalizing ethic and the enactors of a social order which embodies its effects. It is the extraordinary solitary individual,[27] or groups of extraordinary individuals, who are capable of rising to the challenge of creating meaning in an inherently meaningless world. They are Weber's true actors! The historical narrative of their travails is told as the story of the heroic struggle for freedom and rationality. This narrative strategy also articulates well with the logic of history as the emergence of distinctive configurations, found in Weber's methodological writings. It is the creative and revolutionary genius associated with the hero, or the heroic group, that allows novel social configurations or constellations to erupt on to the historical stage. And it is their rationalizing ethic that makes their behaviour understandable to the historian, hence also explainable.

Yet, not unlike in Weber's more formal methodological writings his substantive historical writings are witness to the return of the repressed in the form of charisma as the (ir)rational other of rational heroic action. This is due to the close connotative relationship between the figure of the hero and charisma as Bologh argued in the above quoted excerpt and as the following passage reveals:

> ... the power of charisma rests upon the belief in revelation and heroes, upon the conviction that certain manifestations – whether they be of religious, ethical, artistic, scientific, political or other kind – are important and valuable; it rests upon 'heroism' of an ascetic, military, judicial, magical or whichever kind'. (Weber, 1978: 1116)

Moreover, charisma also connotes the ability of the hero to project on to and institutionalize his conviction in the social world by shaping its material and social conditions: 'The Charismatic belief revolutionizes men "from within" and shapes the material and social conditions according to its revolutionary will' (Weber, 1978: 1116).

Nonetheless, according to Weber, the historical revolutionary potential of charismatic domination[28] lies precisely in its irrationality and its transcendence of rationality:

> Because of this mode of legitimation genuine charismatic domination knows no abstract laws and regulations and no formal adjudication. Its 'objective' laws flow from the highly personal experience of divine grace and god-like heroic strength and rejects all external order solely for the sake of glorifying genuine prophetic and heroic ethos. Hence, in revolutionary and sovereign manner, charismatic domination transforms all values and breaks all traditional and rational norms: 'It has been written ... but I say unto you'. (Weber, 1978: 1113)

In a similar vein Weber writes that

> ... charismatic authority is specifically irrational in the sense of being foreign to all rules. Traditional authority is bound to the precedents handed down from the past and to this extent is oriented to rules. Within the sphere of its claims, charismatic authority repudiates the past, and is in this sense a specifically revolutionary force. (Weber, 1978: 244)

The tension between the irrationality of charisma as the vehicle for the eruption of the new and the rational action of heroic actors receives no satisfactory solution in Weber's writing. Thus as with the instances discussed above, unwittingly irrationality becomes an important vehicle for understanding the development of human history notwithstanding the fact that the logic of historical explanation produced by Weber's writing is premised on the centrality of rational means–ends action. The destabilizing theoretical and explanatory effects of the eruption of irrationality in historical explanation are mitigated and displaced in two ways.

On the one hand, the irrationality is displaced on to the (masses of) individuals who submit to charismatic domination and as such can be relegated to the province of psychology or biology:

> ... charisma [and traditional action] contain the seeds of certain types of psychic 'contagion' and thus give rise to new social developments. These types of action are very closely related to phenomena which are understandable either only in biological terms or can be interpreted in terms of subjective motives only in fragments. (Weber, 1978: 17)

> Where charisma is genuine ... the basis lies rather in the conception that it is the duty of those subject to charismatic authority to recognize its genuineness and to act accordingly. Psychologically this recognition is a matter of complete personal devotion to the possessor of the quality arising out of enthusiasm, or of despair and hope. (Weber, 1978: 242)[29]

And in this way their irrational behaviour remains outside of Weber's historical narrative. On the other hand, when charisma is associated with Weber's heroes of history it is semantically circumscribed in such a way as to connote its creative historical potential which provides the basis for the eruption of new rationalizing ethics. As a result, it becomes an element of the plot structure that narrates historical development as the heroic struggle to create new meanings that crystallize in novel historical configurations.

Notwithstanding the contradictory and the theoretically destabilizing effects of the emergence of charisma as the (ir)rational other of heroic action there is a more fundamental limitation that arises from the fusing together of history, heroic action and rationality in a heroic or romantic mode of emplotment: it creates a theoretical visuality in which it is virtually impossible to conceptualize normal (non-heroic) everyday action and the contribution it might make to the reproduction of social order. To a large extent this modality of action and the types of structures in which it might be grounded are relegated to the sphere of the habitual and the irrational; thus they fall outside of the parameters of a historical dynamic which is driven by the institutionalization of means–ends rationality in social space. Consequently the everyday and the mundane often have little to contribute to Weber's historical narrative. The emphasis is on the emergence of the new and not the reproduction of that which already exists and can be reproduced unreflectively and habitually.[30]

The logic of Weber's historical sociology is for the most part governed by the linear unfolding of a sequence of events that produce historically unique configurations. In this context Weber demonstrates a keen awareness of the range and the complexity of the interrelationship that produce specific events, hence his well-deserved reputation for being the theorist of a radical multi-causality.[31] Still, within this theoretical visuality there are few semantic or conceptual tools for thinking about the social world as being traversed and organized by a plurality of different temporalities, as is the case with Marx's effect of structure in *Capital*. In a certain sense, notwithstanding the fact that Weber is a theorist of complexity, his effect of complexity only exists within the historical telos of the eruption of new configurations of patterned conduct.

The complexity and diverse social temporalities that underpin the organization of everyday life are outside of his historical narrative, they only exist as the supplement of the irrational other. It is true that Roth (Roth and Schluchter, 1979: 166–94) makes a very suggestive comparison between Weber's historical writing and Braudel's *Longue Durée*. But as Roth himself points out, Braudel uses a geological metaphor to think about how different types of historical temporalities can be conceptualized as being layered and in this way can be thought of as co-existing and traversing the same moment. The geological metaphor allows Braudel to think about the interrelationship and the autonomy of the *Longue Durée*, *Generational Events* and *Events* without collapsing them into a narrative dominated by a singular linear historical time. Moreover, Braudel's history is particularly concerned with showing how the rhythms of everyday life feed into larger-scale historical processes. These theoretical effects and their concomitant conceptualization of social structure are difficult to achieve through the discursive and narrative strategies that produce Weber's writing.

CONCLUSION

There can be little doubt that Weber saw the social world as something inherently complex, but not for this reason chaotic. If is true that Weber acquiesced to the centrality of meaning in social life, this did not, in his eyes, banish the need to provide explanations which could be invested with a degree of certainty. Theoretical systems, however, are not just an amalgamation of an author's principles, predispositions and desires. A social theory is not merely determined by the general ontological, epistemological and methodological commitments that a theorist makes, or appears to make. Social theories are written, and as such they are the products of diverse discursive networks, strategies and metaphors. It is not the case that concepts are unproblematically deduced in thought, outside of writing, from general metatheoretical positions.

In this chapter I have tried to show how the effect, if not the concept, of structure emerges at least from three related yet distinct discursive vectors: social structure as the concrete historical configurations of patterned behaviour which always escapes generalizing concepts and is consequently subject to an infinite deferral, social structure as the effect of means–ends rationality, and social structure as the institutionalization of the rationalizing and creative ethic associated with heroic actors. It is in the semantic space produced by these three discursive vectors that the effect of structure is written in Weber's work. And it is the presence of the notion of structure in the volume produced by these vectors that also points to the difficulties associated with Weber's concept of social structure: the reluctance to develop an explicit definition of social structure, the continued irruption of irrationality as a source of patterned behaviour, the predominance of a heroic historical narrative that focuses on the emergence of new historical structures.

However, it is, also, these very difficulties combined with Weber's heroic commitment to empirical research which also provides us with what is most valuable in his attempt to produce the effect of social structure in sociological thought. His dogged reluctance to define social structure in general outside of its specific historical cyrstallizations, while extremely frustrating, does contain the cautionary note that whatever series of discursive strategies one might draw on in order to signify social structure, they had better be flexible and malleable enough to deal with a variety of social configurations, and that any attempt to develop a conception of social structure would best be guided by the friction of a substantive empirical problem. Similarly, the ferocity with which Weber's writing resists the attempt to produce the effect of structure through the metaphor of rationality is suggestive of the pitfalls associated with both putting the burden of patterned social behaviour and other types of social regularities on individuals themselves and thinking about the social world as the embodiment of human rationality. Moreover, the ease with which Weber's sociology flattens his multi-causal theoretical visuality into a narrative dominated by a universal historical time points to the need to develop discursive strategies that might signify social structure not only as the effect of highly complex configurations but also as the effect of heterogeneous temporalities. I would argue that it is very difficult to tackle these questions if one begins with the assumption that the problem of structure is to be resolved within the agency–structure opposition.

CHAPTER 4

Parsons' Structures: Writing Order

INTRODUCTION

Parsons famously began *The Structure of Social Action* with the following citation:

> Who now reads Spencer? It is difficult for us to realize how great a stir he made in the world ... He was the intimate confidant of a strange and rather unsatisfactory God, whom he called the principle of Evolution. His God has betrayed him. We have evolved beyond Spencer. (Brinton, cited in Parsons, 1949: 3)

It cannot be but ironic that the man who claimed to present a theoretical perspective that had 'evolved' beyond the positivist and the idealist positions that he then perceived to divide the sociological tradition, and whose later writings were to be devoted to the evolution of society (Parsons, 1971; 1977b), should be remembered as the theorist of stability, order, consensus and harmony.[1] For a variety of scholars (Dahrendorf, 1959; Mills, 1959; and Gouldner, 1970, to name but a few) Parsons' theoretical, methodological and ideological commitments materialized in a trenchant defence of the status quo, with an emphasis on consensus and the avoidance of conflict.

Habermas (1987: 199), however, has claimed that any contemporary social theory worthy of its name must position itself, be it implicitly or explicitly, with respect to Parsonian theory. Judging by the renewed interest and scholarship linked to Parsons and Parsonian theory, Habermas has certainly been vindicated.[2] Nonetheless, scholarly interest in Parsons' work has by no means produced a unitary evaluation. For some theorists it is precisely the failure of Parsonian theory to link 'action' and 'structure' in a satisfactory synthetic framework that constitutes the fundamental stress points in his work (i.e. Giddens, 1976; Habermas, 1989; Lockwood, 1964). Others claim that it is Parsons' blatant ideological commitments which provide the weak link in his theorizing (Mills, 1959; Gouldner, 1970). Connected with these ideological commitments, but not entirely determined by them, is his alleged inability to engage with the conflictual as opposed to the consensual basis of social life (Dahrendorf, 1959; Lockwood, 1964; Rex, 1961). Alexander

(1982a; 1984), a sympathetic reader, claims that it is the normative and consensual bias, as well as the conflation of distinct theoretical levels, that makes an essentially sound position unsound.

It is not my intention in this chapter to adjudicate between these competing claims, nor to present a definitive interpretation of Parsons. Instead, just as in previous and subsequent chapters, I am going to investigate the ways in which the effect of social structure is written (thought) in Parsons' work. I will do this by examining some of the semantic and conceptual opportunities and limitations that are inaugurated by the instantiation of diverse metaphorical strategies. In doing so, I want to question the significatory stability of the notion of structure (order), which as far as I can tell is taken for granted in the literature devoted to the analysis of Parsonian sociology.[3] In other words, I want to question the notion that it is possible to think or read the concept of structure outside of the specific writing practices and the semantic and conceptual opportunities which they produce. Furthermore, I hope that this will also serve to dislodge the reading of Parsons' attempt to produce a concept of structure from within the economy of scale created by the structure–agency dichotomy.

Perhaps the most frequently repeated statement regarding Parsons' work is its overriding concern with theorizing order at all costs. I would argue that it is not objectionable to hold that Parsons was fundamentally a theorist concerned with the problem of order; this, however, with the proviso that order is not understood as narrowly connoting a conservative political ideology (political conservatism, defence of status quo, etc.). In his most general ontological formulation, under the influence of Whitehead, Parsons was committed to the 'reasonable harmony of being'. Explicit in this conception was the notion that reality was organized in an orderly form; in turn, this order provided the conditions of possibility without which knowledge of its reality would not be possible.

In the words of Whitehead: '. . . there can be no living science unless there is a widespread instinctive conviction in the existence of an Order of Things, and, in particular an Order of Nature' (1967: 3–4). Moreover, as has been highlighted by several commentators[4] as well as by Parsons himself, the question of social order was framed in much the same way as Kant had framed the question of knowledge. Kant's starting point was that we did indeed have valid knowledge, thus the interesting question to pose was how this was possible. Similarly, Parsons was to write: 'I have always assumed that social order in fact existed' (1977b: 69). Consequently, his massive theoretical project must be seen as a relentless attempt to represent the effect of order, structure and organization in social-theoretical thought.

Notwithstanding Parsons' debt to Whitehead's philosophy of the natural sciences, it is clear from his critique of biologism and psychologism in *The Structure of Social Action* that he did not believe that order in the social world was reducible to the order of the natural world. Parsons wrote social order as an emergent property of complexly organized networks of interaction, embedded in the natural world but not reducible to it. As a result, he was faced with the theoretical, hence also discursive, challenge of trying to write the specificity of the *sui generis* quality of social life. Yet, this general ontological statement does not exist in the realm of pure thought prior to its being written; it is only through writing that it crystallizes as text and thought creating certain semantic and theoretical selectivities. Thus the fact that Parsons drew parallels between order in the natural (and social) world and the orderly production of knowledge turns out to be more significant than at first seems. It set up some of the semantic conditions through which Parsons was to produce the discursive and conceptual effect of social structure in *The Structure of Social Action* by creating an opposition between order and randomness (chaos).

In *The Structure of Social Action*, social structure itself exists only as a discursive and narrative effect because it has no clear social-theoretical signified. Nonetheless, it would be wrong to think that the notion of social structure has no meaning at all within the text: that it is subject to an infinite number of deferrals. In fact, the signifier social structure is both produced and stabilized through the metaphorical relationship that is established with the concept of theoretical structure. Among other things, this means that Parsons' convergence thesis, which I will discuss below, and which for too many scholars has held little interest, is also a key discursive strategy through which the effect of social structure is produced. Parsons' 'solution' to the problem of order in the production of knowledge (lack of relativism) provides the metaphorical springboard from which he can begin to write a relatively autonomous level of social complexity as social order. In fact, the relationship between theoretical structure and social structure, order in theoretical systems and order in the social world is one which will continue to be developed throughout Parsons' work.

Nonetheless, it is clearly not the only metaphorical relation to be found in Parsons' work: notions of mechanical systems, equilibrium, homeostasis, cybernetic hierarchies, media of communication, genes, and adaptation are a rich source of metaphorical operations through which Parsons' writing produces a theoretical visuality that provides insightful and penetrating tools with which to explore society as an articulated complex whole. In a certain sense, out of all the theorists examined in this work, Parsons' epistemological position, analytical realism, created the most fertile basis for the deployment of metaphorical strategies in theoretical development.

By arguing for the relative autonomy of theoretical production, while simultaneously grounding knowledge in the order of the world, his 'analogies' and 'homologies' played a crucial discursive role in his theoretical development. Parsons, however, saw these as having only heuristic value; I on the other hand would like to argue that they were constitutive of the many theoretical effects of structure that his writing produced. Therefore, some of the problems associated with Parsons' concepts of structure have to be located in the potential and limitations of the metaphors in which they were grounded.

THEORETICAL STRUCTURE AND 'THE HARMONY OF BEING'

The Structure of Social Action is, without doubt, a complex, insightful and probing theoretical work.[5] Yet, for the purpose of the argument that I am developing in this section, I will focus on two features of the text. In the first place, I would like to examine how Parsons conceptualizes the nature or structure of theory, as well as the centrality of the convergence thesis for his account of theoretical development. Parsons is clearly concerned with attempting to explicate how the development of theory can escape both the randomness and chaos that arise from a strong empiricist position, as well as the relativism springing from a full-blown idealist position. Secondly, I will also argue that in *The Structure of Social Action* the unit act, from which Parsons derives his frame of reference for social structure, is equally defined by its opposition to both randomness and chaos. I believe this is not accidental. It highlights the extent to which Parsons' concepts of social structure and theoretical structure are mutually embedded in a metaphorical relationship produced by a common discursive and semantic space. However, before addressing this second aspect of the text it is necessary to probe further into Parsons' understanding of theoretical practice.

The Structure of Social Action is more than just a critical appraisal of what Parsons believed to be the two major strands underpinning social theoretical development at the time (i.e. positivism and idealism). It allegedly offers a solution through which important elements from both are incorporated. This is achieved by building a bridge across these two positions through an inquiry into the nature of theoretical activity. In so doing, against the empiricist strictures, he argues for the relative autonomy of theoretical development. The practice of science, as understood by Parsons, hinges on the structural articulation of theoretical elements that are used for the organization of the empirical referents. This structural articulation is understood as a 'determinate logical structure' (Parsons, 1949: 7); one which mediates the relationship with possible empirical referents: 'Theory not only formulates what we know but also tells what we want to know, that is, the questions to which an answer is needed' (Parsons, 1949: 9).

The centrality of the mediation of theory is highlighted via the metaphor of the beam of light. Theory illuminates possible empirical facts, and in so doing makes them theoretically relevant. Parsons claims that though facts may be 'known' to exist outside the 'spot' cast by the beam of light (determinate logical structure), '. . . they are not scientifically important until they can be brought into relation with other elements in a theoretical system' (Parsons, 1949: 16).

There have been a number of debates regarding whether Parsons' analytical realism should be seen as positivist or post-positivist.[6] These, however, need not detain us here.[7] I want to suggest that, notwithstanding some inconsistencies with respect to the nature of the connection between theory and fact, the relative independence of theoretical development is a crucial component in the synthesis that Parsons produces in *The Structure of Social Action*. This is so because he posits that facts, even if known, cannot be unproblematically incorporated into a theoretical structure unless there is already a developed category that can accommodate them.

Parsons further elaborates the notion of theoretical structure through his discussion of residual categories. These are *ad hoc* categories not systematically derived from the structure of a theory. The existence of residual categories signals that a theory is not sufficiently comprehensive to incorporate all the significant analytical elements that it requires for theoretical coherence (Parsons, 1949: 16–20). Consequently, what is required is the rebuilding of the theory in such a way that the residual categories become fully integrated elements in the structure of social theory. Theory must strive for closure (Parsons, 1949: 9–10).

As we shall see below, Parsons finds residual categories in both the positivist and the idealist traditions; these indicate the necessity of the *convergence* towards the voluntaristic frame of action. The convergence thesis has been seen by some commentators as a minor aberration. For instance Alexander argues that the convergence thesis is untenable and that it understates the positive and novel elements that Parsons contributed to the synthesis, elements which perhaps Parsons opportunistically read into the four writers dealt with in *The Structure of Social Action* (1984: 154–5).[8]

However, as Bershady (1973: Chapter 1) has convincingly argued, in *The Structure of Social Action*, Parsons was not only dealing with the Hobbesian problem of order in society, he was also addressing the problem of order at an epistemological level. Bershady (1973: Chapter 2) goes on to draw some striking parallels between Parsons and Kant.[9] Just as Kant was ill at ease with the scepticism that emerged from the Humean epistemological position, Parsons was equally disturbed by the chaotic course of a social theory whose rudder was subject to the unmediated vagaries of empiricist navigators. What is more, the open relativism of the German Idealist School, with its emphasis on the uniqueness of the human sciences, did not provide the building blocks for a systematic expansion of social knowledge. Bershady (1973: 68) argues that Parsons, like Kant with his general categories, arrives at a solution to the relativistic strictures of the time, by formulating a series of analytical categories that would be indispensable for empirical explanation (in this way foiling the empiricists), yet general enough to subsume the more specific categories of the idealist tradition, thus avoiding their inherent relativism. This is the core of his analytical realism.

Thus Parsons is able to satisfy himself that the logical structure of theory and the identification of possible pathologies (residual categories) provide the basis for order in the production of knowledge. Theoretical structure and the convergence thesis have to be seen as discursive and theoretical effects which make it possible to represent the orderly development of the production of knowledge as opposed to both chaos and randomness. However, Parsons actually achieves much more. He also introduces the problem of social order, and the theoretical convergence that leads towards its solution, in terms of an opposition between social order and the random and chaotic fluctuation of ends. In this way, he opens up a metaphorical process where he can begin to enunciate the concept of social structure by borrowing signifieds from the signifier 'theoretical structure'.

SOCIAL ORDER AS THEORETICAL STRUCTURE

As is well known, Parsons argues that the residual categories of both the positivist and the idealist traditions converge upon the analytical elements found in his conception of the unit act. The components of the unit act are the actor, the ends, the situation and the normative element. By end, Parsons means:

> An end, then, in the analytical sense must be defined as the difference between the anticipated future state of affairs and that which it could have been predicted would ensue from the initial situation without the agency of the actor having intervened. (1949: 49; emphasis removed)

The situation, for Parsons, is made up of the conditions: those elements, 'over which the actor has no control' (Parsons, 1949: 44) and the means which he defines in the following way:

> Correspondingly, in an analytical sense, means will not refer to concrete things which are 'used' in the course of action, but only in those elements and aspects of them which are capable of, and in so far as they capable of, control by the actor in pursuit of his end. (1949: 49)

Finally, the last element in Parsons' unit act is the normative element:

> ... there is inherent in the conception of this unit, in its analytical uses, a certain mode of relationship between these elements. That is, in the choice of alternative means to the end, in so far as the situation allows alternatives, there is a 'normative orientation' of action. Within the area of control of the actor, the means employed cannot, in general, be conceived either as chosen at random or as

dependent exclusively on the conditions of action, but must in some sense be subject to the influence of an independent, determinate selective factor, a knowledge of which is necessary to the understanding of the concrete course of action. What is essential to the concept of action is that there should be a normative orientation, not that this should be of any particular type. (Parsons, 1949: 44–5)

From the above, it is clear that Parsons thinks of action as taking place in the context of conditions and means that limit the variability of possible outcomes; however, importantly, because there is a theoretical space opened for selection through the introduction of the actor, then action cannot be simply read off from the conditional elements. Parsons argues that this is precisely the problem with theories, operating in the positivist frame of reference, to the extent that they equate social action with either hereditary or environmental factors or both.

The positivistic frame of reference, argues Parsons, begins with the premise that social action is rational action. By this, what is meant is that

Action is rational in so far as it pursues ends possible within the conditions of the situation, and by the means which, among those available to the actor are intrinsically best adapted to the end for reasons understandable and verifiable by positive empirical science. (Parsons, 1949: 58)

However, one of the problems with this approach, Parsons maintains, is that there is no analysis of the ends themselves (Parsons, 1949: 60). Also, inasmuch as action deviates from this rational pattern, then error and ignorance are invoked and the objective reasons for this inadequacy are found in the reduction to hereditary and environmental elements (Parsons, 1949: 67). This eliminates the subjectivity of the actor because both the ends and the means are inscribed in the conditions.

If one attempts to reinsert the actor, within this positivistic framework, then one has to admit that actors play an active role in the pursuit of different ends. Consequently, conditions alone do not explain the actor's ends. If the actor is granted a choice, though, there is no way of explaining why ends should not vary randomly. Parsons refers to this outcome as the utilitarian dilemma:

Thus with respect to the status of ends, positivistic thought is caught in the 'utilitarian dilemma'. That is, either the active agency of the actor in the choice of ends is an independent factor in action, and the end element must be random, or the objectionable implication of the randomness of ends is denied, but then their independence disappears and they are assimilated to the conditions of the situation, that is to the elements analyzable in terms of nonsubjective categories, principally heredity and environment, in the analytical sense of biological theory. (Parsons, 1949: 64)

One of the ways in which the above-mentioned dilemma is overcome is through the invocation of 'metaphysical' elements such as the natural identity of interests (Parsons, 1949: 96). For Parsons this is no solution at all; positivism remains atomistic in so far as it does not consider action within the context of systems of actions where ends are coordinated by attachment to normative values.

Throughout Part II of *The Structure of Social Action* Parsons tries to show how within the structure of the theories of the three thinkers coming from positivist frameworks, Marshall, Pareto and Durkheim, there is a convergence towards this position. I do not want to present a detailed account of these arguments. Instead, I want to highlight that Parsons' solution to the problem of social order is a general one. It relies on the 'structure' of the unit act: the normative fixing of ends by systems of action that prevents both the randomness of ends and chaos. The primary meaning of structure, i.e. the relationship between the analytical elements: actor, conditions, ends and normative orientations, is achieved through its opposition to the random variability of ends which would make order impossible. It is worth noticing that the notion of structure associated with systems of action, upon which the unit act is premised, receives no systematic development. It is vaguely referred to as 'means–ends' chains or 'webs'.

Parsons' discussion of Weber, however, is of a different order. In Weber's writing, Parsons is looking for evidence in the structure of his theoretical arguments which would move him away from the relativist tendencies of the idealist tradition. First of all, Parsons (1949: 640–58) argues that by attempting to create typologies of social action (*zweckrational*, *wertrational*, affectual and traditional) Weber is implicitly trying to produce theoretical categories of sufficient analytical generality with a scope of analytical application beyond concrete historical individuals. However, Parsons argues that in contrasting *zweckrational* to *wertrational*, Weber is opposing two types of action that in reality are analytically indispensable in the context of giving an account of any action. That is to say, a concrete action combines both normative and means–ends rationality.

This leads Parsons to a discussion of the status of ideal types within Weber's theoretical framework, and the solution to the relativistic tendencies inherent in the structure of Weber's theoretical position. Parsons writes:

> An analytical law . . . states a uniform mode of relationship between the values of two or more analytical elements. It is thus likely to be applicable beyond the range of any ideal type. At the same time the kind of generalization about behaviour of the ideal-type units just discussed cannot usually be arrived at by the application of any one analytical law, but only by the application of the combination of several. (Parsons, 1949: 622)

Although Weber is attempting to sketch out a set of categories abstract enough to make comparisons possible across concrete individuals, he is not successful because his categories are not sufficiently abstract and general. Parsons goes on to write that the relativistic implications of this 'mosaic' can be avoided through the formulation of categories that are sufficiently general to encapsulate the lower order ideal types:

> The only means of breaking this mosaic of rigidity without recourse to scepticism is generalized theory which breaks down the particular element combinations in the ideal types, but by seeing in them a manifestation of common elements in constant modes of relationship with each other . . . (Parsons, 1949: 626)

Therefore, in this way once again, Parsons argues that he has presented sufficient evidence for his convergence theory. For my purposes, though, the thing to note is that the importance of incorporating Weber lies not merely in the centrality of normative values found in his work which is also fundamental to Parsons' enterprise in *The Structure of Social Action*. The convergence thesis rests not only on the relative weight of conditional and normative elements within a common frame of reference, but also on the emergence of a common formal theoretical architecture: hence the importance of attempting to demonstrate Weber's search for truly analytical categories via his discussion of ideal types.

His discussion of Weber provides the basis upon which cultural relativism can be avoided in the production of theoretical knowledge. In other words, Parsons incorporates Weber in his argument for the non-relativism of theoretical development by showing that the structure of Weber's theoretical argument is aimed at just such an avoidance of relativism. Surely the conjunction of these two features in *The Structure of Social Action* cannot be 'random': we find structure opposed to relativism, i.e. chaos and randomness in the context of theoretical structure as well as social structure.

To repeat, Parsons' conception of order in the realm of the production of knowledge allows him to demonstrate to his satisfaction that randomness (empiricism) and chaos (relativism) can be avoided. This is done by writing and thinking theory as being a product of a determinate logical structure. In this context, it is pertinent to realize that Parsons conceptualizes theory building along Weberian lines as 'meaning-oriented action' where truth is the ultimate value of the pursuit of scientific knowledge (Schwanenberg, 1990: 116). Theoretical action is itself conceived in terms of the unit act, where the normative values of logic, exhaustiveness, coherence and non-contradiction prevent science from wavering into explanatory chaos. In fact, the account of theoretical production is a paradigmatic case of the unit act.

Similarly, Parsons' conflation of positivist epistemology and utilitarian social theory is very telling. Parsons claims that utilitarianism reduces action to rational action, where rational action is understood as scientific action along the positivist line. Parsons maintains, however, that science cannot be understood as an unmediated encounter with facts. This homology metaphorically resonates with his argument that actors cannot be understood as being merely determined by conditions. In both cases, social action, as voluntaristic action, is seen as the actualization of the normative co-ordination of ends which makes knowledge and social order possible. It is the normative co-ordination of ends which is used to oppose randomness and chaos in both domains. In a certain sense, Parsons' paradigm of action, as with the positivist traditions that he examines, remains scientific action. Except that Parsons has replaced the positivist conception of science by that developed in analytical realism.

Thus the convergence thesis and his conceptualization of theory as a determinate logical structure is not merely accidental, it is constitutive of the notion of social order (structure) presented in *The Structure of Social Action*. What is more, this metaphorical relationship between theoretical structure and social structure is one that persists throughout Parsons' work.[10] Given Parsons' acceptance of the Weberian account of science as being informed by commitments to ultimate values, this initial enunciation of social structure through its semantic relationship with the notion of theoretical structure may go a long way towards explaining one of the tendencies that predisposed Parsons towards his normative–cultural bias. Similarly, understanding the strong metaphorical nature of Parsons' conception of structure in *The Structure of Social Action* also serves to frame questions regarding the early and later Parsons differently. One can argue that the distinction between an early voluntaristic and the later systems-oriented Parsons (action *v.* structure) is difficult to make.[11] If there is a sense in which *The Structure of Social Action* appears to value voluntarism over systemic determination, this is because the concept of social structure remains the effect of a *Modality B* metaphorical operation, without determinate signifieds in the realm of social theory.

SOCIAL EQUILIBRIUM: SIGNIFIED WANTED

In an essay entitled 'Positions and Prospects of Systematic theory in Sociology', we find Parsons' most explicit attempt, after the publication of *The Structure of Social Action*, to enunciate the concept of structure. This attempt arises from a metaphorical relationship between social structure and the concept of structure found in the field of thermodynamics:

> Structure is the 'static' aspect of the descriptive mode of treatment of a system. From a structural point of view a system is composed of 'units', of sub-systems which potentially exist independently, and their structural interrelations. Thus system in mechanics is 'made up' of particles as units. The structure of the system consists in the number of particles, their properties, such as mass, and their

interrelations, such as relative locations, velocities and directions of motion. (Parsons, 1964: 214)

Parsons claims that in mechanical systems, theoretical closure is achieved by the articulation of series of categories that are exhaustive of the system at a descriptive and analytical level. Thus, the consequences of variability in one category, its change of value, can be systematically related to the change of values in other categories. However, the translation of this semantic grid into the realm of social theory presents some important conceptual obstacles and discursive exigencies which Parsons himself acknowledges. For instance, dynamic processes can be dealt with in mechanical systems by use of numerically determined constants. Thus a system's variability can be analytically and descriptively dealt with by using these constants to solve systems of equations. Social systems, though, are not susceptible to the same level of numerical codification (1964: 216–17). As a result, Parsons suggests that structure, in social systems, can be taken to denote elements approaching constants.

Parsons is aware that theoretically and discursively this creates an important bias towards 'static structural categories' incapable of providing an account of the dynamic aspect of a system (1964: 217). To overcome this discursive exigency, he introduces the notion of function to provide a link between social structural constants and social systems:

> This link is supplied by the all-important concept of function. Its crucial role is to provide criteria of importance of dynamic factors and processes within the system. They are important in so far as they have functional significance to the system, and their specific importance is understood in terms of the analysis of specific functional relations between the parts of the system and between it and its environment. (1964: 217)

However, the introduction of the signifier 'function' serves to reconfigure the semantic space through which the concept of system is produced. This is clarified elsewhere when Parsons writes: 'Theoretically [discursively] the concept of equilibrium is a simple corollary to that of the system, of the interdependence of components as interrelated with each other' (Parsons, 1961: 337). Thus the theoretical visuality opened up by the metaphor of the system is characterized by the fact that the terms system, function and equilibrium are locked in a self-referential dynamic, a trinity in which each concept requires the supplement of the other two in order to be complete.

Parsons' exploration of the concept of the social system, a term which he was to later refer to as an 'indispensable master concept' (1977b: 101), was discursively overdetermined by his contact with the work of Whitehead, Schumpeter, Pareto,

Henderson and Cannon. For instance, Parsons maintained that the concept of the social system was the most enduring contribution which Pareto had made to sociology (Parsons, 1977b: 27). However, although Pareto's concept of the social system contained the possibility of creating a semantic space where it might be possible to think about the systematicity of social life, it also contained a fundamental and crippling discursive hence theoretical block. Pareto took equilibrium as axiomatic of social systems (Russet, 1966: 97), thus eliminating the need to attach the signifier equilibrium, hence also social system, to social theoretical signifieds. A social system was by definition an equilibrating and equilibrated process.[12]

Drawing on the work of Henderson, Parsons further elaborated this conceptual space by re-defining the specific form of equilibrium found in social systems in terms of homeostasis. The notion of homeostasis had been developed by Cannon in order to mark a distinction between open and closed systems.[13] The former, which referred to biological organisms, highlighted the fact that these systems were actively engaged in exchanges with their environment, and thus they needed mechanisms to regulate these exchanges in order to maintain their integrity (e.g. the processes by which the body adjusts to changes in environmental temperature). However, as Bailey (1984: 8–10) notes, Cannon's concept of homeostasis was not meant to translate the notion of equilibrium from closed systems into open systems. Closed systems do not receive energy from their environment. Strictly speaking, equilibrium in a closed system does not signify maximum integration, in fact it denotes a system with maximum entropy, a state of complete randomness and chaos.[14] The opposite of what Parsons wanted his concept of equilibrium to connote. Bailey suggests that it was probably Henderson's work which introduced the semantic bias towards equating equilibrium and homeostasis:

> ... he used the closed system model in a study of blood, and apparently simply carried the closed system notion over to social groups where it was inappropriate. That is, the conception of the system that Henderson uses is clearly open as he speaks of disturbances from without the system, but he retains the concept of equilibrium, which is only applicable to closed systems. (Bailey, 1984: 9)

Nonetheless, once the semantic equivalence between homeostasis and equilibrium was established it became possible to see homeostasis as a special case of the general notion of equilibrium (Parsons, 1961: 339). The semantic advantage associated with this equivalence was that it overcame the static bias associated with the notion of structure in mechanical systems. The metaphor of homeostasis connoted regular and orderly dynamic processes through which system integration was produced. In this sense they could be seen as functional for the system as whole.

Within this semantic grid, Parsons proceeded to produce a definition of the specificity of social systems and their constitutive structures:

> A structure is a set of relatively stable patterned relationships of units. Since the unit of the social system is the actor, social structure is a patterned system of social relationships of actors. It is a distinctive feature of the structure of systems of social action, however, that in most relationships the actor does not participate as a total entity, but only by virtue of a given differentiated 'sector' of his total action. Such a sector, which is the unit of the system of social relationships, has come predominantly to be called a 'role'. Hence ... social structure is a system of patterned relationships of actors in their capacity as playing roles relative to one another. Role is the concept which links the subsystem of the actor as 'psychological' behaving entity to the distinctively social structure. (1964: 230)

In many ways, this effect of social structure opens up a theoretical visuality, a way of representing social systems through theoretical language, which is extremely powerful. By defining the role as the unit of the social system it creates the possibility of addressing social processes at a *sui generis* level, in abstraction from actual interaction. Thus the social system can be represented as something more than the arithmetic sum of its individuals. Moreover, it also provides a way of theoretically representing the relationship between individuals through the mediation of the roles which they internalize, and between an individual as a psychological-behaving entity and the social system. Rather ironically, though, it does not actually provide us with an understanding of the way in which roles themselves are structured.

We saw, above, that Parsons likens structure to the set of relationships that inhere between the units of a system and their properties. However, Parsons maintains, that 'in mechanics the structure of the system does not enter in as a distinct theoretical element ... Structure does not refer to an ontological stability ...' (1964: 217). Structure as such does not act; it describes the relationship between acting units: actors guided by roles. Thus in the quotation 'role' is not synonymous with 'social structure'. Rather social structure is the set of systemic relationships which relate the different roles, which 'structure' them.

For example, in a given society we find a number of roles, which, if they are internalized by actors, produce the effect of patterned interaction. Thus a student and teacher are guided in their interaction by drawing on the roles associated with each of these statuses. Any society will contain a plurality of such roles, and inasmuch as individuals internalize these roles and are guided by them they will be able to interact and communicate relatively smoothly. Still, there is another dimension to the social system which the concept of social structure is trying to grasp. These roles have to be aligned in such a way that the expectations which they contain are compatible with one another. That is to say, it is not only the case that the student and teacher have to be guided by their respective roles; the roles themselves have to be compatible both in the context of actual interactions but also in the context of the system as a whole. The question that Parsons' definition of social structure leaves unanswered is precisely what is happening on this level, what are the social systemic mechanisms that integrate roles so that they can be mutually compatible?

The semantic space inaugurated by the mechanical systems metaphor produces the possibility and the necessity of posing and answering such a question. In a mechanical system the relationship (the structure) between the units (the particles) can be represented mathematically through the introduction of constants that makes it possible to balance the equation through which the system is represented. However, in the metaphorical process by which the concepts of the mechanical system are translated into the social system this question is not answered. In fact, it is displaced. This displacement is discursively produced by the connotative resonance established between the significatory chain which links the signifiers system, equilibrium, homeostasis and function to the signifieds denoted by the terms integration and order. That is to say, implicit in the concept of the system as it is produced through Parsons' writing is that the discursive and theoretical act of naming something a system is to represent that entity as something with an orderly structure, thus the basis of the orderliness need not be addressed. This enunciation of system and structure, however, is clearly a *Modality B* metaphorical process. It remains theoretically and conceptually plausible only if we agree to read the concepts system and structure as connoting order and equilibrium.

As a result the only other question that can be asked within this semantic space is the extent to which roles are internalized by a sufficient number of actors. If they are, then these roles can be seen as institutionalized, thus guaranteeing the stability of the system: '... institutionalized patterns do in fact mobilize a combination of forces in support of their maintenance which is of primary significance in the total equilibrium of a social system' (Parsons, 1964: 239).[15] But, to the extent that Parsons' writing remains embedded in the mechanical systems metaphor, then there is a question that can be displaced but not entirely erased from his writing: what social systemic mechanisms (structures) align social roles in such a way that they are compatible or functional? In other words, there is a discursively generated absence that remains unfilled. This, as we shall see in the remaining sections, is made clear by Parsons' own theoretical practice that gravitates towards attempting to pose and answer this very question.

INTERNALIZING ROLES OR SOCIAL STRUCTURES?

In *The Social System*, Parsons continues to work on the concept of social structure by locating its enunciation in the semantic space provided by the mechanical system metaphor.[16] He specifies the 'particles' of the social system as status–role[17] units, and argues these are analogous to 'the particle in mechanics, not to mass or velocity'

(Parsons, 1991: 25). This points to the fact that the concept of social structure cannot be confused with that of the role, nor status–role units; social structure con- notes those systemic relationships that serve to articulate and co-ordinate the moti- vations and expectations crystallized in role systems. Thus the question of the status of the mechanisms and the processes through which they function to align status– role units once again erupts as the discursive effect of using the semantic potential of mechanical systems in order to describe the specificity of social structure as some form of *sui generis* social organization.

In both *The Social System* and *Towards a Theory of General Action* Parsons deploys a number of discursive strategies that deal with this question. However, the question does not receive an adequate answer; instead it becomes discursively displaced. Said differently, the question of the specificity of equilibrium at a systems level is rewrit- ten as the question of 'interactional equilibrium'. This leaves the signifier (term) equilibrium at the systems level unattached to domain specific signified (meanings). It exists and persists as a *Modality B* metaphor connoting integration and order. This in turn acts as a discursive obstacle towards the theoretical development of a con- cept of social structure which it nonetheless presupposes. Before I discuss how this effect is produced, it is necessary to examine the wider argument that Parsons devel- ops in *The Social System*.

Parsons locates the social system between both the cultural[18] and the personality systems.[19] In developing the nature of their articulation he allows for their relative autonomy. In this sense he avoids two possible conflationary tendencies: psycho- logical reductionism and cultural determinism. In order to link the cultural system with the personality system via the social system, Parsons deploys the notion of common values that are rooted in the pattern–maintenance capacity of the cultural system. This is the cultural system's input into the social system. However, if the notion of common values is going to have any analytical purchase *vis-à-vis* the personality system it has to be conceptualized more concretely in terms of value- orientations (Parsons, 1991: 12).

Thus, rather than conceptualizing common values as some entity external to individuals that occasionally crystallize in the form of laws and other cultural arte- facts, Parsons invokes Freudian psychoanalysis to argue that common values are internalized as value-orientations through socialization. Notwithstanding this, Parsons maintains that the structure of the need dispositions in the personality system achieve a certain level of independence. There is no question of creating a relation of symmetry between the personality and the social system. It is precisely because of this under-determination of the structure of the personality by the social system that Parsons devotes a chapter to the analysis of deviance (Parsons, 1991: Chapter 7). Furthermore, he makes it clear that the commitment to the value- orientations is not to be taken as absolute, hence creating a site of possible friction (Parsons, 1991: 28).

Equally, the lack of symmetry between the cultural system and the social system is a source of tension between the two. Nonetheless, if a social system is going to exist and preserve its boundaries, the amount of variation among the systems has to be understood as occurring within certain parameters beyond which the social system would cease to exist. This is ultimately provided by the pattern–maintenance capacity of the cultural system (Parsons, 1991: 27).

Although the role–status bundle is the unit of analysis in the social system, the concept of role has an important semantic and theoretical limitation. It is not sufficiently abstract. It cannot be deployed to distinguish roles that may be similar in some ways, and yet differ in others. For instance, it cannot be used to distinguish the similarities and differences that exist between the professional role of the doctor and the entrepreneurial role of the businesswoman.[20] In *The Social System*, Parsons introduces the pattern-variables to overcome this limitation. In effect, they provide a way of analytically disassembling particular roles into a series of more basic constituent elements.[21]

The pattern-variables refer to the different value choices that any actor has to make in an interactional situation; consequently, they are painstakingly derived by examining the context of actions both from the subjective perspective of the actor as an agent and from the perspective of the actor and his action as an object for other actors. They refer respectively to an actor's value-orientation, and to the values that underpin the social relation which he or she establishes with another actor. For Parsons, the pattern-variables include all the 'action dilemmas' or choices that any actor faces in an interactional situation. Their scope is presented as universal in nature: they can be used to articulate any conceivable role.

The first pattern-variable set, or choice between two value-orientations, is that between *Affectivity* versus *Affective Neutrality*. This refers to the extent to which an actor chooses to invest his or her action with emotional content or maintains a detached impersonal stance (the value-orientation towards a family member versus the value-orientation towards a client). The second set, *Self-Orientation* versus *Collective-Orientation*, refers to whether the goals pursued by the actor are motivated by an orientation towards self-interest or the interest of a particular collectivity (the value orientation of the businesswoman who pursues her own self-interest versus the value orientation of the citizen who would be expected to pursue the interest of the collectivity). The third set, *Universalism* versus *Particularism* refers to whether judgements of the worth of the interactional partner are guided by criteria which are general and potentially applicable to all actors of the same class (all students, all employees, etc.) or by a specific concrete relationship (the teacher who treats all students by the same standard versus the relationship of a parent with his or her child). The fourth set is *Achievement* versus *Ascription*. It refers to whether the interactional partner is judged as a result of what she has achieved, in terms of her performance in some delimited sphere, or in terms of some other quality (does a teacher judge a student by her academic performance or by the fact that she is a woman?). Finally, the last dilemma of action is represented by the *Specificity* versus *Diffuseness* set. Does the actor engage with a limited dimension of his interactional partner or with him or her as a totality (a doctor's interaction with her patient is limited to the patient as an ill person whereas a lover engages with his or her partner in a multitude of diffuse ways)?

A specific role will be defined in terms of the clustering of the selections between each of the choices in the action dilemma. For instance the role of a teacher would be guided by *Affective–eutrality*, *Collective–Orientation*, *Universalism*, *Achievement* and *Specificity*; whereas the role of the parent would be guided by *Affectivity*, *Self-Orientation*, *Particularism*, *Ascription* and *Diffuseness*. Thus inasmuch as the pattern-variables provide the structural elements with which any role can be described it would seem that they might represent the analogues of physical relationships found in mechanical systems. They are not ontological entities; they are structuring principles that describe the relationship between acting units. And it is precisely the permutations which they allow which give rise to structurally described social systems:

> We are therefore justified in taking the possibilities of variation in fundamental value orientations, i.e., in pattern-variable combinations, as a point of departure for developing a provisional classification of generalized types of social systems in structural terms. (Parsons, 1991: 153)

Now it is possible to investigate the adequacy and the theoretical usefulness of the pattern-variables along a number of dimensions: for instance, in terms of the rigour of their derivation, their alleged exhaustiveness, and the stability of their meanings.[22] One might also query whether the modality of attachment with an individual's need dispositions is sufficient to provide an account of the relationship between the psychological and the social domain.[23] Moreover, it is possible to dispute the narrowness with which the articulation of the cultural and social system is produced.[24] However, I want to focus on the way the pattern-variables serve to displace discursively the question of the co-ordination of roles at the systems level and as such do not provide a semantic grid where it is possible to elaborate signifieds for the signifier social structure at the level of the social system.

In *The Social System*, Parsons frames the interactional situation in which the pattern-variables operate via the notion of the 'double contingency'. This notion tries to grasp the fact that a successful interaction requires a mutuality of evaluations, expectations and alignments of need dispositions between ego and alter (the two actors found in the interactional situation): viz., they need to communicate effectively. If anywhere in the discursive fabric of *The Social System* one is to find a *Modality A* signified for 'equilibrium' it is precisely in the semantic space where Parsons develops the concepts necessary to think how communication makes interactional order possible. Parsons describes successful role-guided interaction as a '... stabilized or equilibrated interaction process ...' (Parsons, 1991: 205). Equilibrium or order signifies that ego and alter mutually recognize each other as actors who are guided by role–status relationships and as a result act accordingly, leading to a successful communicative event.[25] Thus, on the one hand the solution to the problem of double contingency requires a theory of the mechanisms through which the internalization of status–role complexes takes place. Parsons uses a variety of psychoanalytical categories for this purpose: reinforcement–extinction, inhibition, substitution, imitation and identification (Parsons, 1991: 209). However, the concept of order at the interactional level also presupposes concepts through which the status–role complexes are aligned such that their instantiation facilitates effective communication, a concept of structure as the relationship between roles. Said differently, equilibrium in interaction is predicated on a prior and more overarching structural equilibrium at the level of the system, because it is the latter combined with adequate socialization which allows the obstacle of the double contingency – the possibility of communication breakdown – to be overcome. To a large extent, *The Social System* contains an impressive and extremely productive development of the unit act framework which Parsons had introduced in *The Structure of Social Action*. The pattern-variables scheme elaborates on the rudimentary notion of interactional structure which Parsons had achieved via the metaphorical relationship between order in the production of knowledge and order in social interaction.

At the level of the system, however, equilibrium remains an assumption which is inextricably linked to the *Modality B* metaphorical operation through which the notion of the system is enunciated, as is clear in an excerpt taken from a contemporaneous text:

> The most general and fundamental property of a system is the interdependence of parts or variables. Interdependence consists in the existence of determinate relationships among the parts or variables as contrasted with randomness of variability. In other words, interdependence is order in the relationship among the components which enter into a system. This order must have a tendency to self-maintenance, which is very generally expressed in the concept of equilibrium. (Parsons and Shils, 1951: 107)

Self-maintenance in the quotation not only denotes successful interaction; it also connotes the systemic alignment of status–role complexes upon which successful interaction is premised. Yet the only candidate we have to structure and align status–role complexes is a notion of structure which is tied to the double contingency of interaction.

In essence what is taking place discursively, hence also theoretically, is that the problem of order at a systemic level is being displaced on to, or rewritten as, the problem of the double contingency of interaction.[26] The deployment of the concept of the system produces, or connotes, the effect of order via the significatory chain that links system, function and equilibrium. This effect, at a certain level, displaces the need to enquire into the origin of order. Its origin is found inextricably tied to its family name: the system. Thus there is no room within this discursive terrain to try to think the specificity of social structure at the level of the system.[27] Because the signifier 'equilibrium' is also used to denote order at the interactional level, it provides a semantic conduit or discursive suture through which it can also connote order at the systems level.[28]

This introduces a number of discursive exigencies which Parsons' texts do not adequately resolve. For instance, the effect of interactional order is produced by the way an actor's behaviour is guided through roles that are structured by pattern-variables. The pattern-variables, however, refer to how individuals orientate themselves towards and interpret social situations. It is not clear how these subjective orientations can be translated into the functional needs at the level of the system. The social system has to be something more than the mere accumulation of a plurality of interactions, otherwise the 'structure' of the system would be the same thing as the 'structure' of the interaction between ego and alter.

The failure of Parsons' writing to generate a concept of social structure at the level of the system produces yet another effect. Given that successful interaction is used to represent discursively the problem of order at the level of the system, his writing establishes a connotative resonance between social interaction and system maintenance. This creates a discursive tendency towards the creation of an identity between structuring principle and actually existing empirical structures. Nowhere is this clearer than when he relates it to the US case: the social structure of a society whose major structuring principle is the universalistic–achievement pattern (the US) must have a concrete social structure that embodies said principle.[29] This has to be the case because Parsons' theoretical visuality lacks the resources with which to produce theoretically specified concepts of *sui generis* mechanisms which are not reducible to interaction. Consequently, there has to be an identity between empirical clusters of structure and pattern-variables (structural elements of the double contingency of interaction).

Since Parsons' theory of socialization links the social system to the personality system by the internalization of value-orientations towards integrated ends, it also demands a correspondence between the structuring principle and concrete empirical clusterings in a society. It is not discursively possible to represent those elements structuring interaction as being at odds with the elements that structure the social system.[30]

I believe that the argument developed thus far might contribute to putting a slightly different spin on the question of whether Parsons represents actors as being cultural 'dopes' or 'dupes'; as a result of the discursive strategies that Parsons deploys actors are not only not dopes, but are actually expected to be inordinately knowledgeable and powerful. Within the semantic grid that his system's visuality inaugurates they have the task of both overcoming the problems of the double contingency of interaction as well as that of systems maintenance simultaneously. Consequently, Parsons' actors internalize both roles and structuring principles.

I also hope that it demonstrates that even for a self-avowed theorist of social systems, success in enunciating the specificity of social structure at the level of the system is in large part dependent on the metaphors and discursive strategies through which the theoretical effect of the system is produced in writing. There is no originary ontological position that can be achieved outside of writing; the actual form in which the ontological position is written inaugurates the theoretical possibilities and not vice versa.

THE FOUR-FUNCTION PARADIGM: GUIDING THE SYSTEM?

The above, however, does not exhaust the different discursive strategies which Parsons deployed in the attempt to attach the signifier social structure to an adequate signified, nor the enunciation of specific social systemic mechanisms of equilibrium. In *Working Papers in the Theory of Action*, the mechanical system metaphor is further developed in relation to a small-group paradigm. Equilibrium, at the level of interaction, is expanded beyond the double contingency between ego and alter: it becomes the resultant of the meeting of the functional exigencies which develop when a small group, under experimental conditions, is asked to solve certain task-oriented problems (Parsons *et al.*, 1953)

As a result of the convergence with Bales' work, Parsons, and his colleagues, were to produce the, now famous, four systems functional exigencies of Adaptation, Goal-attainment, Integration and Latency (Parsons *et al.*, 1953, 180–9). What is more, it was claimed that these functional exigencies could be generalized to all systems and subsystems of action across the micro–macro divide (Parsons *et al.*, 1953: 170–71).

That these functional exigencies are being written through a semantic grid where the signifier equilibrium connotes order is demonstrated by the assumption of system-integration:

> We interpret this to mean that ... there is an imperative placed on systems of action which requires that pattern-elements in the organization of their component should be compatible with each other maintaining the boundaries of the system *vis-à-vis* its external situation. (Parsons *et al.*, 1953: 164–5)

In this sense the equilibrium of the social system remains metaphorically secured through a connotative resonance. It is of interest that the effect of equilibrium that is embedded in this framework, the generation of solutions by group members to specific task-oriented problems, is still couched in terms of successfully overcoming the double contingencies which arise between dyads of alters and egos within the group. Just as in *The Social System*, it assumes a structural functional systemic coordination and alignment whose nature remains unspecified because it secured through a *Modality B* metaphor.

Now it is true that in *Working Papers in the Theory of Action*, unlike in *The Social System*, Parsons and his colleagues define each of the functions in terms of permutations of the pattern-variable schema, in an attempt to translate theoretically the pattern-variables schema to the level of the social system. However, as Dubin (1960) in an influential article pointed out, this attempt was unsuccessful. It produced two different models of society: one was characterized by the perspective of the actor looking out to the system (interactional order), whereas the second was defined in terms of the system (systemic structure) 'looking' down on the actor. In response to this critique, Parsons explicitly admits that 'An action system, however, is not characterized solely by the actor's orientations and the modalities of objects significant to the actor . . .' (1960: 468). In other words the discursive apparatus which produces the effect of order at a systemic level contains a semantic and theoretical absence which the pattern-variables (the structure of interactional order) cannot fill.

The disparity between the two effects of structure, order at the interactional level and order as the product of functional systemic integration, can also be detected in the impressive refinement of the four-function paradigm developed by Parsons and Smelser in *Economy and Society*. Although the economy is presented as the adaptive subsystem of the social system, the economic subsystem can in turn be seen as a social system itself describable by four-functional subsystems.[31] Incorporating the categories of the factors of production from economics (capital, labour and land), and adding a fourth (entrepreneurship), Parsons and Smelser set up boundary interchanges between the subsystems of the economy, itself conceived as a social system along functional lines (Parsons and Smelser, 1957: 24–9). Parsons and Smelser stress that these functional subsystems and the double interchanges that take place across their boundaries are not to be confused with specific concrete organizations (Parsons and Smelser, 1957: 15).

Parsons and Smelser's writing is attempting to enunciate a level of systematicity not reducible to individual interaction: i.e. *sui generis* social systemic mechanisms. Yet they are not entirely successful. If we take the social system as the frame of reference, where the economy is the adaptive subsystem, then it is the polity which is responsible for goal attainment. Now this implies that it is possible to think of the polity as capable of setting the Goal-states of the social system (Parsons and Smelser, 1957: 17). This goal-setting capacity is not reducible to any concrete formal organization such as political parties, government cabinet offices, etc. On close examination, as Savage has persuasively argued, the goal-setting process is conceived in terms of entities capable of 'desire', 'gratification' and 'recognition' (1981: 190–1).[32] Consequently the concepts that refer to mechanisms responsible for social goal setting are the product of *Modality B* metaphors; they establish a semantic equivalence between the exigencies of systemic and interactional order. This effect is further reinforced through the society as an economy metaphor. The social system is broadly conceived as an economic system, where 'interchanges' take place between subsystems (i.e. metaphorical economic agents). *Economy and Society* is underpinned by the assumption that social systems are capable of self-steering and self-regulation; however, this effect is achieved through a theoretical visuality in which subsystems connote human attributes: 'Each subsystem and system must have a *consciousness*, a means by which systemic needs, situational objects and value-patterns can be sifted and arranged in a particular order or pattern. Functional subsystems are therefore conceived as *human subjects*' (Savage, 1981: 191).

GENERALIZED MEDIA, CYBERNETICS AND GENES AS SOCIAL STRUCTURE?

That Parsons continued to search for theoretical enunciations of *sui generis* functional mechanisms at the level of the social system, and systems of action in general, and the discursive basis on which to anchor them, is well documented by the attempt to sever the earlier semantic tie between structure and function. This led him to write that the concept of function was operating at a higher level of abstraction than that of structure (Parsons, 1977b: 104). Among other things, this justifies my claim that Parsons' effect of social structure derived from the unit act is only a structure of interaction which in itself is not capable of producing the theoretical effect of order or equilibrium at the level of the system. The development of the generalized media of interchange, the cybernetic hierarchy and the evolutionary paradigm, can be seen as the deployment of so many metaphorical strategies in order to align his theoretical framework so as to make possible the enunciation of a *sui generis* level of systemic organization.

The concept of the generalized media of communication initially arises from Parsons and Smelser's metaphorical development of society as a social system, modelled on the economy as represented by mainstream economics. If the social system is seen as a market, then something needs to circulate; analogues for money are required. Money is the circulating medium for the economy, power for the political subsystem, influence for the integrative subsystem (societal community) and value commitments for the pattern maintenance subsystem. Parsons' development of the concept of media of communication is provocative and insight-ful.[33] However, even within this semantic space it was not possible to detach rig-orously function from social structure, where the latter is the structure of the interactional order. As Cartwright and Warner argue,

> Although the media analogy subsumes many suggestive and fruitful observa-tions, it also raises many questions and puzzles not least of which is the fact that when examined carefully, most of Parsons' substantive arguments rely on struc-tural conditions rather than media properties, for their basic explanatory vari-ables. (1976: 656)[34]

Some of the reasons for this can be illustrated by looking at the way in which Par-sons' writing incorporated the semantic potential associated with the cybernetic hierarchy and evolutionary theory.

Cybernetic theory is broadly associated with the work of Weiner (1954; 1961) and Deutsch (1951).[35] Essentially, cybernetics is concerned with explaining how systems can be conceptualized as being capable of self-steering as well as self-monitoring. These imply the capacity of controlling the inputs which a system receives from its environment and the way in which these effects will be distributed throughout the system's internal environments. This allows the system to deal internally with changes in the environment. The inputs and its effects are concep-tualized in terms of feedback loops. But also central to the notion of cybernetics is the distinction between energy and information. This depends on the difference between power engineering and information engineering. The former is concerned with the processes through which 'amounts of electricity' are transferred while the latter deals with the transmission of information through the use of codes (e.g. binary). It is not actual events which are transferred, but codes or 'patterned rela-tionships between events' (Deutsch, 1951: 241).

The semantic potential of the concepts of information theory spliced with those derived from the notion of cybernetic hierarchies allows control over lower-order 'energetic' processes to be understood in terms of codes, which are high in informational content. The convergence with Parsons' hierarchical four-function paradigm is striking. Parsons' general framework, as developed in the later evolu-tionary work, is written through a hierarchy with the Cultural System at the summit (high in information), and the behavioural organism at the foot of the hier-archy (high in energy). Contemporaneously, Parsons developed a keen interest in the structuralisms of Piaget, Chomsky, Lévi-Strauss, Jakobson and Halle.

As Rossi has pointed out, however, the alleged convergence with cybernetic theory, as well as with these structuralists, hinges on the development of a con-cept of cultural code compatible with the conceptual networks of these fields (1983: 181–207). Rossi writes,

The notion of code . . . implies a set of rules by which elementary units combine and recombine to constitute larger units. Consequently, the concepts of information and code of information refer directly not to macromolecular and observable phenomena, but to the set of relations among their elemental constitutive units. The emphasis on relationships among terms rather than on the terms themselves is fundamental to the notion of information, code, and grammar as used by biologists, cyberneticians, structural linguists and semiotic structuralists (1983: 187–8).

A close examination of the notions of code, communication and symbol which are found in Parsons' writing, reveals that they are in fact 'pre-structural'; viz., their fundamental units are the already constituted subjective meanings found in the interactional situation: 'events' and not patterned relationships (Rossi, 1983: 191–5). Their orderly mediation of successful interaction points to the existence of codes which constitute them at the level of the system; however, these exist in Parsons' writing as a series of *Modality B* connotative resonances.

For instance, stimulated by his encounter with the biologist Alfred Emmerson, Parsons maintains that '. . . in the human action fields the symbol is analogous to the gene in the organic field' (Parsons, 1977b: 113). Elsewhere, in a footnote, he draws a parallel between the process of social institutionalization and natural selection in the evolutionary paradigm:

We consider the process of institutionalization . . . to be the action-system equivalent of natural selection as that concept has come to be an integral part of biological theory, that is, the theory of the nature and functioning of organic systems. This general action system, and particularly its cultural component, we conceive to be analogous to the genetic constitution of species and the primary source of genetic variation. As such, the cultural system promulgates patterns of what at the value level may be characterized as desirable modes of action. (Parsons, 1977b: 230)

It is through the maintenance of a *Modality B* metaphorical relationship between 'gene' and 'symbol', 'institutionalization' and 'natural selection', that the effect of order is produced at the level of the system. The semantic potential introduced by the term code and its associated semantic fields (e.g. structuralism, biology, cybernetics) did not produce, in Parsons' writing, concepts capable of signifying the operation of the social system at a *sui generis* level. To the extent that the term code was also associated with the already constituted meanings of acting subjects, it relocated the problem of order from the systems level to the interactional level. Once again, it was not that Parsons' writing demanded too little from his actors, but far too much.

CONCLUSION

Parsons' rigorous and fascinating attempt to produce a sui generis concept of social structure through the medium of theoretical language failed on a number of fundamental levels and yet on others it was extraordinarily productive. To the extent that it opened up a rigorous systems visuality, it introduced a number of concepts and theoretical strategies whose semantic and theoretical potential have yet to be exhausted. [36] However, even Parsons' failures are instructive. His work vividly illustrates that the ontological assertion of the existence of social structure does not eliminate the discursive and theoretical exigencies involved in making it a social theoretical sign. In fact, the very possibility of such an ontological assertion is predicated on the simultaneous deployment of writing strategies which inaugurate theoretical visualities, but do so by setting discursive and semantic prices. Parsons' writings also reveal the danger inherent in the seduction of logic and coherence when these are conceptualized as transparent operators for the organization of theoretical statements. It is true that Parsons' writing achieves an effect of systematicity and rigour that was unparalleled by his contemporaries and by subsequent sociologists; however, this effect was, in part, achieved by understanding language as an unproblematic carrier of thought. Parsons' writing produces the effect that it was thought and not written.

Nonetheless, the receptivity towards metaphorical relationships found in Parsons' writing brings to the fore, like the work of no other author in this book, the necessary embeddedness of notions of social complexity in metaphorical relationships with diverse semantic and phenomenological domains. In my reading of Parsons' writing, there is a heterogeneous and multi-layered continuity which centres around the attempt to discursively ground a conception of the social at the *sui generis* level. In this sense his contribution to sociology can be seen as a continuation of Durkheim's injunction to explain social facts in terms of social facts. His theoretical texts prepared the ground for a theoretical visuality which might very well lay the conceptual foundations for a theoretical system capable of signifying the systematicity of the social world.[37]

CHAPTER 5

Althusser's Structure: the 'Epistemological Obstacle' of Complexity

INTRODUCTION

Althusser's ambitious intellectual project included not only the attempt to constitute an adequate Marxist philosophy but also the salvaging of historical materialism
as a non-economistic, non-humanist and non-historicist science (Elliot, 1987: 325).
The project rested on his ability to produce discursively the theoretical effect of the
social formation as a complex articulation of relatively autonomous instances
describable in terms of a non-linear and non-teleological form of causality: structural causality. It is fitting to conclude with Althusser as the last case study for his
work reveals, poignantly and eloquently, the difficulty of translating the effect of
social complexity into a theoretically rigorous system of concepts.

Most now accept that Althusser failed.[1] He recognized this himself in his successive, though not necessarily fruitful retreats. Even so, his work has had a profound
influence in the field of Marxist and neo-Marxist social theory more generally
(Elliot, 1987: 341). This is the case even though Althusser's reading of the Marxist
tradition is often rather superficial.[2] Moreover it is a reading made possible by a
number of non-Marxist elements: French Historical Epistemology, Lacanian psychoanalysis and Spinozian philosophy.[3] Thus, although Althusser saw himself as a
Marxist theoretician,[4] his writing is heavily textured by discursive elements from
domains outside the Marxist tradition.

Perhaps the most common critique levelled at Althusser's work by Marxist theorists is his facile dismissal of a rich and highly nuanced body of Marxist work
under the tricolour banner of anti-humanism, anti-historicism and anti-teleology.
I would argue that the waving of this banner should not be specifically understood
on the basis of the scholarly claims made about the body of work that it purports to
address. Instead it should be seen as a discursive strategy that opens up a semantic
and theoretical space through which Althusser's writing produces the effect of
the complexly structured social formation in writing. Though the terms he rejects

are indeed humanism, historicism and teleology these do not really refer to the traditions which Althusser dismisses, instead they emerge as a result of a basic opposition that he establishes in his writing between simplicity, linearity and reduction, and complexity, non-linearity and structural causality respectively.

In fact, if there is one key discursive organizing effect to which all others can be plausibly connected in Althusser's key texts *For Marx* and *Reading Capital*,[5] it is a fundamental opposition between a simplistic (or reductionist) account of the social formation and the notion of a complexly structured whole. However, this opposition does not codify in theoretical language a prior ontological commitment that exists in the realm of pure thought. It is the product of determinate discursive and metaphorical strategies that make the notion of complexity enunciable as an ontological theme in the first place. The concept of structure is not derived unproblematically from his most general ontological statements: it requires practical language-based work. It is this dimension of Althusser's writing which I shall trace below. In doing so, I hope to show that paradoxically the metaphorical strategies which Althusser deploys both allow him to pose the question of social complexity while simultaneously erecting 'an epistemological obstacle' to a plausible answer.

Althusser's writing is worthy of attention because the perceived failure of his project has been largely read in terms of his over-emphasizing the structural dimension (determination?) at the expense of agency (freedom?). Consequently reaction to his writing, as with Parsons', has played a pivotal role in the theoretical institutionalization of the economy of scale associated with the structure–agency problematic. In this chapter, as in previous chapters, I want to argue for the necessity of understanding some of the problems associated with Althusser's enunciation of the concept of structure in terms of the metaphorical and discursive strategies that produce the effect of structure in his writing. In the next section, I will initiate this process by exploring the links between Althusser's writing and the work of the French Historical Epistemology tradition.

BORROWING AND 'BORROWING' FROM HISTORICAL EPISTEMOLOGY

The centrality of French Historical Epistemology for the development of Althusser's own epistemological position is well known.[6] However, I want to show that Althusser's borrowing from Historical Epistemology cannot be understood exclusively in terms of how it constitutes his epistemological position; it is, also, discursively constitutive of the ways in which Althusser can write questions about social complexity, consequently also social structure. I will briefly list these here and then develop the pertinent arguments more fully in subsequent sections.

Firstly, Althusser uses the semantic potential associated with the conceptual networks pertaining to the historical development of sciences as understood by the
French Historical Epistemology tradition in order to enunciate the historical development of social formations. In other words he establishes a metaphorical relationship between the development of scientific knowledge and the development of
social formations. Both are characterized by an uneven, discontinous and complex
historical unfolding. In doing so, he opens up a semantic space from which he is
able to represent social formations themselves as being constituted by a complex
organization of uneven and discontinous effects.

Secondly, and related to the first point, because Althusser draws so heavily on
concepts and strategies from the discursive domain of Historical Epistemology, the
effect of social structure which he produces through his writing is very closely
linked to the knowledge–ideology opposition. This leads Althusser's writing, as
I will detail below, to produce the effect of social structure, or social complexity, as
that which is necessarily misrecognized by agents through ideology.

In the secondary literature there is an inclination towards treating Althusser's
concepts of (1) structure, (2) science/ideology and (3) subjective ideology (interpel-
lation) as distinct semantic fields which can be dealt with individually. I am going to
argue that there is much to be gained by trying to gauge the 'effectivity', or mode of
articulation, which exists between these relatively autonomous instances in his
theory.[7] Before doing so, I want to examine the most obvious ways in which
Althusser borrows from Historical Epistemology.

In his 'Introduction to Georges Canguilhem', in *On the Normal and the Pathological*, Foucault wrote: '. . . take away Canguilhem and you will no longer understand
much about Althusser, Althusserianism and a whole series of discussions which
have taken place among French Marxists . . .' (1978: ix). Foucault goes on to
argue that one can identify two intellectual streams in French post-World War II
thought: one, the existential philosophy associated with Sartre and Merleau-Ponty,
the other the Historical Epistemology associated with Cavaillés, Koyré, Bachelard
and Canguilhem.[8] Tiles has argued that the first stream begins with the subject in
order to ask questions about knowledge and social reality, whereas the second
inverts this order by focusing on the 'formations and deformations of knowledge'
in order to speak of the subject (1987: 142–3). Now, Althusser's acknowledge-
ment of this tradition can be found scattered throughout his work.[9] However, he
does not anywhere, as far as I know, systematically spell out the nature and extent
of this debt.

There are at least three obvious debts which can be highlighted. First there is
Althusser's concern with theoretical language, and the way in which concepts are
understood as being embedded in networks of other concepts within determinable
structures which he calls a problematic. It is the structure of the problematic which
assigns meanings to concepts. For instance, he deploys this argument in order to

argue for the break between Marx and Feuerbach (Althusser, 1969: 46–7) and later the break between Marx and Hegel (Althusser, 1969: 93). By this he means to demonstrate that although the same terms (signifiers) appear throughout Marx's texts, they have radically different meanings (signifieds).[10]

Although Althusser calls a reading that sought to discover the problematic in which concepts were operating a symptomatic reading, in clear reference to Freud,[11] the debt is more clearly one to Bachelard and Canguilhem. As Lecourt points out:

> For Gaston Bachelard it is incumbent on the epistemologist to get to the secret of the sciences ... starting from a principle which was to remain one of the corner-stones of his philosophy: a word is not a concept; which implies the definition of the concept by its function in a system of inter-conceptual relations. (Lecourt, 1975: 39)

Bachelard's concept of 'epistemological value' and Canguilhem's interest in the 'history of concepts' immediately come to mind. Both authors stress that the mere empirical appearance of the same words (signifiers) in different discursive fields is no guarantee that they have the same meaning (signified). Bachelard makes this point with respect to the signifier space and its Euclidean and non-Euclidean signifieds in *L'Expérience de l'Espace dans la Physique Contemporaine*, and Canguilhem with respect to the concept of reflex in *La formation du Concept du Réflexe aux XVIIe et XVIIIe siècles*.

The second debt is intimately connected with the first. It is the notion of the epistemological break or the 'coupure'. For Bachelard it has a dual sense. On the one hand it represents the break of scientific experience from commonsense everyday experience (i.e. epistemological obstacles); for instance, our everyday experience of a table is different from how a table is conceptualized at the atomic level by physicists. The latter demands a break with the former.[12] On the other hand, it represents breaks within science as a result of new developments: for instance thermodynamics involved a substantial break with the worldview of Newtonian physics.[13] Althusser shadows Bachelard in the first sense with his distinctions between science and ideology; the second distinction is constitutive of Althusser's reading of Marx in terms of a pre-Marxist ideological problematic (the humanism of Marx's early works), and a mature scientific Marxist problematic (Marx's analysis of the capitalist social formation in *Capital*).

Finally, the third debt arises from the way in which the relationship between objects of knowledge and real objects is conceptualized: ' ... for Bachelard theoretical conceptions are not abstractions from the full reality of objects but the way of reaching this reality beyond the vagueness and incompleteness of our sense experience' (Gutting, 1989: 30):

... the true scientific phenomenology is therefore essentially a phenomeno-
technics. It instructs itself by what it constructs ... Science raises up a world no
longer by a magical force immanent in reality, but rather by a rational force
immanent in the mind (Bachelard cited in Lecourt, 1975: 76–7).

If this is compared with Althusser's statement of the relationship between theoretical concepts and real objects the similarity cannot be missed:

> The process that produces the concrete-knowledge takes place wholly in theo-
> retical practice: of course it does concern the concrete real, but this concrete-real
> 'survives in its independence after as before, outside thought' (Marx) without it
> ever being possible to confuse it with that other 'concrete' which is knowledge
> of it. (Althusser, 1969: 186)

Implicit in the notion of the debt, is the related idea that it can be cancelled. In
Althusser's case, however, the discursive debt to Historical Epistemology is not
only not cancelled, it is augmented, as I will show in the next section.

BORROWING A THEORY OF HISTORY FROM HISTORICAL EPISTEMOLOGY

Thus far, I have explored the explicit links between Althusser's epistemology and
the approach developed by Historical Epistemology; for those familiar with
Althusser's work there is nothing new here. But Althusser's writing contains
traces which suggest that there is something more going on; he is also incorporating its logic of historical explanation. That he does this is not immediately obvious.
This is because Althusser constructs his argument in *For Marx* and *Reading Capital*
in opposition to what he identifies as a Hegelian notion of history, and the break
with historicism, teleology and humanism which Marxism allegedly embodies. For
instance, Althusser criticizes the Hegelian notion of history as follows:

> ... the structure of historical existence is such that all the elements of the whole
> always co-exist in one and the same time, one and the same present, and are
> therefore contemporaneous with one another in the same present. This means
> that the structure of historical existence of the Hegelian social totality allows
> what I propose to call an 'essential section' (coupe d'essence), i.e., an intellectual
> operation in which a vertical break is made at any moment in historical time, a
> break in the present such that all the elements of the whole revealed by this sec-
> tion are in an immediate relationship with one another, a relationship that imme-
> diately expresses their internal essence. (Althusser and Balibar, 1970: 94)

A few pages later, Althusser argues that this critique of Hegelianism can be attributed to Marx (Althusser and Balibar, 1970: 97). It seems to me that Althusser is right in suggesting that one can read Marx as having a complex notion of the articulation of social formations and their historical development, and this is found not only in substantive historical texts such as the *Eighteenth Brumaire*, but also in *Capital*. Yet it is certainly not unequivocally enunciated, hence there is some warrant for those authors who read Marx as being teleological. However, take the following citation where Canguilhem outlines the uneven effects of an epistemological break:

> Often ... the effect of a break is presented as global, affecting the totality of a scientific work. But we need to know how to uncover even in the work of a single historical figure, successive breaks and partial breaks. In a theoretical fabric, certain threads can be entirely new, while others are taken from earlier weavings. (Canguilhem, in Gutting, 1989: 40)

One of Historical Epistemology's central tenets is that there can be no such thing as a general history of science; there are only histories of science, that is to say histories of determinate concepts and the conceptual interrelations in which they exist. For Historical Epistemology scientific activity is highly localized and specific both diachronically and synchronically, thus it presupposes unevenness, discontinuity and rupture. The history of science cannot be conceived as one unitary movement, nor captured by 'an essential slice'; and it is precisely these ideas of rupture, unevenness and discontinuity which Althusser's critique of Hegel invokes.

Thus the discursive and semantic matrix through which Althusser develops his anti-Hegelian conception of history can with a certain degree of plausibility be linked to the semantic and discursive potential associated with the logic of historical explanation contained in the theoretical visuality made possible by Historical Epistemology.[14] For instance Althusser writes:

> We are thereby obliged to renounce every teleology of reason, and to conceive the historical relation between a result and its conditions of existence as a relation of production, and not of expression, and therefore as what in a phrase that clashes with the classical system of categories and demands the replacement of those categories themselves, we can call the necessity of its contingency. To grasp this necessity we must grasp the very special and paradoxical logic that leads to this production, i.e., the logic of the conditions of production of knowledge, whether they belong to the history of a branch of still ideological knowledge, or to a branch of knowledge attempting to constitute itself as a science or already established as a science. We can expect many surprises from this series, like those we have had from Canguilhem's work on the history of the

production of the reflex concept . . . like those we owe to Michel Foucault's studies of the disconcerting development of that complex cultural formation which
in the seventeen and eighteenth centuries grouped around the over-determined
word of 'Madness' . . . (Althusser and Balibar, 1970: 45)

Now, the use of the term 'production' suggests that we are dealing with a Marxian
notion of knowledge production. This is, however, far from clear.

A few pages later Althusser lists four types of practice: economic, political, ideological and theoretical, and then claims that there can be no such a thing as a practice
in general (Althusser and Balibar, 1970: 58). Despite this, what is common to all
practices is that they can be represented as distinctive modalities of production:
'We think the content of these different practices by thinking their peculiar structure, which, in all cases, is the structure of a production . . .' (Althusser and Balibar,
1970: 58). The connotative intent and discursive function of deploying this Marxist
term is obvious. It is an attempt to position discursively the concept of theoretical
practice within a Marxist semantic field.

Marx's concept of economic production represents two facets of production
simultaneously: the labour process itself and the relations of production in which
production is embedded at the level of the social formation (e.g. capitalist, feudal).
Althusser's notion of theoretical production elaborates the first dimension but not
the second. Althusser conceptualizes the production of knowledge as a process
where *Generality I* (raw materials: scientific facts, ideological concepts such as freedom in the market) is acted upon by *Generality II* (the actual theoretical structure
that processes and organizes the facts such as historical materialism) in order to
produce *Generality III* (i.e. a scientific knowledge of social formations) (Althusser,
1969: 182–200). However, Althusser's transfer of the metaphor of economic production into the domain of theoretical practice does not produce the analogues for
relations of production in this domain.[15] This leads Glucksmann to ridicule the
primacy of production as follows:

> The basis for the whole tripartite Althusserian architecture thus arises fully
> armed from the simple but somewhat forced use of a dictionary. It 'happens'
> that everything is production, it 'happens' that every production is divided
> into three. That is how it is. This conceptual empiricism is never questioned in
> the Althusserian reflection. (1972: 71)

Now, the use of the concept of production does not really derive from the forced
use of a dictionary definition (no doubt Glucksmann was aware of this); it derives
from Bachelard's distinction between scientific and everyday experience. The
former is characterized by the use of instruments (or materialized theories as Bachelard likes to call them); thus 'phenomeno-technics' designates the fact that the
production of knowledge presupposes an active intervention, not only conceptual

but also material. However, as Lecourt argues, although Bachelard was aware that 'the scientific city' (the different sites where scientific knowledges were produced) was embedded in wider social conditions of possibility, he never explored them in any detail (1975: 138–9). Similarly, this second dimension is absent from Althusser's notion of production even though it is explicitly presupposed by its metaphorical connection with the Marxist variant of the term.[16]

Consequently, the concept of production crystallizes as a semantic node between, or a gateway towards, two discursive networks. On the one hand it establishes a metaphorical relationship with the Marxist concept of production. Yet this link remains a *Modality B* metaphorical process due to its failure to develop the notion of relations of production. It produces a connotative resonance with the former which does not adequately specify what social relations of knowledge production might be. On the other hand, it draws on the semantic potential associated with the concept of knowledge production as developed by Bachelard, but it also reproduces the limitation inherent in it: it does not embed knowledge production in a wider social context.

It could be argued, nevertheless, that although Althusser accepts the account of the historical development of theoretical practice inherited from Historical Epistemology, his enunciation of the development of social formations does not. But things are not quite so simple. Althusser takes seriously the fact that theoretical practice, though relatively autonomous, takes place within social formations; this is the case despite his inability to conceptualize fully the actual relationship between the social formation and theoretical practice. Therefore, the way in which he conceptualizes the different practices which constitute the social formation cannot be at odds with the way he represents knowledge production as a practice.

In the best-case scenario, the metaphorical relationship between the history of scientific practice and the history of the social formation would generate a semantic field wherein a concept, or concepts, of social structure capable of conceptualizing the historical development of social formations in terms of ruptures and discontinuities would crystallize. In this way his writing would transcend the discursive exigency of enunciating a history of social formations metaphorically in terms of a history of knowledge production. In the worst-case scenario, a mere connotative resonance, a *Modality B* metaphorical operation, would be established between theoretical and other social practices.

There are a number of discursive elements which push Althusser's writing towards the latter case. For instance, as we saw above one of Althusser's fundamental objections is aimed at a conception of history which is understood in terms of the 'teleology of reason'. Now this can be taken to mean two closely linked but distinct things. First, it can be taken as a critique of a linear and cumulative account of the development of knowledge that ignores the ruptures and the emergence of new problematics which is at the heart of Historical Epistemology. Equally, though, it can be taken to refer to the simple totality which Althusser argues is constitutive of the Hegelian notion of history. The thing to note is that this very semantic ambiguity allows Althusser's discourse to switch almost seamlessly from the domain of the history of ideas to that of social formations.

We can observe the same discursive tendency elsewhere. In the essay from *Reading Capital* entitled 'The Errors of Classical Economics: Outline of a Concept of Historical Time', Althusser argues that the Marxist 'structured whole' is characterized by a certain complexity of relatively autonomous levels (ideological, political and economic) which are in the last instance fixed by the level of the economy. He also claims the following:

> Of course, we still have to define more exactly the structural nature of this whole, but this provisional definition is sufficient for us to be able to forecast that the Hegelian type of co-existence of presence (allowing an 'essential section') is incompatible with the existence of this new type of totality. (Althusser and Balibar, 1970: 97)

A few pages later he adds: 'As a first approximation, we can argue from the specific structure of the Marxist whole that it is no longer possible to think the process of the development of the different levels in the same historical time' (Althusser and Balibar, 1970: 99). However, if one follows the text carefully it is apparent that Althusser immediately switches over to illustrate this different non-Hegelian conception via the historical development of philosophy (i.e. theoretical practice), and not of social formations. It is true that Althusser mentions *Capital*, and he points to the operation of a non-linear and complex time, 'a time of times', to be found there (Althusser and Balibar, 1970: 101);[17] but he does not make visible the Marxist conceptual architecture which would elucidate the nature of the articulation of the complex whole.

A little later he writes:

> I think that I have said enough to suggest what direction the construction of the concept of history in its different domains must take; and to show that the construction of this concept incontestably produces a reality which has nothing to do with the visible sequence of events recorded by the chronicler. (Althusser and Balibar, 1970: 103)

Given that the preceding paragraphs contained an account of the history of philosophy, it becomes ever clearer that Althusser is speaking from within the discursive domain of Historical Epistemology. After all it was the chronicle of ingenious and cumulative events which Historical Epistemology precisely sought to undermine.[18] What is more, immediately after writing this, Althusser turns to Foucault. And rightly so, because the conception of history developed by Althusser is strikingly similar to that developed by Foucault in *The Archaeology of Knowledge*: a text concerned with understanding the social and historical conditions of the production of knowledge located broadly in the Historical Epistemology tradition.

In highlighting the similarities between Althusser's conception of history and that of Bachelard and Canguilhem I am not simply trying to draw attention to the resemblance between the two. Instead, I think that it is important to realize that the conceptual networks associated with Historical Epistemology allow Althusser to enunciate a conception of the social formation in terms of the complex articulation of different levels, each containing different rhythms or times. It provides the semantic and discursive tools through which Althusser can write his most general ontological vision of the nature of social formations. It rests on the opposition between a linear and cumulative historical logic which Althusser associates with Hegel and one that highlights discontinuities, ruptures and unevenness which he associates with Marx but which can be more plausibly related to Historical Epistemology. What is more, to the extent that Historical Epistemology's object is ostensibly concerned with networks of relationships between scientific, or pseudo-scientific, concepts, it is not semantically tooled up to produce the effect of social structure. It is for this reason that when Althusser tries to write the uneven and discontinuous nature of the form of organization characteristic of the social formation his writing discursively slides towards a discussion of theoretical practice and the history of ideas. His writing is not able to translate the logic of theoretical practice into the logics of the other practices (economic, political and ideological) that constitute the social formation. Therefore the relationship between the concepts in the domain of Historical Epistemology and Althusser's science of social formations is best conceived in terms of a *Modality B* metaphorical operation. To be sure Althusser's debt to Historical Epistemology inaugurates a powerful theoretical visuality in which the social formation can be represented as a complexly articulated whole, but it also introduces the discursive exigency of enunciating a concept of social structure capable of theoretically representing this complexly articulated whole. In the next section I want to examine Althusser's attempt to do so. I will show that Althusser is not entirely successful in this endeavour. Moreover, I will argue that his appropriation of the Spinozian notion of 'Structural Causality' serves to further cement the enunciation of social structure in terms of ideology and knowledge, reinforcing the *Modality B* metaphorical relationship between Historical Epistemology and Althusserian structuralism.

ENUNCIATING STRUCTURE 'SANS' BACHELARD AND CANGUILHEM?

The effect of social structure in Althusser's writing is inextricably embedded within a discursive strategy where structure is enunciated as a complexly articulated whole.

Therefore, first and foremost, structure is that which is not simple; it is a certain type of complexity. Yet as Glucksmann was to write: 'To express the need for a concept is not to provide the concept of this need' (1972: 77). One of the most striking things about Althusser's texts is the extent to which most of his writing is oriented towards highlighting the need rather than fulfilling it. In *For Marx*, Althusser ostensibly draws on Spinoza, Freud, Mao and Lenin in order to begin to deploy discursive resources which might make the complexity inherent in the structured whole thinkable and theoretically representable (i.e. the concepts of overdetermined contradiction and structural causality).[19]

From Lenin and Mao, Althusser invokes the notion of uneven development. He quotes Mao approvingly: 'For as Mao puts it in a phrase as clear as dawn, nothing in this world develops absolutely evenly' (Althusser, 1969: 201). Althusser goes on to claim that the concept of unevenness is not only relevant for thinking the relationships between social formations (i.e. Lenin's Imperialism Thesis of Uneven Development); it is constitutive of individual social formations and their different levels (Althusser, 1969: 212–13). This, of course, goes against the grain of the so-called Hegelian notion where it is possible to identify one 'essential' contradiction. However, in offering a decentred account of social formations anchored in the concept of unevenness, Althusser clearly does not want to sacrifice the elimination of economism and historicism[20] on the 'altar of pluralism':

> ... the unity discussed by Marxism is the unity of complexity itself, that the mode of organization and articulation of the complexity is precisely what constitutes its unity ... In the last resort this specific structure is the basis for the relations of domination between contradictions and between their aspects that Mao described as essential. (Althusser, 1969: 201–2)

Following Mao,[21] Althusser goes on to distinguish between principal and secondary contradictions, principal and secondary aspects of contradiction, and antagonistic and non-antagonistic contradictions. Nonetheless, these analytical distinctions are perhaps better understood as a discursive strategy whose purpose is to further sustain the opposition between Althusser's emphasis on complexity and Hegel's alleged emphasis on the simple and homogeneous historical totality. Similarly, although notions of fusion and displacement are crucial to Althusser's account, they do not receive systematic treatment or analysis.

This is perhaps not obvious because of Althusser's use of concepts such as overdetermination, condensation and displacement. On closer examination, however, the *Modality B* metaphorical status of these terms can be unveiled. They remain plausible only to the extent that they manage to invoke signifieds from the domain of psychoanalysis. They do not have determinate meanings or signifieds within historical materialism. This indicates that the metaphorical relationship has not served to generate new concepts, but to import meanings from the domain of psychoanalysis. For instance with respect to overdetermination, Althusser writes the following in a footnote:

> I did not invent this concept ... it is borrowed from existing disciplines ... In these disciplines it has an objective dialectical 'connotation', and – particularly in psychoanalysis – one sufficiently related formally to the content it designates here for the loan not to be an arbitrary one. (Althusser, 1969: 206)

To say the least, this is a surprisingly casual statement from a theorist who stressed the importance of understanding the meaning of specific concepts in terms of the determinate theoretical structure in which they were embedded.

As is well known, Freud develops the concepts of overdetermination, condensation and displacement as a means of theorizing the relationship between dream-thoughts and dream-contents. Like Althusser, Freud was keenly aware of the necessity of formulating concepts adequate to his object of study. Freud's first approximation is via the metaphor of weaving:

> Here we find ourselves in a factory of thoughts, whereas in the 'weaver's' masterpiece:
>
> ... a thousand threads one treadle throws
> Where fly the shuttles hither and thither
> Unseen the threads are knit together
> And an infinite combination grows! (Freud, 1991: 388)

In analysing the dream-contents of a specific dream, Freud moves on to theoretically specify the nature of the complexity made possible by the metaphor of weaving. He writes:

> ... the elements ... found their way into the content of the dream because they possessed copious contacts with the majority of the dream thoughts, because, that is to say, they constituted 'nodal points' upon which a great number of dream-thoughts converged, and because they had several meanings in connection with the interpretation of the dream. The explanation of this fundamental fact can also be put in another way: each of the elements of the dream's content turns out to have been 'overdetermined' to have been represented in the dream thoughts many times over. (Freud, 1991: 388–9)

For Freud the elements found in the dream-thoughts are characterized by a certain psychic value which determines their entry into the dream-contents: 'It thus seems plausible to suppose that in the dream-work a psychic force is operating which on the one hand strips the elements which have a high psychical value of their intensity

...' – i.e. displacement – '... and on the other hand, by means of overdetermination creates from elements of psychical value new values, which afterwards find their way into the dream content' – i.e. condensation (Freud, 1991: 417). To be sure, there is in Freud a certain ambiguity with respect to terms such as psychic energy and psychic value, however the mechanisms underpinning the displacement and condensation of the elements are clearly of symbolic nature. Consequently overdetermination is enunciated as the flow of symbolic elements whose respective psychic values are censored via the mechanisms of displacement and condensation.

In Althusser's writing the term overdetermination is, despite his denial, more easily associated with the notion of 'pluralism'. This is so because even though he insists that the economic level is determinant in the last instance and assigns a hierarchy of dominance to the other levels, it is not clear how the articulations of the different levels might be understood. Above I made reference to Glucksmann's critique of the use of the term production in the context of the production of knowledge; the critique also applies to production at the political level. The specificity of political practice as a form of production and its mode of effectivity are never elucidated. Althusser qualifies Mao's statement on the existence of a principal contradiction which plays a leading role by suggesting that 'this principal contradiction produced by displacement only becomes "decisive", explosive, by condensation (by "fusion")' (Althusser, 1969: 211). But this does not take us very far as Smith argues:

> Althusser never tells us what are the equivalent contradictions – equivalent, that is, to that between the forces and relations of production that arise within the superstructure. It is hardly adequate to assert that all the elements of the superstructure evolve and develop according to their 'own differential historicity' without giving some further specification of what this might mean. (1984: 163)

In the Freudian discursive space, although there is some ambiguity with respect to the meaning of psychic energy, all the elements are symbolic: more specifically, they form a system or network of symbolically associated elements with differing psychic values. Thus it is possible to enunciate the operations between them. In Althusser's writing, in contrast, there is no sense of a 'value' that could be displaced or fused from one level to the other. There is of course the notion of 'contradiction', but no analysis of its effectivity or its mode of operation. If each level has its autonomous form of effectivity, how are we to understand the interaction of these levels? How are effects translated? What is absent is, in fact, a specification of structure beyond the discursive strategy by which it is merely opposed to a simple Hegelian totality.[22]

In *Reading Capital*, Althusser addresses the question of the complexity of the structured whole again, but this time he does so via a different conception of causality, the notion of structural causality derived from Spinoza. Benton has quite correctly suggested that this amounts to no more than a restatement of the need to think the effectivity operating among the different structures of the complex whole (1984: 64). Nonetheless there is a sense, and this is far from obvious, in which the concept of structural causality goes further than merely restating the problem, yet still not providing an adequate solution. In a well-known passage in *Reading Capital*, Althusser writes:

> ... the effects are not outside the structure, are not a pre-existing object, element or space in which the structure arrives to imprint its mark: on the contrary, it implies that the structure is immanent in its effects, a cause immanent in its effects in the Spinozist sense of the term, that the whole existence of the structure consists of its effects, in short that the structure, which is merely a specific combination of its peculiar elements, is nothing outside its effects. (Althusser and Balibar, 1970: 188–9)

This passage follows a section where Althusser is arguing that we cannot think the relationship between structure and economic objects as one of exteriority. As such, it is meant to provide the framework for thinking the links between the different levels in the social formation.[23]

However, if we examine the relationship between Althusser and Spinoza it is clear that there is much more at stake than the mere importation of a new concept of causality. If we return to the first reference to Spinoza in *Reading Capital*, it is made in the context of the development of the concept of a symptomatic reading. There exists in Spinoza, Althusser argues, a crucial awareness of the embeddedness of the social production of knowledge in wider historical conditions of possibility:

> The first man ever to have posed the problem of reading, and in consequence, of writing, was Spinoza, and he was also the first man in the world to have proposed the opacity of the immediate. With him, for the first time ever, a man linked together in this way the essence of reading and the essence of history in a theory of the difference between the imaginary and the true. (Althusser and Balibar, 1970: 16–17)

Now it would seem that Althusser borrowed two sets of ideas from Spinoza (i.e. structural causality and reading/writing). Yet it is important to highlight the fact that for Spinoza the concept of structural causality is inextricably linked to knowledge production, as well as to the production of erroneous knowledge – what Spinoza calls 'knowledge of the imagination'. In the words of Norris

> In Spinoza, this argument [that the existence of structure consists in its effects] is conjoined with the strong (metaphysical-determinist) claim that the highest

form of knowledge consists in perceiving the entire order of causal relations sub specie aeternitatis, or as they might appear to a pure (indeed a God-like) rational intelligence, one that has somehow managed to transcend all merely contingent limitations of time and place. It is remarkable indeed that Althusser should find such thinking amenable to the purposes of Marxist criticism. But in fact he takes this whole metaphysics on board, including the doctrine at the heart of Spinoza's Ethics: namely that our time bound or localized perceptions of cause and effect belong to mere 'knowledge of imagination' and are therefore not to be confused with the order of self-evident, a priori things. (1991: 37)

The concept of structural causality, of Spinozian derivation, allows Althusser to further anchor the effect of structural causality within the discursive domain of Historical Epistemology. This is so because for Historical Epistemology and for Spinoza, indeed also for Althusser, the notions of structure, of the subject and of history are intimately connected with the possibility of the production of scientific knowledge (true knowledge) against the structurally inscribed selectivity (epistemological obstacles) towards ideology (everyday knowledge or knowledge of imagination).

For Althusser, as is the case with Spinoza, the necessary misrecognition of knowledge is grounded in a functionalist rationale. For instance, in criticizing the prophets of the Old Testament for their recourse to divine interventions, Spinoza simultaneously accepts that these errors were necessitated by political and social contingencies, not reducible to individual error or will to power.[24] In Althusser this is most clear in the essays on the *Ideological State Apparatuses*, where he is unable to link their functioning except by an implicit functionalist reasoning.[25] Perhaps the crucial discursive link between Althusser and Spinoza (and also with Historical Epistemology) is provided by the most powerful metaphor to be found in Althusser's writing: vision as ideology. It is by examining the semantic potential and limitations contained in this metaphor, as it is developed in Althusser's writing, that we can further grasp another order of discursive, hence theoretical, problems associated with Althusser's attempt to produce the effect of structure in writing. Paradoxically, as we shall see in the next section, for the champion of anti-humanism, structure is ultimately defined as that which the subject cannot 'see'.

VISION AND ANTI-VISION

As we saw above, Spinoza defines true knowledge by opposing it to the effect of 'imagination'. By imagination, Spinoza has in mind ' . . . the idea wherewith the mind contemplates a thing as present; yet this idea indicates rather the present disposition of the human body than the nature of the external thing' (Spinoza, cited in

Norris, 1991: 38). In *For Marx*, Althusser writes: ' "Men live" their ideologies as the Cartesian "saw" or did not see – if he was not looking at it – the moon two hundred paces away: not at all as form of consciousness, but as an object of their "world" as their "world" – itself' (Althusser, 1969: 233). This excerpt is interesting for a number of reasons. First of all, it serves to locate Althusser in a discursive current which has produced the effect of ocularphobia which has been surprisingly vital in French thought ranging from the writings of Bergson to Levinas and Foucault.[26] The debates and literature dealing with the historical emergence of different scopic regimes cannot be summarized here.[27] Nonetheless, there are some relevant points worth drawing out. Descartes' inclusion in Althusser's discussion of ideology is certainly not accidental: 'he [Descartes] is after all ... a quintessentially visual philosopher, who tacitly adopted the position of a perspectivalist painter using a camera obscura to reproduce the observed world' (Jay, 1994: 69). Cartesian perpectivalism and its ocularcentrism has, therefore, been an important target for ocularphobes.

Now it is well known that empiricist evangelists such as Bacon were unrepentant in their grounding of truth in the domain of vision: 'I admit nothing but on the faith of the eyes' (Bacon cited in Jay, 1994: 64). But Descartes does not easily slot into this position. There is both a 'sensationalist' and 'rationalist' (therefore a potentially anti-visual tendency) grounding Descartes' notion of vision (Jay, 1994: 81). Nonetheless, it is widely accepted that Descartes' writing sought to produce a positive link between what the 'organs sensed' and what the 'mind saw' (Jay, 1994: 76).

Althusser is without doubt critical of both alternatives. The rationalist position would be vulnerable as it is oblivious to the embeddedness of knowledge production in wider social structures, the sensationalist position, because it relies on a naive empiricism, which Althusser, following Historical Epistemology and Spinoza, rejects.[28] Frustratingly, Althusser never actually confronts the question of vision head on. When, in the passage cited above, Althusser writes that the 'Cartesian saw' and did not realize that this seeing was a form of consciousness, Althusser is suggesting that it is possible to account for this seeing as a socially mediated practice. However, this theme is never developed. Vision remains a polyvalent signifier that connotes scientific ideology (empiricism), but also ideology in general (more on this below). 'Empirically', the focus on vision as the fundamental modality of ideology is explicit throughout his writing, but it is never analysed. As such I want to argue that it is the product of a *Modality B* metaphorical operation: it is embedded in a larger discursive network which remains unacknowledged and undeveloped. It does not lead to the elaboration of signifieds specific to the realm of historical materialism or Marxist philosophy. Instead it relies on a connotative resonance, on the ability of the signifier vision to find signifieds elsewhere. I am first going to examine this assertion with respect to his comments on scientific ideology, and then with respect to ideology in general.

As is well known, Althusser identifies empiricism as an epistemological position which is not aware of its conditions of possibility, as an epistemology that believes that knowledge comes from abstracting and purifying some essence already contained in reality. In an essay entitled 'Theoretical Practice and Theoretical Formation', he writes:

> ... theoretical work is not an abstraction in the sense of empiricist ideology. To know is not to extract from the impurities and diversity of the real the pure essence contained in the real, as gold is extracted from the dross of sand in which it is contained. To know is to produce the adequate concept of the object by putting to work means of theoretical production ... (1990: 15)

In this excerpt, it is not clear that the notion of apprehending the essence of reality is produced through the metaphor of vision, but if we move up a few paragraphs in the text, it becomes clearer.[29] He writes, and he italicizes this passage for emphasis, '*In an existing science, the theoretical work that produced it is no longer visible to the naked eye; it has completely passed in the science as constituted*' (Althusser, 1990: 14).

In *Reading Capital*, where Althusser distinguishes between political economy as a scientific ideology and Marxism as a science, he constantly uses terms such as 'seeing', 'oversight' and 'vision':

> ... what classical political economy does not see, is not what it does not see, it is what it sees; it is not what it lacks, on the contrary, it is what it does not lack; it is not what it misses, on the contrary, it is what it does not miss. The oversight, then, is not to see what one sees, the oversight no longer concerns the object, but the sight itself. The oversight is an oversight that concerns vision: non-vision is therefore inside of vision, it is a form of vision and hence has a necessary relationship with vision. (Althusser and Balibar, 1970: 21)

Of course the centrality of vision as a discursive strategy for producing the notion of ideology or ideological knowledge in Althusser's writings has been noted. Elliot, for instance, writes that for Althusser, 'Knowledge was not vision, but production, not abstraction (or purification) but appropriation' (1987: 97), and a few pages later he reiterates, 'Theoretical ideology is a knowledge, but in the form of recognition, not cognition ... (1987: 99). Commentators have also drawn attention to the fact that Althusser is operating with an excessively wide and vague notion of empiricism.[30] Connected with this is the fact that Althusser does not offer a workable criterion for distinguishing between science and ideology.[31] In both *For Marx* (Althusser, 1969: 231) and *Reading Capital* (Althusser and Balibar, 1970: 52) he suggests that theoretical ideology can be distinguished from science by its 'practico-social function' as compared to the 'theoretical function' of theoretical practice. However, these are just appended notes receiving no systematic treatment.

Althusser also tries to produce the distinction by moving in the opposite direction, that is by trying to discover the conceptual criteria used by an already constituted science, mathematics, and argues that criteria are 'purely internal' (Althusser and Balibar, 1970: 59), but this creates an insurmountable problem. If it is the case that theoretical objects are internal to theoretical practice and that theoretical practice polices knowledge through internal criteria, then how is one to understand this knowledge as being knowledge of the real object? Althusser's unsatisfactory answer to this problem is in the form of an unspecified and untheorized mechanism referred to as appropriation via the 'Knowledge-Effect' (Althusser and Balibar, 1970: 78–8). As Elliot has pointed out, this solution only works if a fundamental homology is established between reality, which is a product of practices, and theoretical practice, such that they must necessarily be isomorphic and synchronic (1987: 105).[32]

Commentators have seen this problem as arising from the simultaneous use of a conventionalist (i.e. Historical Epistemology) and a realist theory of science in which the tensions between the two have not been resolved (Benton, 1984: 23–31). Elliot however argues that

> ... if Bachelard assigns theory primacy over experience and considers scientific progress to reside in increasing conceptual coherence and progressive mathematization, he does not adopt a purely rationalist position; rectification of a theory on the basis of new evidence is envisaged. (1987: 92–3)

Gutting suggests that 'Bachelard's position collapses into either idealism or metaphysical realism' (1989: 32). Tiles (1987), on the contrary, argues that Bachelard successfully transcends the dichotomies between externalist and internalist accounts of science.

Clearly, scholarly opinion on Bachelard's success is divided. Nonetheless, however much Althusser's problem is inherited from Bachelard and from Historical Epistemology in general, what is distinctive about Althusser's posing of the problem is the way he produces the idea of empiricism (scientific ideology) through the metaphor of vision. I believe it is only if we take account of the metaphorical strategies underpinning this usage that we can understand Althusser's extension of empiricism to all sensuous experience, with vision as its fundamental modality. Moreover, it is only then that we can understand Althusser's obstinate refusal to engage with activities through which empirical evidence can be used to test theoretical practice.[33] It is worth pointing out that Bachelard was also firmly entrenched in an ocularphobic discourse, 'Sight says too many things at the same time. Being does not see itself' (Bachelard, cited in Jay, 1994: 388). However, one cannot but agree with Jay when he writes that Althusser's distinctiveness is that ' ... he jettisoned the distinction between an occluded and clear vision, and identified ideology with a reliance on sight of any kind' (1994: 374).[34]

VISUALIZING IDEOLOGY

Without doubt, the reliance on vision and specularity in order to characterize ideology is most forcefully expressed in Althusser's appropriation of Lacanian psychoanalysis. In 'Ideology and Ideological State Apparatuses', he writes

> ... all ideology is *centered* ... the Absolute Subject occupies the unique place of the Centre, and interpellates around it the infinity of individuals into subjects in a double mirror-connexion such that it *subjects* the subjects to the Subject, while giving them in the Subject in which each subject can contemplate its own image (present and future) the *guarantee* that this really concerns them and Him, and that since everything takes place in the Family (The Holy Family: the Family is in essence Holy), 'God will *recognize* his own in it', i.e. those who have recognized God, and have recognized themselves in him, will be saved. (1984: 54, italics in original)

The embedding of ideology in the Lacanian discursive semantic space opened up by the idea of the 'mirror phase' makes possible the enunciation of vision as the fundamental mechanism through which ideology can be conceptualized.[35] Despite this, Althusser's use of Lacanian psychoanalysis not only does not provide an accurate reading of Lacan; it, as Barrett (1993) has argued, does not create a field for the conceptual integration of Lacanian psychoanalysis with historical materialism. For instance, Althusser sees the family only in terms of the reproduction of labour power: 'Scarcely a meeting of the Marxist and psychoanalytical minds!' (Barrett, 1993: 172). Barrett goes on to argue that there are, in a sense, two theories of ideology at work in Althusser's writing – one that deals with social reproduction, the second with subjectivity – but their relationship is never conceptually developed (Barrett, 1993: 170).[36]

Even the use of the mirror phase, which is so central to Althusser, is problematic. For Althusser it is the source of social cement, for Lacan it is not the imaginary but the symbolic order that provides relative stability.[37] Barrett concludes that Althusser's use of Lacanian psychoanalysis is fundamentally metaphorical (1993: 181). Althusser's writing in this context is clearly embedded in a *Modality B* metaphorical process, not because it does not adequately appropriate Lacan's conceptual schema, but because the borrowings themselves are not developed consistently and systematically within his own work. Vision, as the fundamental modality of ideology, persists through connotation rather than through denotation.[38]

Beyond the analytical utility of specific psychoanalytical concepts, psychoanalysis plays a more general discursive role in Althusser's writing, and once again vision and non-vision are at the centre. In 'Freud and Lacan' Althusser highlights the difficulties that Freud had to confront in his attempt to inaugurate a new continent of knowledge:

He had to cope with the following situation: to be himself his own father, to construct with his own craftsman's hands the theoretical space in which to situate his discovery, to weave with thread borrowed intuitively left and right the great net with which to catch in the depths of blind experience the teeming fish of the unconscious . . . (Althusser, 1971: 148)

This excerpt is taken from a section in the text which deals with the concept of the problematic. For Althusser, there are important similarities between the founding of psychoanalysis and historical materialism, but the phrase '. . . to catch in the depths of blind experience the teeming fish of the unconscious . . . ' is worth highlighting. It suggests in strong terms the anti-visual basis which Althusser believes any truly scientific problematic should have. The metaphor is powerful; it suggests that social formations are as inscrutable to the human eye as is the unconscious. The unconscious by definition is that which is beyond the conscious grasp of individuals. Similarly, the structured whole is enunciated precisely as that which individuals do not 'see' by seeing. Its condition of possibility resides in its seamless effectivity. I will elaborate on this last point, but before doing so I think that it would be useful to draw together the strands of the arguments that I have been developing in this chapter.

I have traced the centrality of Historical Epistemology for Althusser's writing, not merely as an epistemology but as a semantic and discursive space that allows Althusser to produce the effect of the social formation as an uneven complex whole underpinned by the historical logic of Historical Epistemology, a logic of ruptures, uneven development and discontinuities. I then proceeded to show the centrality of the metaphor of vision throughout Althusser's work, but also to show that vision provides the discursive and semantic networks through which the functioning of ideology can be written. In a sense, I have written about Althusser almost as if he were not a Marxist theorist.[39] Yet there is no doubt in my mind that Althusser was in fact working within a broadly defined Marxist problematic. However, as I have argued in the chapter on Marx, the concept of structure is never clearly nor unproblematically enunciated in Marx's own work. The discursive possibilities of enunciating the concept of structure in Marx are not there to be found ready-made as it were. Rather they need to be discursively 'produced'. Althusser's recourse to discursive networks outside of Marxism (Historical Epistemology, Spinoza and psychoanalysis) demonstrates that reading is never a passive activity; it is an active construction of meaning. I will return to this point in the concluding chapter.

In drawing on these diverse discursive resources, Althusser makes possible a theoretical visuality in which social reality and social structure are represented as the effect of a complexly structure whole. The structured whole is that (unfilled?) conceptual space which is created when it is opposed to a Hegelian notion of structure, which is most fundamentally, in the use that Althusser makes of it, a historical logic – a unilinear historical logic of the development of reason. Notwithstanding Althusser's recourse to Mao and Lenin and strategic citations from Marx's work, the logic and the yet to be enunciated concept of structure, which Althusser tries to deploy against historicism and humanism, is more plausibly found in Canguilhem's critique of the precursor.[40]

Althusser's borrowings from psychoanalysis can be divided into two discursive strategies. The first is identified with the metaphorical borrowings of overdetermination, displacement and condensation. Althusser is not able, however, to overcome the discursive exigency of providing the equivalents (or the signifieds) in the domain of historical materialism of Freud's symbolic mechanisms that form the backbone of his discussion of the relationship between dream-thoughts and dream-contents. The second strategy is to be found in Althusser's so-called appropriation of the Lacanian mirror-stage. Althusser does not successfully integrate psychoanalysis with historical materialism, rather he establishes *Modality B* discursive relations. I expanded this point further by highlighting the centrality of anti-visualism in Althusser's work. I have also tried to trace the metaphorical status of vision as the primordial modality of ideology. In this sense, although it is common to refer to the non-Marxist influences on Althusserianism in terms of Historical Epistemology, Spinozian philosophy and psychoanalysis, I would argue that the French ocularphobic discourse, which cross-cuts disciplinary boundaries, should also be included.

Althusser's borrowings from Spinoza are often presented in terms of the notion of structural causality. Yet 'structural causality' in Spinoza, no less than in Althusser, is also conjoined with both a rejection of everyday 'vision', and with a notion of structural complexity where complexity is characterized by its opacity. In 'Theoretical Practice and Theoretical Formation', Althusser writes 'The opacity of the social structure necessarily renders mythic that representation of the world which is indispensable for social cohesion' (1990: 29). Ultimately the complexity of Althusser's structured whole is defined by an invisibility which is inscribed in a certain type of seeing which is not fully specified:

> The relations of productions are structures – and the ordinary economist may scrutinize economic 'facts': prices, exchanges, wages, profits, rents, etc., all those 'measurable' facts as much as he likes; he will no more 'see' any structure at that level than the pre-Newtonian 'physicist' could 'see' the law of attraction in falling bodies, or the pre-Lavoisierian chemist could 'see' oxygen in 'dephlogisti-cated' air. (Althusser and Balibar, 1970: 181)

Thus the defining features of social complexity are the epistemological obstacles to its apprehension. It also reveals the semantic seductiveness of psychoanalysis as the fellow problematic for historical materialism. Implicit in much of Althusser's writing is the equivalence between 'complexity' and the 'unconscious'. The relationship of a conscious individual to the depths of the unconscious is paradigmatic of the relationship Althusser wants to draw between subjects and the structured whole.

Keeping the above in mind, Althusser's writing could be plausibly categorized in terms of its emphasis on discursively conveying the effect of process, rather than on representing those mechanisms that make the process possible. It is the logic of the movement rather than the mechanism which is central to his account. Thus, for instance, Althusser does not give us the components of the structured whole, instead he metaphorically highlights their movement.[41] Also, it is the process of misrecognition that Althusser identifies, rather than the object which is being misrecognized or the mechanisms responsible for the misrecognition.

Elliot has recently written about the most comprehensive French collection of Althusser's work to be published to date. In texts such as 'Machiavelli and Us' and 'The Subterranean Current', Althusser develops what he calls 'aleatory materialism' or 'materialism of the encounter'. He argues for

> ... a materialism of the encounter, hence of the aleatory and of contingency, which is opposed ... to the various registered materialisms, including the materialisms commonly attributed to Marx, Engels and Lenin, which, like every materialism in the rationalist tradition, is a materialism of necessity and teleology, that is to say, a transformed and disguised form of idealism. (cited in Elliot, 1998: 27)

In tracing the source of this alternative materialism, Althusser omits to mention Historical Epistemology, though he does mention Spinoza. This is surprising because it is precisely the notion of 'irruption', of contingency and non-teleological development that underwrites the historical logic of the unmentioned historical tradition. Moreover, Althusser is content to continue addressing the question in terms of movement and process, rather than enunciating the mechanisms that make this movement possible.

CONCLUSION

I have argued that Althusser comes closest to defining the structured whole, that is the social formation, in terms of two discursive processes. First in terms of a certain historical logic, derived from within the discursive networks of Historical Epistemology, which could be characterized precisely in terms of, to use his latter formulation, the 'materialism of the encounter' of 'irruption', 'contingency' and 'the aleatory'; secondly in terms of a discursive strategy where 'seeing' is written as the fundamental modality of ideology. This second approach is most paradoxical: the champion of anti-humanism defines complexity (the structured whole) as *un humanisme-du-non*. In other words, structure is that which subjects must necessarily misrecognize, that which they do not 'see' by 'seeing'.

That this should be the case is linked to the fact that the discursive resources which his texts draw on in order to produce the effect of structure as a complexly organized whole are taken from the field of Historical Epistemology. The persistent slippage to be found in Althusser's work from social formations to theoretical practice is indicative of his failure to escape the *Modality B* metaphorical relationship that he establishes with Historical Epistemology. The social formation and its historical development are akin to knowledge production and its development(s). It also explains the discursive tendency towards enunciating social structure in terms of the ideology–knowledge opposition. Thus, paradoxically, Historical Epistemology simultaneously allows Althusser to enunciate the concept of structure as a complexly articulated whole while foreclosing its adequate theoretical specification.

As is the case with the four other authors in this book, the enunciation of a notion of social organization or structure does not take place in a pristine field of pure thought. The very possibility of enunciating social organization arises from the existence of cross-cutting statements from a number of discursive fields. The space produced by this interweaving (writing) of discursive elements on the one hand provides a field in which we can cultivate our theoretical desires (thinking the social as a complexly structured whole), and on the other also creates demands and limits the ways in which we might fulfil our desires. It creates *sui generis* discursive exigencies which can be ignored but not erased. Thus, the 'founding act' of enunciating social complexity does not guarantee the production of appropriate social scientific signs. About this Althusser was surely right. Knowledge production is a theoretical practice, but perhaps a deeper awareness of the unavoidable discursive nature of this practice would have served Althusser better.

Reading Texts, Writing Theory: Against the Illusion of Transparency

INTRODUCTION

To engage with social theory is to engage in the practice of reading texts. Social theories exist and persist only inasmuch as they are embodied in texts. No one would deny this. Thus, it is surprising that so little effort has been devoted to actually theorizing and empirically investigating what reading social theory as a practice presupposes. This absence, however, does not only function as a marker that points to a need that might be filled; the absence itself discursively participates in displacing the need for developing an understanding of the specificity of reading theoretical texts. If there is no knowledge of this activity (reading theoretical texts), if it is not an area of investigation in its own right, it must be because the activity itself is unproblematic. Thus, the language of social theory is taken to be transparent for the reader; it is the relatively unproblematic embodiment of thought and it can be read as such.

It is precisely this issue which I want to address in this concluding chapter, where I will argue for the necessity of developing a theory of reading theoretical texts which considers their language-borne nature. In doing so I will briefly discuss the role that literary criticism might contribute to this enterprise. Although it is beyond the scope of this chapter to formalize a theory of reading theoretical texts proper, I will show how my examination of the language-borne nature of attempts to enunciate a concept of social structure in previous chapters might be seen as a contribution towards this task.

READING SOCIAL THEORY

Ironically, the idea that theoretical language is transparent to the reader is unwittingly reinforced precisely by those theorists who have made various attempts to represent the reading of theory as a specific and determinate type of practice. This is so because they have been predominantly concerned with reading social theory only as an effect of its logical architecture (e.g. Alexander, 1982a; Althusser, 1969; Althusser and Balibar, 1970; Hindness, 1977; Parsons, 1949; Savage, 1981). To be sure, these authors have in different and fruitful ways demonstrated that theoretical systems exist in texts as complexly organized (and disorganized), multi-tiered networks of statements which cannot be reduced to a single and coherent unity. Thus Savage prefaces his critical reading of Parsons by writing that

A text may be a purely arbitrary unity in which any number of discrete propositions may occur – it may reflect the author's conception of knowledge-in-general, his 'worldview', his 'philosophy', or whatever, in addition to his substantive concepts ... (Savage, 1981: 58).

Consequently, the task of reading theoretical texts must be understood as a critical inquiry whose aim is to uncover and specify 'a set of concepts and the relations between them' where the latter are understood as being 'strictly logical' (Savage, 1981: 58).

In arguing thus, Savage also highlights the fact that as Althusser put it '. . . there is no such thing as an innocent reading . . .' (Althusser and Balibar, 1970: 14). To read is to '. . . distinguish the existence or non-existence of a concept behind a word, to discern the existence of a concept by a word's function in theoretical discourse . . .' (Althusser, 1969: 39). It is to intervene in a text, to unpack the structure of its statements and the hierarchies in which they exist. In other words it is to recognize that theoretical texts are not merely constituted by a series of logical relations between statements and concepts that can be grasped innocently or effortlessly; they always contain an excess of meaning, a certain quantity of distorting semantic noise. The task of reading is to filter out this noise for the purpose of identifying and amplifying the alleged logical structure of a theory in order to make judgements about its logical (in)stability.

Although this framing of reading theoretical texts has the virtue of problematizing the transparency of texts by showing that they connote more than just a logical structure, it nonetheless reproduces the effect of the transparency of theoretical language itself in so far as it equates the latter with logical closure and coherence. In this context, reading is concerned with overcoming the opaque language of texts for the purpose of extracting a(n) (il)logical core whose (in)coherence can be examined. Critical reading makes (il)logical thought available for judgement through the mediation of a transparent theoretical language. The challenges and obstacles that language itself poses to writing and reading remain unexplored; the text loses its innocence but theoretical language emerges untainted and pure.

Although sociology as a discipline has not, for the most part, been concerned with theorizing the relationship between the text and its reader the same cannot be said of literary criticism (Ekegren, 1999). Literary criticism has problematized the practice of reading and its relationship to literary texts and in so doing has generated a number of conceptual and theoretical resources through which reading practices can be represented. Thus, it could be argued that it is both possible and desirable for sociologists to borrow from this field as a stepping-stone towards understanding the specificity of reading social-theoretical texts.

Although it is certainly true that sociologists might learn much from this engagement there are also a number of obstacles that cannot be ignored. In the first place, it is not the case that literary criticism operates with a single model of reading. Quite the contrary, positions vary from those theorists who conceptualize the activity of reading as being driven by a reader who projects his or her meaning on to the text, to those who have argued the texts are structured in such a way as to produce determinate interpretive effects through the reader.[1]

At one end of the continuum we find a number of literary theorists who broadly maintain that meaning is not something which exists in the text ready-made: it emerges as a result of the semantic potential created by the act of reading. For instance Ingarden (1973) argues that readers need to suture the indeterminacies contained in texts in order to establish their inherent harmony, while Iser (1989) argues that texts are sufficiently malleable to ground multiple readings as long as these readings are articulated in a coherent way. In a similar vein, Fish (1980) has argued, under the banner of 'reception theory', that meaning is not inherent in the text; it is produced by 'interpretive communities' who in 'reading' texts also 'write' them. For Gadamer, as Eagleton has written: '. . . all interpretation of a past work consists in a dialogue between past and present' (1993: 71). The effect of the hermeneutic dialogue is to make the text part of our present-day interpretive framework: 'To understand it [the literary text] does not mean primarily to reason one's way back into the past, but to have a present involvement in what is said. It is not really a relationship between the reader and the author . . . but about sharing in what the text shares with us' (Gadamer, 1989: 391).

On the other side of the continuum, we find authors who have stressed that, although the act of reading necessitates an active reader, the meaning itself lies embedded in the text. Thus, for Hirsh (1967) meaning is secured via the intentionality of the author which the reader must identify, while for Frye (1973) meaning arises through the instantiation of fundamental narrative codes (comic, romantic, tragic and ironic) that structure texts. In a more structuralist vein, the Prague school of linguistics (e.g. Jakobson and Halle, 1956) draws on Saussure's structuralist linguistics in order to argue that the meaning of a text is the effect of the internal relations between its signs or its meaning structure, whereas Potter (1999) has argued that the meaning of the text (and its referentiality) is secured through the social embeddedness of both its production and reading.

Some literary critics have even gone as far as to argue that reading should not be understood as an act of orderly interpretation at all since texts themselves do not provide the basis for this type of practice. For instance Barthes begins *The Pleasure of the Text* as follows:

> Imagine someone … who abolishes himself all barriers, all classes, all exclu-sions, not by syncretism but by simple discard of that old spectre: *logical contra-diction*; who mixes every language, even those said to be incompatible; who silently accepts every charge of illogicality, of incongruity; who remains passive in the face of Socratic irony (leading the interlocutor to the supreme disgrace: *self contradiction*) and legal terrorism (how much penal evidence is based on a psychology of consistency!). Such a man would be the mockery of our society: court, school, asylum, polite conversation would cast him out: who endures contradiction without shame? Now this anti-hero exists: he is the reader of the text at the moment he takes his pleasure. (Barthes, 1975: italics in the original)

For Barthes, what characterizes the practice of reading is the potential of subvert-ing all manner of social and logical conventions; the purpose of reading is not the search for a meaningful unity, logical consistency or coherence, but is a search for pleasure. De Man (1979), in a different way, displaces the search for mean-ing as the goal of reading by arguing that the metaphorical nature of all language makes the distinction between the literal and the figural undecidable thus making texts 'literally unreadable' (Eagleton, 1993: 145), while Derrida (1979), as is well known, has argued that it is the very structure of language and writing which makes all meaning subject to an infinite deferral.

This brief mapping of the diversity and the contradictory nature of the different theories of reading which exist in the field of literary criticism clearly illustrates that there is much more at stake than simply borrowing a ready-made theory of reading practice. There is, however, a more fundamental obstacle that has been identified by Ekegren (1999) in his pioneering attempt to incorporate the insights of literary criticism into the development of an understanding of the specificity of reading social-theoretical texts: literary criticism's diverse theories of reading are located in a semantic and conceptual space where the opaque and ambiguous language of literature is inserted in opposition to the alleged transparent and clear language of scientific writing. Consequently, it is possible to identify a number of opposi-tions such as the literary and the scientific, the metaphorical and the literal, the poetic and the referential, the polyvocal and the univocal, the polysemic and the unisemic, the connotative and the denotative, the opaque and the transparent, the subtle and the crude, the centripetal and the centrifugal, internal and external reference, etc. which discursively reproduce the difference between the two and the transparency of theoretical language (Ekegren, 1999: Chapter 3).

SOCIAL THEORY AND LITERATURE

Ironically, then, the importation of models of reading from literary criticism may very well lead to the reproduction of the opposition which the process of importation was initially meant to overcome. For this reason, any attempt to develop an understanding of the specificity of theoretical language must begin by accepting that there is no *a priori* reason for asserting that the language of social theory has any special status *vis-à-vis* literary language. As Ekegren argues,

> ... the clear-cut-dichotomy between 'literary' and 'referential' language (or whatever terms one uses) is a myth, contrary to what many literary theorists and linguists claim, and that the scientific text is as polysemic, polyvocal and opaque as the literary, contrary to 'conventional' wisdom in literary theory and linguistics. Likewise, we may with some assurance say that language – 'scientific' as well as 'literary – is centripetal, pointing towards itself, signs getting their meaning from within language systems, as both Derrida and Saussure argue, and that thus the author's control of his or her language must be questioned: every word is always 'impure', 'contaminated'. (1999: 70)

To assert that the language of social theory is like literary language, however, is not to assert that social theory is literature. For instance, if it is true, as I have tried to demonstrate throughout this book, that the writing of theoretical texts is not possible despite the existence of metaphorical strategies but precisely because of them, then the presence of metaphors and other narrative strategies is not an exceptional state of affairs for social theory. It is through their effects that distinctive theoretical visualities can be creatively crafted. To deny this is to hold on to a conception of social theorizing that ignores the productivity and effectivity of language. This, however, should not lead us to lose sight of the fact that social theorizing is not, or at least tries not to be, an open-ended creative activity. It is not an imaginary musical instrument capable of signifying on all conceivable ranges. Social theorizing is not writing in general, it is a particular type of writing which aims to represent conceptually different dimensions of how the social world functions. Thus in the realm of social theory, as in all language-borne activities, the range of possible metaphors and the meanings that they can convey depends on the one hand on historical and social conditions, and on the other on the semantic fields with which they are aligned. Some metaphors cannot be thought in some social sites, or in particular historical periods. Some, though possible, just make no sense at all. Others cannot be thought within the discursive space where social theorizing unfolds.

This is necessarily the case because as Foucault argues, in *The Archaeology of Knowledge*, the meanings made possible through scientific discourse are not the effect of the general structure of language or *langue* in which both scientific and literary languages participate. The general structure of language refers to a '... system for possible statements, a finite body of rules that authorizes an infinite number of performances ...', whereas serious talk or scientific discourse is located in a field (i.e. the crystallization of rules of discursive formations) of enunciative events which

> ... is a grouping that is always finite and limited at any moment to the linguistic sequences that have been formulated; they may be innumerable, they may, in sheer size, exceed the capacities of recording, memory, or reading: nevertheless they form a finite grouping. (Foucault, 1992: 27)[2]

Consequently, the historical, social and semantic institutionalization of different forms of writing (e.g. sociological, psychological) and the embeddedness of concepts in 'fields of discursive events' set limits to the semantic promiscuity of theoretical texts,[3] though they certainly do not succeed in making these texts univocal or unisemic (McCanles, 1978; 191–2).

The polyvocal and polysemic character of texts is grounded in the fact that concepts – along with the theoretical strategies and logical architectures which they presuppose – obtain their meanings by the way in which they are located in determinate semantic and discursive fields. As Ekegren argues,

> An isolated term or word has no *value* although it has potential meanings; it receives its specific identity, its value and function and specific meaning only when it becomes a concept, i.e., when it is related to other concepts in a language practice ... it is in need of contextualisation ... (1999: 156)

The space of contextualization, however, is never a singular and homogeneous space; it is a complex, uneven and heterogeneous field which contains a number of historically and socially grounded semantic possibilities (e.g. labour as creativity, labour as the concrete originary action, labour as the historical basis of political and ideological superstructures, labour as the trans-historical basis of all social formations, labour as exploitation, labour as an abstract social mediation). It achieves its unity through the possibility of its dispersion: it necessarily points simultaneously to a number of semantic networks which may reinforce as well as undermine its meaning:

There is not a statement that does not presuppose others; there is no statement that is not surrounded by a field of coexistences, effects of series and succession, a distribution of functions and roles. If one can speak of a statement, it is because a sentence (a proposition) figures at a definite point, with a specific position, in an enunciative network that extends beyond it. (Foucault, 1992: 99)

Thus the meaning of a particular proposition or a concept exists neither in a field where all meanings are possible nor a in a field where only one meaning is possible. A theoretical text cannot exist 'uncontextualized'; it cannot exist outside of a field of co-existences; however, '. . . no context can ever be saturated, since no text can say everything' (Ekegren, 1999: 157).

There is always a disjunction between what is actually written, and what might have been written, between what is meant and what the text might mean. As Derrida claims, '. . . the writer writes in a language and in a logic whose proper system, laws and life his discourse by definition cannot dominate absolutely. He uses them only by letting himself, after a fashion and up to a point be governed by the system' (1976: 158). In other words, theoretical language is not a neutral vehicle for thought. We think theoretically by intervening in semantic spaces through our writing; we attempt to demarcate concepts by relating them to other concepts and by integrating them into theoretical strategies which are both logical and coherent. We try to stabilize semantic spaces (e.g. by defining concepts and relating them to other concepts, by giving concepts and models empirical content) in order to prevent them from communicating constellations of infinite possibilities, we want to communicate 'something' and not 'everything'. However, at every step of the way, we work with a material, theoretical language, which is semantically polychromatic and whose discursive and non-discursive connections are multi-layered and effective in complex ways. Theoretical writing resists our desire for clarity and transparency by denoting and connoting more than what we intend. It engenders connections that we have not consciously or actively willed, connections that may very well undermine the theoretical effect we are trying to achieve or perhaps achieve more than what we thought was possible.

THEORIZING THROUGH METAPHORS

Theorizing thus not only challenges our ability to think, it challenges our ability to produce determinate theoretical effects (e.g. of logic, coherence, non-contradiction, explanation) through writing. At every turn we encounter the resistance of language with its *sui generis* possibilities and limitations of which our writing is only a particular instance. I think that this dimension of theoretical practice, this active working on and through language is fundamental to an understanding of the possibilities and the challenges which the deployment of metaphorical strategies present to theorizing.

As a language-borne practice, theorizing depends on a certain permeability that allows the circulation of meanings not only in its immediate field but also in those of other disciplines or domains. Metaphorical linkages make the latter possible. They open up specific theoretical systems to new semantic and theoretical effects and in this way provide the foundation for new theoretical visualities, new ways of signifying some aspect of social reality. Nevertheless, precisely because theoretical writing attempts to say something about the objects in its own domain it must attempt to translate this semantic and theoretical potential into systems of concepts and theoretical strategies that are domain specific. It is crucial that these refer to its own subject matter (i.e. the social world however this might be defined). The semantic potential is only a theoretical potential to the extent to which this is achieved; otherwise social theory would have no identity at all. It would have no basis of regularity or grounds for intelligibility.

This theoretical practice, however, cannot be understood as somehow taking place outside of language. It is through language that social theory takes concepts and meanings from other domains and attempts to refurbish or rebuild them for its own purposes (i.e. to explain the nature of social life). The irony of social theorizing is that on the one hand it needs to establish metaphorical relationships with other disciplines or phenomenological domains in order to import new signs with their corresponding signifiers (terms) and signifieds (meanings); on the other hand, it needs to work on these signs in order to attach them to signifieds in its own domain. For instance if one imports the sign 'body' into social theory one needs to give this sign a distinctively sociological signified or meaning. One needs to erase the trace of its 'foreignness' (its biological origin) and 'naturalize' it (give it a sociological content). It is in the fractured and creative space engendered by these types of semantic relationships that theorizing as writing unfolds, and it is this complex dynamic that any theory of reading must grasp.[4]

Moreover, if our theoretical practice demands reflexivity, then we cannot be complacent about the discursive tools which we use to produce theoretical effects. We must recognize that metaphors constitute our writing and we must endeavour to use them and not let ourselves be used by them. This of course does not mean that we must attempt to eliminate every single *Modality B* metaphorical effect from our writing. These effects at times function like windows which remain shut but nonetheless allow us to see vistas of potential semantic opportunities. As I will argue in the next section, one of the limitations of theoretical language is its linear structure: not everything can be said at the same time. A *Modality B* metaphor not only provides a possible starting point for the process through which it might be developed towards a *Modality A* status, it allows us to connote possibilities that we cannot directly incorporate into the structure of our arguments. However, if all the metaphors in our writing functioned in this way, then we would be communicating possibilities and not information. It is for this reason that we must work on our metaphors.

In this book I have also drawn on a variety of metaphors, the most important of which is the metaphor which I have applied to metaphors themselves: the metaphor of the circulation of meaning through transfers and transformations. I have attempted to work on its metaphorical potential by developing it as a theoretical sign, by giving it a meaning which is specific to theoretical practice and deploying these meanings in my analysis.[5] However, no writer is ever in complete control of his writing and I invite the reader to attempt to see through my theoretical visuality, but also to see beyond and around it in order to see what I have not been able to see. We cannot delude ourselves into thinking that we can write exactly what we mean. All we can do is to follow Bourdieu (1988) and ask that the 'objectifiers' submit themselves to 'objectification'.

READING SOCIAL STRUCTURE

That the notion of theoretical language as a relatively transparent embodiment of thought is hegemonic in current conceptualizations of social theory is not only demonstrated by the lack of discussion on the language-borne nature of social theory,[6] it is also revealed by the way social theory is taught to students. As far as I know there is no empirical work in this area, but surely any sociology of sociology is radically incomplete if it does not address the way in which students learn to read theoretical texts. I think that the following vignette will allow me to illustrate the point I want to make.

After an attempt to read a theoretical text a student confesses that he or she just does not understand it. The teacher then asks the question: 'but how many times have you read the text?'. The student confused replies: 'once'. The teacher responds: 'Only once! You must read it more than once. I have been reading this same text since my undergraduate days and only now am I beginning to understand it!' Who has not baited a student or as a student been baited in this way?

The implication is that, yes, texts are difficult: in part because they challenge us to look at the social world in new ways and in part because they are couched in an abstract (and foreign) language. However, if one works on the text sufficiently, then its meaning will become clear. Thus an introductory text to social theory for the 'real world' gives the following advice which I think would be shared by most social theory teachers: (1) *read* the text more than once, *read* patiently and do not assume that the intended meaning will be self-evident; (2) *read* with others to allow you to contrast your interpretations with theirs; (3) *read* secondary sources that will allow you to put the text in a wider context, though secondary sources are no substitute for *reading* the original; and finally (4) as you *read*, write notes, identify themes and flesh them out in subsequent *readings* (Miles, 2001: 13). It is difficult to disagree with this advice: it is good advice. However, the meaning of the verb *to read* remains unspecified. Moreover, in so far as the meaning of the term *reading* is not problematized, it serves to reproduce the notion that theoretical language is the transparent embodiment of (il)logical thought. The onus falls on the reader to understand the language, but it is not possible to understand the language if one is not aware of the ways in which writing produces theoretical effects.

In this book, I have continuously put the transparency of theoretical language in question by trying to show that one does not think the concept of structure: one writes it. I have argued throughout that this has important implications for how we read the concept of social structure. I have refused to read the concept of social structure through the economy of scale associated with the structure–action opposition precisely because it economizes too much. It reduces all attempts to produce a concept of structure to the development of a morally acceptable balance between determination and freedom, involuntarism and voluntarism, reproduction and transformation. It is premised on the assumption that once an author's ontological commitments have been identified (his or her location on the structure–agency continuum), it is possible to identify economically what is wrong with the specific concept of social structure without incurring the added cost associated with dealing with the writing effects that produced the concept in the first place. These are seen as externalities best left to philosophers and literary theorists. Against this position, I have argued that an ontological statement is not a concept of social structure and that ontological statements do not embody some pure thought prior to writing.

The problems with concepts of social structure cannot be understood in isolation from the discursive and metaphorical strategies through which they are produced. Thus an ontological statement does not represent an originary moment in thought that guides the deduction of concepts and relations between concepts. Ontological statements themselves are the effect of writing: they produce demands and challenges and contain potentials and limitations.

For instance Durkheim's general ontological position is not primarily geared up to produce a concept of social structure, instead it is concerned with the enunciation of the social at a *sui generis* level. The organismic metaphors, and the metaphors of emergence allow him to do this, but they simultaneously curtail the ways in which the concept of social structure can be written. Moreover, his ontological position places the development of the concept of social structure on the periphery of his theoretical writing. Much the same can be said with respect to Althusser and the effect of the social formation as a complexly structured whole which his writing attempts to produce. The semantic potential associated with Historical Epistemology and its understanding of the development of scientific ideas as a heterogeneous historical process which is characterized by unevenness and ruptures allows him to enunciate not only an epistemology but an ontology of the social formation which shares these attributes. However, it also introduces a discursive tendency towards thinking about all social practices (economic, political and ideological) as if they were theoretical practices.

Similarly, Parsons' discursive and semantic linking of the problem of social order (social structure) with that of the orderly production of knowledge, when it is combined with the assumption of equilibrium, ironically leads not to an over-socialized conception of women and men (Wrong, 1961), but to a conception of actors that are inordinately powerful and knowledgeable. Thus it is not that his writing demands too little from them, but far too much.

The absence of a general concept of social structure in Weber's writing can to some extent be explained by his principled refusal of a *sui generis* ontology for society – his methodological individualism; however, it is also the effect of a defer-ral mechanism connoted by his methodological writings and by the metaphorical relationship between rationality and order. Finally Marx's grounding of the struc-ture of society in the labouring activities of the individuals that comprised the social formation created a discursive and semantic tendency towards material reduction-ism. However, this reductionism must be understood not as a general ontological commitment, but as the effect of the semantic and conceptual networks in which his writing was inserted. This is particularly clear when in *Capital* his writing is able to overcome many of the semantic, hence theoretical, limitations associated with his earlier work and with the base–superstructure model.

An understanding of the way in which these general ontological commitments are positioned through writing provides important avenues for exploring the potentiality and the limitations of the concepts of social structure produced in these texts. Theoretical writing, however, does not produce texts that are governed by a single writing strategy, a single metaphor, from which all its theoretical effects can be derived. Texts are multi-layered and determined by a variety of different discursive effects and exigencies. This book has been an attempt to write about the challenges that this conception of theoretical writing poses to attempts to pro-duce and think concepts of social structure. In the writings I have examined, I have tried to show how their distinctive theoretical visualities are grounded in the rela-tionships between myriad discursive and metaphorical strategies: that it is through these that concepts of social structure are written and thought. Notwithstanding the limitations and the problems associated with the texts I have examined, I have tried to illustrate that they clearly do much more than merely establish a relation-ship between structure and agency. Consequently they also provide a different con-text from which to engage with current debates on social structure. In so far as these are anchored in the structure–agency opposition, they ignore the extent to which the challenge of producing a concept of social structure is tied to a theoretical practice which is underpinned by creative metaphorical thinking and writing.

It is precisely this focus on the creative-theoretical practice of trying to develop concepts of *sui generis* social organization which is, as Woodiwiss argues, lacking in my many contemporary discussions on social structure (2001: 62–92). We can conceptualize the strategies that agents (whether individual or collective) deploy, but we have much difficulty in theoretically imagining the processes through which social systemic effects are produced. On the one hand, we have agents strategizing, on the other we have unintended systemic effects. In between, we have a 'black box'. I believe that it was precisely this 'black box' that the authors I have dealt with here tried to illuminate. This was achieved, in part, through the deployment of broad discursive strategies that served to generate concepts that tried to grasp in theoretical thought *sui generis* forms of social organization. I believe that it is only by recognizing the discursive features of our theoretical effects that we can search for more powerful metaphors of social organization, thus also of social structure and in this way dislodge current discussions outside of the structure–agency problematic.

I think that these arguments provide the basis for a much more productive way of reading and writing the concept of social structure. To be sure, I have not developed a theory of reading or of theoretical practice but I hope that this book is taken as a step in this direction. While on the subject of reading, I think that it is worth reiterating that no reading is innocent. One always reads with and for a purpose. If there is one theme that has driven my analysis in this book it has been a concern with understanding the variety of discursive resources that are used in order to write or think the notion of society as a complex organized whole. I think that the attempt to achieve this effect can be plausibly attributed to the writings of the five theorists I have analysed. In doing so, however, I do not want to replace the economy of scale associated with the structure–agency opposition by a new one of my own making. I have only followed some of the discursive and theoretical threads contained in the texts; I do not claim to have exhausted all of their potential. There are many more ways of reading the concept of social structure that acknowledges its language-borne nature.[7] Moreover, the texts with which I have dealt are no doubt concerned with more than just producing a concept of social structure.

Thus my readings have been partial, and perhaps even misreadings. However, a theory of reading that recognizes the polyvocality and opaqueness of theoretical language must surely strive to overcome the simplistic opposition between reading and misreading. As Culler argues,

> Given the complexities of texts, the revisability of tropes, the extendibility of context and the necessity for a reading to select and organize, every reading can be shown to be partial. Interpreters are able to discover features and implications of a text that previous interpreters neglected or distorted. They can use the text to show that previous readings are in fact misreadings, but their own readings will be found wanting by later interpreters, who may astutely identify the

> dubious presuppositions or particular forms of blindness to which they testify.
> The history of readings is a history of misreadings ... (Culler, 1986: 176)

Similarly, Rasch drawing on Luhmann's theory of communication contextualizes interpretation and understanding as follows:

> The goal of understanding, then, becomes not the elimination of noise but the exploitation of difference between noise and code, 'the construction and reproduction of order out of order and disorder' ... 'Meaning, therefore, involves focusing attention on one possibility among many'; it is 'actuality surrounded by possibilities. The structure of meaning is the structure of this difference between actuality and potentiality'. (Rasch, 2000: 67)

To recognize this is not to undermine the task of reading, it is to read with the realization that this practice demands that we actively engage with the semantic and theoretical texture of a text, that we make choices and that we attempt to justify these choices by reference to the text. It is also to accept that the purpose with which we read (e.g. the challenges that language poses to the enunciation of a concept of structure) will affect our reading. To accept all of this is to acquiesce to the fact that theoretical language is not the transparent embodiment of thought. I believe that this has to be the starting point of any theory of reading theoretical texts.

WRITING SOCIAL STRUCTURE

In this book I have been concerned with exploring some of the challenges associated with the writing of diverse concepts of social structure. In doing so I have focused on the potential and limitations associated with the deployment of particular metaphorical and discursive strategies. This focus has meant that I have had to adopt a strategic and not a principled indifference towards other dimensions associated with the production of concepts of social structure, above all the way in which research informs theorizing. Although I stated it on the first pages of this book, I think that it is worth restating. Social theorizing is concerned with producing knowledge about the social world. This process cannot be understood in isolation from the procedures through which our representations are related to the social world which exists outside of our discursive practices. If it were, it would be impossible to say anything meaningful about the social world. Theorizing would be locked into a game characterized by the infinite deferral of meaning or the search for aesthetic effects; it would involve a paranoiac reflexivity that would lead to idealism, explanatory paralysis and self-referential sterility. We write social structure not only by producing language-mediated models, but also by injecting our models with language-mediated empirical content.

Our theoretical representations have to be developed in conjunction with the friction produced by social objects. It is true that in producing our theoretical models we must aim to be coherent, non-contradictory and logical if we are to be able to use them to say something meaningful about the world. Since these effects cannot be produced outside of language, we must be vigilant and reflexive with regard to our language use. Yet it is, also, crucial never to lose sight of the fact that a near perfectly constructed model is just that. Its integrity, whether logical or aesthetic, is no guarantee that it is an adequate explanation of anything.

An emphasis on the language-borne nature of social theorizing has implications for how we conduct empirical work. If it is the case that the meaning of terms and the coherence of theoretical models are produced through discursive effects then we should not be looking for a one-to-one correspondence between our theories and the social world. A powerful alternative is provided by Woodiwiss' reworking of the scientific realism elaborated by Bhaskar (1975): '. . . observation should be theory-driven; causal modelling and testing are better means of articulating theory and data than hypothesis testing for generalisations; and because of the irreducible difference between our minds and what they seek to comprehend, results are always ultimately fallible . . .' (Woodiwiss, 2001; 19).

The notion of theoretical visuality, as opposed to that of theoretical vision, is premised on the fact that we have no direct access to what is taking place in the social world; our access is always produced through language (Woodiwiss, 2001). Our social theorizing is not mediated through a naturalistic sociological eye which can capture the social world exactly at it is. This is not only, as Durkheim, Marx, Weber, Parsons and Althusser were surely right to point out, because the social world is far too complex and our theoretical discourse positions us in such a way that we must say something and not everything, but also because we are always working within the potentialities and constraints of language.

Against Stehr and Grundmann's (2001) claim, to say that the social world is complex is not an act of resignation. It is to recognize the obstacles that theoretical language and explanation face. As Law and Hetherington (2001) argue, the fact that discourse is 'more or less linear in structure' sets important limitations to our representations of the social world.[8] For instance a 'simple' interaction between a black female lecturer and her white male student in a tutorial would require a far from simple theoretical and empirical representation. It would involve among other things gender relations, power relationships based on cultural capital, generational relationships, communicative practices and commitments to normative ideals, the positioning of knowledge in the current economy, the organization of universities as the site for the transmission of knowledge, the regulation of equity practices and quality control, the expectations of employers, the institutionalization of didactic techniques, race relations, the economic and social background of both actors, etc. However, the question of complexity impinges not only on the level of exhaustiveness (have we covered all the relevant elements?), but also on the way in which these different dimensions can be linked conceptually in a meaningful way in order to specify their mode of effectivity.[9]

To the extent that theoretical language aspires to mimic the social world, it will fail. The opacity of social life cannot be understood by attempting to reproduce its opacity detail by detail in theoretical language.[10] Social theorizing must be understood as an activity which takes place in and through language. The goal of theorizing is to construct conceptual models that are then used to align how we look at the social world for the purpose of testing them. To use Luhmann's terminology, it is to make a distinction that allows us to observe some aspect of the social world, and to use our observations to refine and transform our distinctions. It is precisely in this context that metaphorical thinking has much to offer social theorizing. It provides a way of introducing and organizing new conceptual systems, of internally tooling up our theoretical visualities so that we might observe the social world with more explanatory resources. In order to do so it is necessary to understand how we use language and how language uses us.

Notes

1. As this work will demonstrate, I am particularly indebted to Tony Woodiwiss, both in print and in person, for his championing of the importance of understanding the language-borne nature of theoretical practice.
2. See Holmwood and Stewart (1991) and Holmwood (1996).
3. See Barnes' (2000) critique of the theoretically underdeveloped status of accounts of agency notwithstanding their current hegemonic moment in social theory. Also see Emirbayer (1997: 284) for a similar argument from the perspective of Relational Sociology.
4. It is also necessary to recognize that the discursive space in which sociology unfolds is different from that of philosophy. Consequently, it is not necessary to solve the perennial freedom/determination problem before tackling the question of social structure.
5. An example of this type of analysis is found in the 'history of concepts' approach developed in the history of science by Bachelard (1937), Canguilhem (1994) – see Gutting (1989: Chapter 1), Lecourt (1975), and Tiles (1987). Also see López and Scott (2000).
6. Parsons (1949) and Alexander (1982a, 1982b, 1983, 1984) both developed penetrating critical readings of classical social theory that paid close attention to the autonomy of theoretical language; however, their conception of theoretical discourse as systems of logically coherent statements excluded the consideration of the constitutive role played by metaphors and other narrative strategies.
7. See Woodiwiss (1990, 2001) and Woodiwiss and Pearce (2001) for an insightful and provocative reading of Foucault.
8. By arguing in this way, Foucault was explicitly drawing on the ideas of Bachelard (1937) and Canguilhem (1977). In their work on the development of concepts in the natural sciences, both authors stressed the ways in which concepts obtained their meanings by their location in wider conceptual networks. Although Foucault's archaeology is concerned with analysing the ways in which specific concepts obtain their meanings through their location in wider conceptual fields, its analytical scope is far broader.
9. Very briefly, they comprise the following: 'The rules with respect to "objects" are: the 'surfaces of emergence' or the institutional sites where they appear; the 'authorities of delimitation who predominate within these sites; and the "grids of specification" such as the "body", "psyche" or "soul" that the latter authorities use to demarcate their areas of expertise. The rules with respect to mode of statement or "enunciative modalities" are: the identity of the qualified speakers; the institutional sites where they speak; and the modes of "interrogation" they take up (listening, questioning or looking, for example). The rules with respect to "concepts" are: their order and forms of succession; their fields and forms of coexistence; and the "procedures of intervention" or working within the conceptual field as instanced by "rewriting", "transcribing" and "translating". Finally,

the rules with respect to themes or "strategies" are: the determination of their points of "diffraction" and "equivalence" or differentiation and systematisation; the identification of thematic authorities whether these are located within the field of discourse involved or external to it and are therefore authorities by analogy; and the identification of "the *function* that the discourse under study must carry out *in a field of non-discursive practices*"' (Woodiwiss, 2001: 149–50).

10. For the centrality of the non-discursive, see Foucault (1992: 68, 162, 172); see also Woodiwiss and Pearce (2001) and Woodiwiss (2001).

11. In my opinion, those authors who read the *archaeological* period as being frustrated by its untenable structuralism (e.g. Dreyfus and Rabinow, 1982; Privitera, 1995) fail to grasp the significance of the spatial metaphor underpinning Foucault's *archaeology*.

12. One of the reasons why the arguments I will be developing cannot be considered an archaeology is because I am bracketing off the non-discursive dimensions which as we have already seen are presupposed by an archaeological analysis.

13. See López and Scott (2000: 2–3).

14. Foucault does mention that metaphors and analogies have an important role to play in this context, but he does not develop this idea further in *The Archaeology of Knowledge*.

15. The specialized literature on metaphors has grown at an astonishing rate. For instance two successive, though not comprehensive, bibliographies (Noppen *et al.*, 1985; Noppen and Hols, 1990) contain over 6,000 entries. Noppen has referred to this as an intellectual 'metaphormania' (Maasen, 1994: 11). Many of these texts make important distinctions between 'metaphors, images, analogies, models and systems of thought'. In this study, I am not going to be concerned with hair-splitting distinctions or highly specialized debates regarding the use of the aforementioned terms. Following Maasen *et al.* (1994), I will maintain that many of the important implications of the functioning of metaphors in theory can be examined without recourse to a specialist vocabulary. Consequently I am going to use metaphor, model and analogy almost interchangeably. Nonetheless, below I will provide the working definition of metaphorical processes that informs this study.

16. For instance: Bhaskar (1975), Boyd (1993), Harré (1970), Harré and Madden (1975), Harré and Martin-Soskice (1982), Hesse (1966) and Lewis (1996).

17. See Bono (1990), Johnson (1981), Leatherdale (1974), Maasen (1994), Nerlich and Clarke (2001) and Ortony (1979).

18. I want to reiterate that Foucault understands systems of statements as arising from non-discursive as well as discursive practices, and though I bracket off this question for the purposes of this study I in no way deny its validity or its centrality. The selectivity towards specific metaphors has to be understood as both discursive and non-discursive. However, this is certainly not the same as equating metaphors to ideology. It has been pointed out, for instance, that Darwinian selectionist theory was used to legitimize European colonialism, and social inequality. However, recent historical work by showing 'the tortuous paths by which metaphors enter and transgress a discipline' suggests that a crude causal connection between metaphors and ideologies obscures more than it reveals (Maasen *et al.*, 1994: 5). See for instance Bowler (1994) on the metaphor of 'struggle', Hejl (1994) and Vergata (1994) on the metaphor of 'organism' and Mitchell (1994) on the metaphor of the 'superorganism'. Also see, Bannister (1970), Kelly (1981) and Morgan (1994) where the commonsensical connection between Darwinism and Economic theory is subject to a trenchant critique.

19. See Lakoff and Johnson (1980).

20. A related *Modality B* metaphor which has been more influential in the development of theories of social organization is the metaphor of equilibrium drawn from both the fields of biology and thermodynamics; see Russet (1966) and Bailey (1994).

21. Frequently, when sociologists refer to a metaphor pejoratively, it is this variety which they normally have in mind.

22. Consequently, the study of metaphors can, also, provide important co-ordinates for the study of cultural change in diverse yet related social domains (Bono, 1990).

23. As Venuti has argued, the translator and translation as a particular form of writing has for too long enjoyed the privilege of invisibility: 'Current pedagogy implicitly conceives of translation as communication unaffected by the language that makes it possible, or in Derrida's (translator's) words, "governed by the classical model of transportable vocality or formalizable polysemia" ' (Venuti, 1998: 92). Venuti also insists that it is necessary to explore the way in which translated texts are domesticated and the function which this domestication fulfils: 'Translations, in other words, inevitably perform a work of domestication. Those that work best, the most powerful in recreating cultural values and the most responsible in accounting for that power, usually engage readers in domestic terms that have been defamiliarized to some extent, made fascinating by a revisionary encounter with a foreign text' (Venuti, 1998: 5). For instance, see Sica (1988: 28–39) for a discussion of how the irrational elements (see Chapter 3) in Weber's writing were sanitized through a translation framework that emphasized nominalism and positivism.

Chapter 1: Durkheim's Structures

1. The charge of evolutionism and teleology is one that is often directed towards Durkheim. However, it is not so simple to uphold this claim. For instance, in *The Division of Labour in Society*, Durkheim writes that a mechanistic theory of progress or of social determination is not synonymous with the end of history or the end of contingency (1984: 344). See also Lukes (1992: 388). In *The Rules* in his discussion of 'social types' he criticizes the simple linear and teleological conceptions of historical development found in the work of Comte and Spencer by writing that 'If ... social types exist which are qualitatively distinct from each another, it would be vain to seek to juxtapose them together exactly like the homogeneous segments that constitute a geometrical straight line' (1982a: 109). A little later in the text he reiterates the same point: 'If historical evolution is envisaged as being moved by a kind of *vis a tergo* (vital urge) which impels men forward, since a dynamic tendency can only have a single goal, there can exist only one reference point from which to calculate the utility or harmfulness of social phenomena. It follows that there exists, and can only exist, a single type of social organisation which fits humanity perfectly, and the different societies of history are only successive approximations to that single model. It is unnecessary to show how such a simplistic view is today irreconcilable with the acknowledged variety and complexity of social forms' (1982a: 141). Gane (1988) recognizes that Durkheim's concepts of morphology and physiology (more on these below) depend on some type of evolutionary understanding, but he denies that it should be understood in terms of teleology. For instance he remarks that 'Durkheim constantly reiterated that the advanced societies have not the elementary societies as their cause, for they cause themselves *causa sui*' (161).

2. For the extent of the similarities, see Braudel (1972a, 1972b) and Lukes (1992: 394). Traugott (1978), in a note, comments that Durkheim had a profound influence on Henri Berr, a philosopher/historian around whom the first *Annales* group crystallized; moreover Lucien Febvre and Marc Bloch were regular readers of *L'Anné Sociologique* (255).

3. See Schmaus (1994: Chapter 2) for a discussion of the importance of the intellectual division of labour for the Durkheimian sociological project.

4. This of course does not mean that Durkheim's analysis is free of a normative focus. For instance in *The Rules* he suggests that a statesman enlightened by a scientific understanding of society would have a role analogous to that of a doctor: 'The duty of the statesman is no longer to propel societies violently towards an ideal which appears attractive to

him. His role is rather that of the doctor: he forestalls the outbreak of sickness by maintaining good hygiene, or when it does break out, seeks to cure it' (1982a: 104).

5. Here as elsewhere in this book I am not analysing those extra-discursive elements that also serve to constitute discursive systems. In doing this, I am not denying their importance; I am merely bracketing them. With respect to the organismic metaphor, one could cite for instance the social-political context in which the emergence of sociology was located. France's defeat at the hands of Germany in 1871 was conceptualized by intellectuals, at the time, in terms of the defeat of 'French Individualism' by 'German Collectivism' (Hejl, 1994: 157). The resonances between this political climate and Durkheim's emphasis on social solidarity are clearly too important to ignore. The intellectual debates following France's defeat and their relationships to Germany are documented by Digeon (1959) and Guiton (1968). For an account of the emergence of the social sciences in the French university system see Clark (1973). For an introduction to the Durkheimians in their institutional setting see Besnard (1983).

6. Here I am speaking of the organismic analogy in a general sense. However it is, in fact, possible to find two related but distinct metaphors. On the one hand Durkheim conceives of society as a functioning body, on the other he employs the body–mind distinction in order to describe the emergence of psychic life. Although in general terms it is sufficient to speak about the organismic analogy, below I will show the importance of analysing them separately

7. The centrality of the organismic metaphor has, of course, been noted in the secondary literature: Giddens (1971); Lukes (1992); Nisbet (1952, 1965); Szacki (1979); Tiryakian (1978); Wallwork (1972); Zeitlin (1994); Hirst (1973a, 1975); and Pearce (1984). However, its implications for how we read Durkheim have received little attention with the notable exception of Lehmann (1993).

8. The ambiguity that exists between the concept of organization and occupational specialization points to another metaphor, which, to my mind, has not received sufficient attention in the secondary literature. Curiously, there is a basic similarity between the Marxist conception of labour, as the mechanism that makes it possible to bridge the conceptual space between individual action and social organization, and Durkheim's tendency to conflate function with occupation. Specifically in the *Division of Labour in Society*, social organization is, often, narrowly conceived in terms of work as opposed to broader institutional organization.

9. It can, of course, be legitimately objected that one narrows the field too quickly if social structure is conceived only in terms of social morphology. Among other things, this would prevent the realm of 'representations' and the 'conscience collective' from being understood in structural terms. I will pick up this second objection in a section below.

10. In this chapter I am not dealing with the specificity of Durkheim's method, but it is worth highlighting that it is much more sophisticated than many have claimed. See especially Schmaus (1994).

11. See Némedi (2000) for a discussion of the relationship between the concepts of morphology and representations in Durkheim's writing.

12. See Hirst (1973b), Benton (1974), Canguilhem (1994) and Prigogine and Stengers (1985) for the context of these debates.

13. See López and Scott (2000: 82–8) for an illustration of how this relational conception of social organization is developed in the work of Bourdieu and Foucault.

14. As Gane quite rightly points out: 'It is also an error to suggest that because Durkheim became critical of analyses which assumed a one-to-one relationship between morphology and collective representations he was no longer interested in the role of morphology after 1898' (1988: 110). See also Schmaus (1994).

15. See essays in Pickering (2000) for a number of interesting contributions relating to the concept of representations in Durkheim's works.

Chapter 2: Marx

1. Implicit here is a discursive strategy that serves to fix the meaning of 'human' via an opposition with the animal world which is by no means unquestionable. See Benton (1993: Chapter 2) for a critique and a possible theoretical reconstruction of Marx's negative representation of animals and nature.
2. This last connection is developed in Löwith (1993).
3. On this point also see Colletti (1975).
4. See Erich Fromm (1966) and Heller and Fehér (1991).
5. I am not suggesting that Marx set out the manuscripts with this purpose in mind. The process of reproducing large portions of text was central to how Marx worked. Nonetheless in this case his mode of presentation and his thought strongly reinforce each other, even though this might be unwittingly so.
6. It is worth noting that Habermas believes, incorrectly to my mind, that this problem plagues all of Marx's work and not just his early writing. Habermas argues that the reduction of action to the paradigm of production is excessively narrow and fails to capture the communicative dimension of social life. Consequently Habermas' project is an attempt to derive the ethical consequences of the centrality of communication within a trans-historical and evolutionary framework (Habermas, 1987; Vol. 2). For a cogent critique of Habermas' misreading of Marx's later conception of labour and his immanent critique of capitalism see Postone (1996: Chapter 6).
7. Engels of course pioneered this defence (Engels, 1978: 475–6), but it has also been taken up by McLellan (1973: 40).
8. As Schimdt (1971: 86–9) argues, this stress on the centrality of physiological processes is derived from the influence of German Materialists – who also held an anti-idealist position – specifically the 'metabolic' metaphors of Moleschott. This is the case notwithstanding the strong tensions that existed between Marx and the group to which he referred to as 'vulgar materialists'; see Rabinbach (1992, 319–20). Also see Gregory (1977) for a study that maps the relationships between Ludwig Feuerbach, Karl Vogt, Jakob Moleschott, Ludwig Büchner and Heinrich Czolbe.
9. This simple positional thinking is not even sufficient to give an account of the relationship between the base and the superstructure in the physical domain itself. The solution to the base–superstructure problem in engineering required that this simplistic model of an above and below be abandoned. In terms of Newtonian physics, it was clear that the solution lay in finding a way of thinking how it was possible for the base to push back in order to counterbalance the downward pull of gravity. That is to say, it was realized that the opposition between base and superstructure had to be resolved in terms of the balancing of forces: what needed to be understood was under which conditions the force of the superstructure was reciprocated by that of the base. It suggested the need to think about the relationship between the base and superstructure in terms of the equalization of two opposing forces, and not one of determination by the base. The solution was arrived at through the metaphor of the 'springiness' of solids from which the modern-day concept of elasticity has been developed – see Gordon (1978: 34–7).
10. See also Jakubowski (1976), Hall (1970) and López and Scott (2000: 66–74).
11. As is well known, the two fundamental laws of thermodynamics deal with the processes that underpin the conversion of energy. 'The first law of thermodynamics deals with the conservation of energy. It states that the total amount of energy in a process is conserved despite complex forms and changes' (Adam, 1990: 61). The second law, which deals with entropy, states '... that all systems tend towards disorder; that things, just like people, are impermanent; and that every time something occurs, some amount of energy will be unavailable for future work' (Adam, 1990: 62). See Prigogine and Stengers (1985) for an accessible introduction to thermodynamics.

12. However, see Postone (1996) for a critique of this position where he argues that advanced industrial production is internally related to capitalism; it is not an objective technological process which exists outside of capitalist social relations. Consequently neither the intensification of production nor the idealization of proletarian work provide the basis for emancipation from capitalism. Nonetheless, Postone does highlight that the notion of abstract labour differs from Marx's earlier conception of labour in a way that is in broad agreement with the argument I am developing here.

13. Engels (1940), of course, makes the link to Helmholtz explicit, and argues for the unity between the natural and the social world. However, we need not accept Engels' scientistic account of Marx's work in order to recognize the productive discursive and theoretical labour that the energeticist metaphor makes possible.

14. From this point onward, I am going to be using Vol. 1, Vol. 2 and Vol. 3 in the text to refer to Marx's *Capital* (1983).

15. It is fair to say, however, that though Marx makes reference to these things he never develops the connection at the same level of abstraction and sophistication with which he deals with labour. I will return to this in the concluding section.

16. See Postone (1996) for a penetrating and powerful reading of Marx's *Capital* along the lines suggested here.

17. I think that the conceptual and theoretical richness contained in Marx's discursive attempt to re-spatialize capitalism as a complexly structured social system is missed by the essentialism of commentators such Laclau and Mouffe (1994) who focus exclusively on the lack of tenability of the economic determinist thesis, and who seem to read Marx exclusively as a political theorist.

18. In this sense, it is not surprising that much of the interesting work which has been done within the context of the conceptualization of social space has a strong Marxist debt, for instance, Harvey (1985), Soja (1989), Lefebvre (1974), Glucksmann (2000) and Gregory and Urry (1985) to name but a few.

19. For instance, some of the conceptual tools provided by Foucault (1979; 1991a; 1991b) and Burchell *et al.* (1991) could be crucial for a systematic theory of political structure, notwithstanding Foucault's own protestation to the contrary; see for instance Marsden (1999). Similarly, structuralist and post-structuralist accounts of meaning, identity, culture and discourse provide powerful theoretical tools for a richer, more complex, and simultaneous embedding of socio-economic processes as described in *Capital*, in other social spheres. Moreover, Marx's account of the capitalist system as a field of complexly co-ordinated processes can also be seen as providing important points of contact with the systems notion of communication found in the work of Luhmann (1998; 1995) and theorists who are exploring a theoretical rapprochement between social theory and complexity theory. Finally, the concept of social structure as a 'field' and the notion of structure as 'virtual depth' found in the work of both Bourdieu and Foucault (López and Scott 2000) also contains important points of contact with Marx's later model.

Chapter 3: Weber's Structures

1. See for instance Craib (1997), Benton (1977), Rex (1971), Turner (1981) and Scaff (1989). For a critique see Kalberg (1994).

2. Löwith sees the lack of a substantial definition of social structure as an effect of the process of secularization and disenchantment: 'Along with the transformation of reality into something entirely secular and without an "objective" meaning, the emanatistic conceptualisation also becomes an ideal-typical "construction", and all "substantial definitions" of "social structure" vanish. The constructivist and "nominalistic" character of Weber's basic methodological concepts and the whole style of his scientific

approach do not arise from an immediate demand of science as such . . . The ideal-typical "construct" is based upon a human being who is specifically "free of illusions", thrown back upon itself by a world which has become objectively meaningless and sober and to this extent emphatically "realistic" ' (Löwith, 1993: 60). In a similar vein, Aron (1967: 185–258) characterizes Weber's sociology as existentialist. For an account of the importance of Löwith's reading of Marx and Weber see Turner (1999: 48–71).

3. This notion of complexity as is well known is the product of two distinct, yet related networks of philosophical thought. On the one hand, it arises from the Protestant worldview and the philosophy of Kant that sees the individual as the bearer of meaning in a chaotic and meaningless world; see for instance Albrow (1990: Chapters 1 and 2). On the other, it emerges from Nietzsche's reluctance to accept that the systematizing of our knowledge of the world was anything other than the production of anthropo-morphic tropes: 'that the collective character [*Gesamtcharakter*] of the world . . . is in all eternity chaos – in the sense not of a lack of necessity but a lack of order, arrangement, form, beauty, wisdom, and whatever other names there are for our aesthetic anthropo-morphisms [human weakness – *Menschlichkeiten*]' (Nietzsche in Spivak, 1976: xxiii). On the effect of Nietzsche's thought on Weber see Albrow (1990), Eden (1983), Gerth and Mills (1991), Hennis (1988), Stauth and Turner (1988) and Turner (1995; 1982).

4. Textually and stylistically this effect is also written through the deployment of a situated casuistic mode of exposition. Situated casuistry is a form of moral argumentation that among other things privileges the development of ethical doubt, and produces a complex, qualified and cautious form of argumentation. It is also characterized by the 'Avoidance of transcendental arguments or universal formulas to carry the burden of examination, resulting in a typically episodic, fragmentary presentation of materials' (Green, 1988: 198). All of which are clear in Weber's writing.

   In his study of the centrality of the genre of situated casuistry for Weber's writings, Green argues that 'Weber's concern to break the hold of collective reifications on socio-logical theory, his resistance to all doctrinal-isms, master principles and "world-formu-lae" . . . his aversion to the bureaucratic petrification of conduct and the modern rule of formal rationality . . . his rejection of all save an ethics of responsibility – all follow the same pattern of opposition as situated casuistics' (Green, 1998: 188). Moreover, the effect of the casuistic genre is also evident in the actual structure of Weber's writing: it can be seen in 'the inclusiveness of the substantive discussions; their failure to move decisively towards a definite conclusion (*Economy and Society* does not conclude; it simply trails off); the proliferations of cautionary connectives and qualifiers – perhaps, but, yet that – yields the entwining tangles of statements; the placement of so many ordinary terms in quotation marks; and the striking contrast between its stylistic defi-ance of straightforward reading and the lucid simplicity and eloquence of his extrascho-larly writings and from all reports his spoken presentations' (Green, 1988: 264–5).

5. See for instance his scathing critique of Hegel and 'emanatism' in Weber (1975).

6. See Burger (1976) for a discussion of the parallels and divergences between Rickert and Weber; see also Benton (1977).

7. As Hughes rightly claimed in his influential *Consciousness and Society*: Max Weber's great-est challenge was to attempt 'to combine the Germanic sense of history and philosophy with the Anglo-French and positivist notion of scientific rigor . . . a task that he, more than any other of his contemporaries, was qualified by temperament and training to confront (Hughes, 1959: 285).

8. See also Weber (1975: 122–3).

9. This is precisely what Weber is doing in the first chapter – 'Basic Sociological Terms' – of *Economy and Society*. However, see Burger's argument of the special status of Ideal Types as a class of generalizing concepts *vis-à-vis* other generalizing sciences (1976: 115–29).

10. The question of the status of Ideal Types in Weber's writing and in sociological expla-nation in general has long been the subject of debate. See for instance Albrow (1990:

Chapter 8), Bruun (1972), Burger (1976: Chapters 3, 4), Freund (1968), especially Kalberg (1997: Chapter 7; 1994: Chapters 3, 4 and 5), Mommsen (1989: Chapter 8), Parsons (1949), Roth and Schluchter (1979: 195–206), Runciman (1972) and Watkins (1973).

11. In this context, Sica is surely right to assert that 'in his [Weber's] effort to defuse teleologies of right and left, with their entelechies and organic relations, he very nearly empties the social world of any *telos* whatever, of any functional relations. He is left with a social ontology so bereft of order that it resembles more than anything else what one might imagine the interior perceptions of a psychotic might be' (1988: 155).

12. And it is for this reason that the historical sciences will remain eternally youthful: '... there are sciences to which eternal youth is granted, and the historical disciplines are among them all those to which the eternally onward flowing stream of culture perpetually brings new problems' (Weber, 1949: 104).

13. This of course should not be taken to mean that Weber is constructing a sociology of individualistic systems of values: 'It is a tremendous misunderstanding to think that an "individualistic method" should involve what is in any conceivable sense an individualistic system of values' (Weber, 1978: 18).

14. It has to be noted that there is some degree of ambiguity regarding Weber's mentalistic concept of action. For instance, Runciman has pointed out that, although Weber is clearly committed to thinking about meaningful actions as causally efficacious, he never developed the mechanics of this in any detail (1972: 62–3). Similarly, the post-Wittgensteinian school of action have argued that Weber's conception of social action is excessively mentalistic, hence it does not provide the basis for the development of the concept of action (Blum and McHugh, 1971; Melden, 1961). Another critic of the Weberian conception of action, Rubenstein (1977), argues that if one develops the notion of intentional action found in Weber to its logical conclusion then most social actions fall outside of the Weberian schema.

    With this I am not suggesting that reasons cannot be causes; rather I am merely highlighting that inasmuch as Weber left his conception underdeveloped, probably as a result of the *Modality B* metaphorical plausibility of rationality as the basis of social order, he produced a rather descriptive and mechanistic notion of causality. For an overview of these debates and a possible but to my mind not very convincing solution see Porpora (1987: Chapter 4).

15. An explicit assumption of Weber's 'means–ends' rationality is that it is capable of transcending all meaning systems (Holmwood and Stewart, 1991: 66). For instance, Weber writes that '... the successful logical analysis of the content of an ideal and its ultimate axioms and the discovery of the consequences which arise from pursuing it, logically and practically, must also be valid for the Chinese' (1949: 58).

16. However, as Rossi persuasively argues, there are problems with the way in which 'Weber considers subjective meaning, ideas, and statistical uniformities to be self-evident and self-contained data of analysis' (1983: 67), see also Holmwood and Stewart (1991: 67) and Benton (1977).

17. See Sica (1988) for Weber's ambiguity with respect to irrationality and for an analysis of the social and theoretical factors that have excluded this ambiguity from mainstream interpretations of Weber's writings.

18. Weber also highlights the irrationality of traditional action and charisma by suggesting that these types of behaviour might best be explained as the persistence of 'animal' instinctive behaviour: 'This is particularly true of all "traditional" action and of charisma, which contain the seeds of certain types of psychic "contagion" and thus give rise to new social developments. These types of action are very closely related to phenomena which are understandable either only in biological terms or can be interpreted in terms of subjective motives only in fragments' (Weber, 1978: 17). This admission is particularly problematic as it has the potential for undermining the entire explanatory edifice of the logic of scientific historical explanation that is premised on the possibility of

reconstructing the subjective (rational) states of mind of historical actors. However, as I will argue in the next section, some of the problems associated with this discursive exigency are overcome through the deployment of a heroic mode of emplotment.

19. This is precisely the position held by the German Historical School, which Weber so scathingly criticized (Weber, 1949; 1975).

20. See López and Scott (2000: Chapter 6) for a discussion of the limitations associated with trying to enunciate the embodiment of social structure through purely mentalistic metaphors.

21. Moreover it also alerts us, as Mitzman (1970) has argued, to the psychological impact of the positioning of Weber's generation in post-Bismarkian Germany.

22. As Turner has argued, 'Weber was in fact profoundly ambiguous about the nature of rationality and modernity, being specifically conscious of the irrational drive behind the growth of rational values' (1999: 21).

23. Marianne Weber suggests that it was Weber's paternal uncle, Karl David Weber, who served as a model for this type of heroic entrepreneur: 'In his nephew's work on the spirit of capitalism, this uncle served as a prime example of the modern entrepreneur, the affirmation of whose creative energies contrasted sharply with Weber's lifelong condemnation of the eudemonistic ethic represented by his own father' (Mitzman, 1970: 16).

24. See Scott (1996) for an attempt to construct a theory of stratification around Weberian lines.

25. In this context it is worth noting that, although Weber makes theoretical distinctions in virtue of which individuals can be mapped into three different spheres of stratification (class, status and party) in terms of being positively or negatively privileged, his substantive writing tends to focus more often than not on the former.

26. For instance in *The Religion of China* the accentuation of this type of action produces, as Alexander (1983) has argued, an instrumental account of the emergence of the literati.

27. In this context it is important to realize that even Weber's conceptualization of bureaucratic structure relies on the notion of the solitary and heroic individual as the source of patterned action. As Luhmann has written, Weber's bureaucratic organizations are written from '. . . the standpoint of a single participant: the founder, entrepreneur and ruler. The organization is, in some sense, an extension of the rationality of the leader's actions' (Luhmann, 1982: 31). Similarly, Bologh has argued that 'Weber looked to the heroic individual, a strong political leader, who can take charge of the state bureaucracy and master it, subordinating bureaucratic rules and methods to substantive, political ends' (Bologh, 1990: 92).

28. As is well known Weber argued that charismatic domination was fundamentally unstable and in its myriad historical manifestations revealed a tendency towards routinization (Weber, 1978: 1111–57). This has led one of Weber's interpreters to represent the dynamic between charisma and routinization as the 'essential origins of all social change as such' (Mommsen, cited in Schroeder, 1992: 10). However, given Weber's multi-causality and his commitment to the radical heterogeneity of concrete social configurations, I think that this position is not very convincing. I think that it might perhaps be more useful to understand charisma as an element of Weber's heroic mode of emplotment.

29. See Baeher (1990) for a critique of Weber's conceptualization of the irrationality of the 'masses'.

30. It is perhaps for this reason that Weber concludes his study of the emergence of the protestant ethic with such pathos: 'To-day the spirit of religious asceticism – whether finally, who knows? – has escaped from the cage. But victorious capitalism, since it rests on mechanical foundations needs its support no longer . . . Where the fulfilment of the calling cannot directly be related to the highest spiritual and cultural values, or when, on the other hand, it needs not be felt simply as economic compulsion, the individual generally abandons the attempt to justify it at all' (Weber, 1992: 181–2). Thus, once

capitalism is established and can be reproduced in a mundane and unreflective way it loses the heroic gloss that characterized it during its eruption on to the world stage. Tellingly, Weber goes on to pose the question of whether some new prophet may not yet arise (1992: 181).

31. See Kalberg (1994: 50–78).

Chapter 4: Parson's Structure

1. See *Appendix: Conflation and Reduction in the Interpretation of Parsonian Theory* in Alexander (1984) for a brief, yet comprehensive, ordering of the major strands of Parsonian critique, and also Turner (1974), Turner (1986) and Savage (1981).

2. For instance, Holmwood (1996), Alexander (1984; 1985), Adriaansens (1980; 1989), Barber (1989), Bourricard (1981), Buxton (1985), Hamilton (1983; 1992), Holton and Turner (1988), Lemert (1995: 123–9), Luhmann (1982), Munch (1987), Robertson and Turner (1991; 1991), Rocher (1974), Sciulli and Gerstein (1985) and Wearne (1987).

3. For instance, the fact that the term structure is not even listed in the subject index of Alexander's impressive work of scholarship on Parsonian theory, *Theoretical Logic In Sociology, Vol. 4: The Modern Reconstruction of Classical Thought: Talcott Parsons*, is an important index of the alleged significatory stability of the concept of structure.

4. See, for instance Schwanenberg (1990), Munch (1987) and Bershady (1973).

5. A fairly extensive bibliography of the debates surrounding this work can be found in Camic (1992) where the author argues that *The Structure of Social Action* has to be seen as a political intervention in the academic world in the form of a charter for sociology. Hence, the theoretical argument is structured in such as a way as to allow for the emergence of a distinct disciplinary space for sociology among both economics and behavioral psychology. It is perhaps the case that a similar argument could be made for Durkheim. Although Camic presents some very interesting insights, a strong argument, as the one made by Camic, would deprive theoretical development of any autonomy because it would be overdetermined by extra-theoretical elements. See Alexander and Sciortino (1985) for a rejoinder.

6. For a general introduction to positivism and related debates see Potter (2000) and Benton and Craib (2001).

7. For instance, both Alexander (1984) and Savage (1981) argue that in Parsons' writings we find a harbinger of a post–positivist understanding of science. However, Alexander claims that it remains just a harbinger because of the paradoxical way in which Parsons combines assertions of the autonomy of theoretical development with strongly flavoured positivist statements (1984, 152–6). That Parsons can be seen as sitting on the fence with respect to the positivist–post-positivist divide, is also strongly indicated by the fire that he draws from the positivist camp; see the essays in Black (1961).

8. Others have seen this as a major aberration, hence the need to de-Parsonize Weber, and the Utilitarian tradition; see Cohen *et al.* (1992) and Camic (1979) respectively. Still others have seen this merely as a strategy for academic legitimation, for instance Parker (1997).

9. Parsons in his later writings also stressed the centrality of Kant (Parsons, 1977b). Munch (1987: 8–30) argues that the Kantian core is crucial for an adequate evaluation of Parsonian action theory. However, Munch's argument stresses the similarities between the Kantian philosophical questions of 'How is knowledge possible?'; 'How is judgment possible?'; 'How is moral behaviour possible?'; and the Parsonian sociological counterpart: 'How is social order possible?'. Münch takes the epistemological solution as given in its Kantian form; consequently the metaphorical role played by the epistemological convergence theory is not examined.

10. For instance the notion of theoretical convergence, and its modalities outlined in *The Structure of Social Action*, emerge in the context of Bales' work on small groups (Parsons *et al.*, 1953), in the convergence of economic theory and the general theory of action (Parsons and Smelser, 1957), as well as the dramatic convergence that Parsons claims between the latter and evolutionary biology, to name but a few (Parsons, 1977b). Moreover, in *Theories of Society* Parsons draws on the notion of cybernetic hierarchy to account for order both in the social world as well as in the realm of knowledge production. Finally, if one looks at Parsons' later evolutionary theory, it is quite suggestive that the process of evolutionary differentiation understood in terms of adaptive-upgrading, integration, inclusion and value generalization (Parsons, 1977a) could easily be used as a framework for an account of Parsons' theoretical development, particularly as developed in his intellectual biography essay (Parsons, 1977b). Other issues regarding the parallel unfolding of social order and epistemological order are explored in Schwanenberg (1990).
11. For instance this argument is made by Scott (1963).
12. See Russet (1966) and Bailey (1994) for an account and critique of the centrality of the concept of equilibrium in American sociology.
13. See Cannon (1939).
14. As Bailey writes: 'The way sociologists used equilibrium was unique in the scientific community. They seemed driven chiefly by its perceptual or conceptual level ... connotations of balance, harmony and stability ... Such perceptual-level ... value judgments of equilibrium were generally absent from thermodynamics. It did not connote stability, but system death or disintegration (maximum entropy) according to the second law [of thermodynamics] (1994: 117).
15. See also Parsons (1964: 148).
16. Though Parsons puts a certain emphasis on the boundary maintenance aspect of the social system, he has not yet begun to describe this in terms of interchanges between a system and its external environment, as well as the interchanges between internal subsystems.
17. Parsons uses the couplet status–role in order to parallel two simultaneous features of interaction. Status refers to that facet of interaction where the actor is a possible object of orientation for other actors, and role refers to the facet where the actor orients herself to other actors as social objects (Parsons, 1991: 25).
18. The cultural system is made up of '... relatively stable symbolic systems where meaning is not predominantly contingent on highly particularized situations' (Parsons, 1991: 11).
19. For Parsons, personality is '... the relational system of a living organism interacting with a situation. Its integrative focus is the organism-personality unit as an empirical entity' (Parsons, 1991: 17).
20. On this point see *Towards a General Theory of Action* (Parsons and Shils, 1951: 49).
21. It should be noted that three of the pattern-variables make their debut in two of the essays collected in *Essays in Sociological Theory* (*The Professions and Social Structure* and *The Motivation of Economic Activities*); however at this stage they are not systematically derived from the interaction frame of reference as they are in *The Social System*.
22. For a critique of Parsons' derivation of the pattern-variables along these lines see Rocher (1974: 166–7), Dubin (1960), Black (1961: 283–8), Savage (1981: 160–65) and Williams (1961: 93).
23. Parsons elaborates on the articulation of psychoanalysis and social systems theory in Parsons *et al.* (1953: Chapter 1). Notwithstanding the fact that Parsons writes on this issue extensively throughout his career, it is unfortunately the case that his contribution to psychology has not been seriously examined by practitioners of this discipline.
24. The cultural system is narrowly conceived in terms of the linkage between culture and the individual being mediated through the social system. This means that all elements of culture are distilled to those capable of being understood in terms of pattern

maintenance. As Habermas writes, 'Evidently it is a question of the standards against which the validity of descriptive, normative, evaluative and expressive statements are measured within the framework of a given cultural tradition. But the substantive richness of a culture is not exhausted by such abstract standards of value and validity' (1989: 218).

25. For instance, Parsons and Shils write 'The need for order is seen in its simplest and most elementary form in the complementarity of role expectations' (Parsons and Shils, 1951: 175).

26. Holmwood (1996) via a different argument arrives at a similar point, though he certainly draws different conclusions with respect to its importance for general theorizing. See also Luhmann (1976: 510).

27. Admittedly, Parsons and Shils write '... institutionalization itself must be regarded as the fundamental integrative mechanism of social systems' (Parsons and Shils, 1951: 150). However, earlier in *The General Statement*, we find 'By institutionalization we mean the integration of the expectations of the actors in a relevant interactive system of roles with a shared normative pattern of values' (Parsons and Shils, 1951: fn. 27, 20). Hence institutionalization is a crystallization of the already existing compatibility between different role–status complexes; therefore it serves to explain why communication is possible at the level of individual interaction against the background of an already existing, yet unspecified, order.

28. This same problem can be identified with reference to the question of collectivities: 'A collectivity may be defined as the integration of its members with a common value system. This integration implies that the members of the collectivity will, under appropriate circumstances, act in defense of the shared values' (Parsons and Shils, 1951: fn. 2, 192). Now, presumably it would be the social alignment of status–role complexes underpinned by relations (social structures) that allows solidarity to emerge in collectivities. But elsewhere, Parsons writes '... affective attachments of individuals to the collectivities ... are constitutive of the structure of the social system ...' (1977b: 220). But surely it is the social structure that is constitutive of the attachment and not the other way around. Without social structure in the first place, interaction would not be possible.

29. There is clearly an ideological dimension at work here. In this respect Woodiwiss' (1993, Chapter 3; 1997) genealogy of the emergence of the 'social-scientific' discourse of modernity from a specific ideological framework is of interest, especially its connection with the pattern-variables.

30. I particularly have in mind the work of Bourdieu. In Bourdieu's concept of habitus we have a series of generative mechanisms that do not rely explicitly on the attachment to concrete value-orientations, rather the reproduction of structural relations depends on a certain disjunction between the actual structuring elements, and the concrete values held by actors (Bourdieu, 1977: 19). Moreover the same could be said regarding socialization or social learning. For Parsons, learning is ultimately dependent on an identity between what is learnt and the basis for social order. For Bourdieu, this is clearly not the case. Structuring principles are 'embodied' and not necessarily known (Bourdieu, 1977: 94–5).

31. This of course produces the often derided 'Russian dolls' effect where any system can be represented as both being one of the four subsystems in a wider system and as having four subsystems of its own. The elegance of this model cannot be denied, however; see Mouzelis (1995: Chapter 7) for a well-founded critique.

32. See Morse (1961: 148–9) for a similar critique grounded in the exigencies of empirical research.

33. Parsons develops and expands the notion of media of communication in Parsons (1967), Parsons (1977b: 204–73) and Parsons and Platt (1973). See also Alexander (1984: 110–18).

34. See also GanBmann (1988).

35. See Kay (1995) for some of the wider discursive conditions of possibility associated with the development and dissemination of the cybernetic framework.
36. For instance the concept of the social system is far from dead in contemporary theorizing. The assumption of equilibrium was the effect of the particular discursive strategies through which Parsons wrote this concept. Consequently a number of theorists have been able to open up systems-based theoretical visualities that do not rely on this assumption (e.g. Bailey, 1994; Habermas, 1989; Luhmann, 1982, 1995, 1998; Oliga, 1996).
37. In this sense, one cannot help but be disappointed that theorists who have allegedly continued the Parsonian functionalist project have done so precisely by reneging on the theoretical task of finding adequate signifieds for the signifiers' function, communication, and code. Instead, they have turned the system perspective to 'an actor-based model of interests'. Thus for Alexander (1988), Eisenstadt (1985), Colomy (1990) and Colomy and Rhoades (1994), equilibrium and function are redefined along a pluralist model, where these signifiers are taken to refer to competition among different interest groups. See Schwinn (1998) for a development of this argument.

Chapter 5: Althusser's Structure

1. Opinions on the nature of the failure vary quite significantly. Some have seen in Althusserianism a theoretical and political pathology to be excised at all cost (Thompson, 1978; Clarke et al., 1980), others have seen in Althusser a mutation leading to a new and invigorating state for Marxist theory (Resnick and Wolf, 1993). Yet other scholars' positions have changed at a lightning pace from, in the words of Elliot (1987: 5), 'hyper-Althusserianism' (Hindness and Hirst, 1975) to 'post-Althusserianism' (Cutler et al., 1978: 79). Fortunately, there have been others who have offered a sympathetic, yet critical and more nuanced account of Althusser's theoretical work (Benton, 1984; Callinicos, 1976; Smith, 1984; Freedman, 1990; Elliot, 1987; and Kaplan and Sprinker, 1993).
2. A reading of Marxism anchored in 'the expressive totality' he fought to remove from Marxist theory (Elliot, 1987: 45)!
3. See Benton (1984: Chapter 2), Barrett (1993) and Norris (1991: Chapter 1) respectively for some of the implications of these borrowings.
4. See Althusser (1969: 21–39). For a penetrating analysis of the political background against which Althusser's work must be interpreted see Elliot (1987). Anderson locates Althusser firmly in the Western Marxist tradition (Habermas, Colletti, Sartre, Goldmann, Williams, etc.), a tradition fundamentally concerned with 'second-order' problems such as scientific method and epistemology, as well as issues relating to the 'super-structure' (1976: 52–3). Also see Smith's Reading Althusser for further elaboration on this point.
5. Most of my comments are going to be centred on these two earlier works. This can be justified for two reasons. First it is in these two works that Althusser most self-consciously attempted to produce the effect of social structure. Also, although Althusser was to modify his position with respect to theoretical practice and philosophy, he never did so, as far as I know, with respect to the conceptualization of a social formation in terms of a complex structured whole.
6. On Historical Epistemology see Gutting (1989: Chapter 1), Lecourt (1975), Major-Poetzl (1983: Chapter 3) and Tiles (1987).
7. Naturally, Althusser's concept of structure cannot be explained exclusively in terms of its genealogical origin in Historical Epistemology; there are other elements that I shall explore below.

8. Furthermore, Foucault argues that this division can be traced back further. It is seen operating between Comte and Maine de Brian, between Lachelier and Courturat, and also between Bergson and Poincaré (Foucault, 1978; Gutting, 1989: Chapter 1; and Tiles, 1987).

9. For instance in a note in *Reading Capital* he writes ' ... I feel bound to acknowledge the obvious or concealed debts which bind us to our masters in reading learned works ... Gaston Bachelard and Jean Cavaillés and Georges Canguilhem and Michel Foucault' (Althusser and Balibar, 1970: 16). Also Althusser (1969: 25–6) and Althusser (1971: 33–4).

10. This argument is broadly compatible with the argument that I am developing in this book. However, Althusser, not unlike Parsons, focused too narrowly on the logical architecture of theoretical practice to the exclusion of its semantic and metaphorical dimensions.

11. Nonetheless, in *Reading Capital* Althusser argues that his model for the symptomatic reading is Marx's reading of political economy (Althusser and Balibar, 1970: 28).

12. Canguilhem, however, is much more reluctant to make a strong distinction between everyday experience and scientific experience; see Gutting (1989: 43).

13. See for instance Adam (1990), Prigogine and Stengers (1985) and Kuhn's notion of revolutionary paradigm shifts in scientific development (1970).

14. It is worth noting in this context that although it is possible to produce Hegelian readings of Marx, it is not possible to produce Hegelian readings of Historical Epistemology.

15. See Benton (1984: 41–5) and Glucksmann (1974: 135–37).

16. Of course it is true that in *Eléments d'Auto-Critique* and 'Reply to John Lewis', Althusser was to modify this position with the notion of political intervention in the realm of theory. However this can be seen as a retreat rather than a substantive advance. See Benton (1984: 83–95) and Elliot (1987: 198–207).

17. On this point I am in agreement with Althusser; see my discussion of Marx's *Capital* in Chapter 3.

18. In the words of Lecourt, 'The history of science is not a chronicle. Georges Canguilhem attacks a tradition in the history of the sciences which can itself be said to reflect on itself in the form of tradition: the transmission (from one scientist to another or from one period to another) of truths acquired and problems unsolved along the thread of a linear and homogeneous time whose only virtue is to pass (or to be past)' (1975: 167).

19. It is important to note that there is a tendency in Althusser's writing to present the terms structure, structural causality and contradiction as being interchangeable, though in *For Marx* structure is associated with the notion of overdetermination and contradiction whereas in *Reading Capital* it is associated with the notion of structural causality (Lipietz, 1993: 104).

20. By economism Althusser means economic determinism. Historicism refers to 'a linear view of time susceptible to an essential section into a present at any moment. The knowledge of each moment is then the self-consciousness of each present' (Althusser and Balibar, 1970: 314).

21. I am only mentioning Mao here in passing, but the importance of Mao to Althusser's political interventions is crucial. This is analysed in depth in Elliot (1987).

22. In this context Laclau and Mouffe's reading of Althusser is surprising. They write that the concept of overdetermination ' ... comes from psychoanalysis, and its extension had more than a superficially metaphorical character'; they cite the quotation that I gave above and take Althusser at his word that the borrowing is unproblematic. They do not attempt to show that Althusser did in fact manage to find signifieds for this signifier in the context of historical materialism: this, to say the least, is surprising from discourse analysis! They go on to argue, rightly I believe, that '... the concept of

overdetermination is constituted in the field of the symbolic, and has no meaning what-soever outside it' (1994: 97). However where they err is in attributing a 'potential pro-found meaning' to Althusser, which only exists as a potential, which in any case Althusser does not clearly develop.

23. It might be argued that Balibar's contribution to *Reading Capital* represents an attempt to overcome the lack of specification of the nature and operation of the 'effectivities' oper-ating in the social formation, among the different levels and instances, via his Althusser-ian theorization of historical materialism. Notwithstanding Balibar's attempt, the need for a concept of structure remains unfilled.

Balibar's contribution is both insightful and potentially quite fecund, if relatively inconsistent. It deserves more attention than can be given here. Fortunately this has been done (Benton, 1984; Smith, 1984; Hindness and Hirst, 1975; Glucksmann, 1972, 1974; Lipietz, 1993; Elliot, 1987 and Callinicos, 1976). There are perhaps two key fea-tures which can be skimmed from these critiques. First, Balibar does not provide histor-ical materialism with the requisite concepts to distinguish different modes of pro-duction. A striking feature of *Reading Capital* is the abrupt shift from the language of complexity found in the chapters leading up to Balibar's section, and the schema of three elements and two modes of connection of the elements. Glucksmann (1972), for instance, argued that Balibar is able to distinguish the *Capitalist Mode of Production* from other modes of production, but is not able to distinguish between the remaining modes of production (81). Moreover, Balibar does not clearly specify how we are to understand the connections between the different levels beyond the fact that they are complexly articulated, nor does he provide the key for understanding how different modes of pro-duction might be articulated within the social formation: 'In different structures, the economy is determinant in that it determines which of the instances of the social struc-ture occupies the determinant place. Not a simple relation, but rather a relation between relations; not a transitive causality, but rather a structural causality' (Althusser and Bali-bar, 1970: 224).

I think that Benton is right to point out that this deficiency is, in fact, connected with the ambiguous, and inconsistent, use that Balibar makes of the concept of mode of pro-duction (1984: 73–4). Moreover, this is connected with a second problem identified in the various critical appraisals of Balibar's efforts. His attempt founders on his inability to provide a convincing non-teleological and anti-humanist account of the transition from one mode of production to another. Related to this is the prevalent criticism of the over-extension of the concept of reproduction. For instance Balibar writes, 'The concept of reproduction is thus not only the concept of "consistency" of the structure, but also the concept of the necessary determination of the movement of production by the perma-nence of that structure; it is the concept of the permanence of the initial elements in the very functioning of the system, hence the concept of the necessary conditions of produc-tion, conditions which are precisely not created by it. This is what Marx calls the eternity of the mode of production (Althusser and Balibar, 1970: 272). As Lipietz argues, this leads to making the mode of production the concept of historical continuity, so that transitions are virtually unthinkable (1993: 115).

The authors listed above provide a variety of explanations for the sources of these aforementioned problems. However, I would argue that this over-extension of the notion of reproduction is symptomatic of the lack of specification of what counts as structures, as well as modalities of production. To use production to describe the wider social reproduction of the conditions of production is surely to use the term as a *Modality B* metaphor if the specificity of political and ideological production is not made clear. The perilous over-extension of the mode of production to signify the social for-mation allows Balibar to remain with a notion of structure centred on complexity with-out actually explicating the mechanisms that underpin the said complexity. In this sense, the space opened up for the concept of structure remains empty.

24. 'The prophets had recourse to fallacious modes of argument, not merely (as Spinoza is careful to add) out of power-seeking motives or a will to deceive, but in order to maintain social cohesion and the rule of law among a people as yet incapable of reasoning clearly on their own account' (Norris, 1991: 26).
25. In using the term functionalist reasoning I would not like to be taken as suggesting that functionalist reasoning has no role to play in social theory. In fact, investigating functions remains, often implicitly, one of social theory's substantive tasks. The point is to distinguish between the investigation of functions, their historical emergence, genealogies, etc. as well as the possibilities of other functional alternatives. If functions are solutions to specific problems, these problems need to be identified; moreover the agencies, whether human or not, that make them a possible solution equally need to be specified. One asks questions about functions, one does not assert them as explanations. However, I am afraid it is the latter that Althusser does in the aforementioned essay.
26. In this sense it is interesting that Althusser shares some unacknowledged ocularphobic positions with philosophical enemies such as Bergson and Sartre. This of course does not eliminate strong disagreements as well.
27. See Jay (1994) for a typically comprehensive framing of the literature and debates.
28. Moreover it is no surprise to discover that Bachelard had also ferociously critiqued Cartesian perspectivalism; see Gutting (1989: 25).
29. The argument is substantially the same in *For Marx* (182–93) and *Reading Capital* (34–43). Moreover, in his later writings when Althusser tries to exorcise his latent theoreticism by bringing class struggle into the very core of his philosophy, he continues to operate with the same metaphor of vision as the basic modality of the existence of ideology.
30. Benton remarks, 'For Althusser, empiricism appears to be a very broad tradition indeed, seemingly including virtually every tradition in epistemology except his own' (1984: 38). Similarly, Elliot writes 'Conflating the empirical and empiricist, Althusser furthermore equated the experiential with the ideological realm of the imaginary and "false conceptions" – antithesis of conceptual science and objective knowledge' (1987: 110).
31. This leads Callinicos to argue that for Althusser 'There is no general criterion of scientificity' (1976: 59).
32. Similarly, Glucksmann pointed out that Althusser's position requires a 'secret correspondence between a theory and its object' (1972: 74).
33. It is also worth stressing that by posing the problem of evidence in terms of a crude distinction between vision and non-vision, Althusser reproduces an epistemological logic that he had sought to overcome. Like Bachelard, Althusser wanted to transcend the opposition between the knowing subject and the object. This is done by arguing that subjects, in fact, never confront real objects, just objects in thought. However, because Althusser's framing of the notion of production is grounded in terms of the 'labour process', it leads to an excessively 'mentalistic' development that isolates the moment of conceptual production from the effectivity of the real. But perhaps more importantly, a temporal framework of succession structures the question. What I have in mind is actually quite prevalent in discussions that attempt to adjudicate between realism and idealism in scientific practice. Much energy is devoted to arguing back and forth about the temporal primacy of real objects versus concepts. Thus emphasis is put on temporal succession rather than on simultaneity.
     Surely, the production of knowledge takes place in the domain of the real, not outside of it. Hence it is constitutive of theoretical practice. The real world is already implicated in the concept; it underpins the very possibility of speaking about the social or natural world. I take Foucault's work to be drawing attention to precisely this point when he writes about the co-presence of discursive and non-discursive processes in any discursive formations (Woodiwiss, 2001). Due to his excessively 'mentalistic' conception of

knowledge production, and in this he follows Bachelard (see Gutting, 1989: 26; and Lecourt, 1975: 155–61), Althusser ends up opposing subject and object, and this primarily because he is not able to enunciate the effectivity of the structured whole on theoretical practice.

34. In this sense, it would seem that Althusser almost has a mystical view of scientific practice as a blinding light, where the scientist thus blinded becomes a true seer! I would like to underscore, however, that I am not suggesting that there is no value in Althusser's anti-visual position. Quite the contrary, the notion that the structured whole is too complex to be seen or that sight says too many things at once is in fact a very useful starting point for understanding the language-borne nature of social theory. But the concept of seeing needs to be specified, its *Modality B* metaphorical status overcome in order to form a suitable basis for social theory. See Woodiwiss (2001).

35. Lacan, drawing on Freud, uses the idea of the 'mirror phase' to conceptualize the process through which a child begins to develop his or her ego by having some sense of him or herself as a unified entity separate from the mother. As Eagleton argues, this sets up a number of interesting semantic opportunities for Althusser's theory of ideology: ' . . . the relation of an individual subject to society as a whole in Althusser's theory is rather like the relation of the small child to his or her mirror image in Lacan's. In both cases, the human subject is supplied with a satisfyingly unified image of selfhood by identifying with an object which reflects this image back to it in a closed, narcissistic circle. In both cases, too, this image involves a misrecognition, since it idealizes the subject's real situation. The child is not actually as integrated as its image in the mirror suggests; I am not actually the coherent, autonomous self-generating subject I know myself to be in the ideological sphere, but the "decentred" function of several social determinants. Duly enthralled by the image of myself I receive, I subject myself to it; and it is through this "subjection" that I become a subject' (1993: 173).

36. Moreover, as Rose (1986) has also argued, theories of ideology that borrow from psychoanalysis often tend to displace the unconscious as a serious object of study. This is certainly true of Althusser. No doubt this is in part due to the fact that, although Lacan provided insights that have been valuable in other fields, he was essentially a clinician and his work was concerned with psychoanalytical practice; see Benvenuto and Kennedy (1986).

37. The imaginary is doubly seductive to Althusser: first because of its visual resonances, but second because it no doubt connects with Spinoza's notion of imagination as defined above. In fact, Spinoza's imagination as 'lived experience' seems to me much closer to Althusser's notion of ideology than does the Lacanian version.

38. If vision or anti-visualism is going to have any theoretical importance then 'scopic regimes' have to be delineated and their mode of operation elucidated. In this respect the essays contained in Foster's *Vision and Visuality* are of interest. See also Jay (1994) for a discussion of the development of different scopic regimes. Lyotard's search for a formulation of vision that does not reduce it to signification also provides some interesting insights; see Readings (1991) and Barth (1996). See also Woodiwiss (1990; 2001) who argues that sociology's visual bias is due to its representationlist paradigm.

39. This leads to the paradox as expressed by Séve: 'one of the strongest Marxist thinkers of this century . . . was doubtless never exactly a Marxian' (Séve cited in Elliot, 1998: 24).

40. For instance Canguilhem writes that 'Strictly speaking, if precursors existed the History of the Sciences would be meaningless, since science itself would only apparently have a historical dimension . . . A precursor is supposed to be a thinker, an investigator who once made a few steps on the road more recently completed by another. The willingness to search for, to find and to celebrate precursors is the clearest symptom of an inaptitude for epistemological criticism. Before putting two distances on a road end to end, it is advisable to be sure that it really is the same road' (Canguilhem, in Lecourt, 1975: 168). Thus as Lecourt suggests: 'This passage shows . . . Each science has its own movement,

its rhythm, and to put it better, its specific temporality: its history is neither the "lateral fiber" of so-called "general run of time" nor the development of a germ in which lies "preformed" the still un-filled-in outline of its present state; it proceeds by re-organizations, ruptures and mutations; it turns around "critical" points . . .' (1975: 168).

41. Though Althusser speaks about both levels and instances to characterize the structured whole, the first is clearly geological whereas the second is temporal and it is in fact the latter which is more applicable to Althusser's schema.

Conclusion: Reading Texts, Writing Theory

1. In what follows I will be singling out some examples for illustrative purposes. The actual positioning of the different theorists is much more complex. For critical overviews of these debates see Culler (1981; 1986), Eagleton (1993), Ekegren (1999) and Potter (1999).
2. Put slightly differently, since social scientific discourse aims to communicate knowledge about the social world, it has to be understood as designating 'information as opposed to possibilities' (Luhmann, 1998: 47). Thus communication requires 'operative closure' and in so doing '. . . claims indifference to everything else and can there concentrate on itself . . .' (Luhmann, 1998: 48). At the general level of language, the set of possible signifieds that can be attached to a chain of signifiers is virtually infinite, but since social-theoretical discourses aim to communicate 'something', specific discourses are governed by the principle of exclusion and not open-ended inclusion.
3. In the introduction I argued that Foucault's rules of discursive formations provide a powerful theoretical visuality through which the discursive and non-discursive elements which make discourses possible can be represented. Nonetheless, to say that particular discourses or theoretical texts exist as the effect of discursive formations is not to say that the former narrowly determine the latter. As Woodiwiss (2001: 155–6) points out, it is crucial not to confuse discursive formations with specific discursive events. The rules of formation of sociology's discursive formation make possible a variety of competing 'knowledges' about similar and dissimilar objects (e.g. the individual, the group and social structures) via different methods (e.g. the questionnaire, the analysis of the written text and listening) in diverse institutional sites (e.g. the university, the think tank and the professional journal) through the deployment of concepts with diverse semantic links both within and across the discursive formation (e.g. the semantic relationship between rationality and social order, and between social systems and general systems theory respectively) and a variety of different theoretical strategies (e.g. rationalization, differentiation, modernization).
     A specific discursive event crystallizes a dynamic relationship between the rules of formation of objects, types of statements, concepts and theoretical strategies. The 'rules' are the actual systems of relations among the elements of a discursive formation, hence they cannot be understood as static rules of construction.
4. In this context, see Ekegren (1999) for a very promising start to the development of a theory of reading social theoretical texts.
5. One of the devices which I have deployed in this context is the use of the terms *Modality A* and *Modality B* which I suspect the reader has probably found quite unpalatable. I initially introduced these terms as an aid in my attempt to break away from the general connotations associated with the notions of transfer and transformation. I have kept them in the text in the hope that precisely because of their cumbersomeness they might have the same effect on the reader.

6. Sociologists continue to work with the explicit assumption that the actors whose activity they are trying to describe or explain depend on a universe of unacknowledged conditions of possibility. However they like to think of their own actions and language as relatively transparent. This receives its most ironic rendition in the current fashion for self-identification which is *de rigueur*. In the preface to a work, an author locates him/ herself biographically, politically and intellectually. In this way, a gesture is made towards making the author's writing more transparent. The possible bases for distortions have allegedly been clarified. However, by understanding distortion only at the level of the author's subjectivity and intentions and factoring these out, the effect of the transparency of language is reproduced. See for instance, Mouzelis (1995: 160–72).

7. For instance see Kontopolos (1993) and López and Scott (2000).

8. See also Woodiwiss (2001: 166–8).

9. It is among theorists who are sensitive to the challenge that this exigency poses that we find an active exploration of metaphors and semantic systems that might signify this type of complexity through theoretical language. For instance: 'The base and super-structure model depicts a one-to-one relatedness, while the system model depicts a many-to-one relatedness between subsystems and the larger system. Kontopolos, on the other hand, develops what he calls a model of many-to-many relatedness: a plurality of fields at one level connects in complex ways to pluralities of fields at other levels, and it is the network of criss-cross connections that constitute the ontological depths at which social structures operate' (Scott, 2001: 19). Adam's discussion of the metaphor of the holograph as a tool for understanding the relationships between the different times of social life is also particularly relevant (1990: 157–69). See also López and Scott (2000: Chapter 5) for an exploration of the potential associated with the metaphor of space.

10. The error of many postmodernist writers; see López and Potter (2001) and Woodiwiss (2001: Chapter 4).

References

Adam, B. (1990) *Time and Social Theory*, Philadelphia: Temple University Press.

Adriaansens, H. (1980) *Talcott Parsons and the Conceptual Dilemma*, London: Routledge and Kegan Paul.

Adriaansens, H. (1989) 'Talcott Parsons and Beyond: Recollections of an Outsider', *Theory Culture and Society*, 6: 613–21.

Albrow, M. (1990) *Max Weber's Construction of Social Theory*, London: Macmillan.

Alexander, J. (1982a) *Theoretical Logic in Sociology: Vol. 1*, London and Heney: Routledge and Kegan Paul.

Alexander, J. (1982b) *Theoretical Logic in Sociology, Vol. 2: The Antinomies of Classical Thought – Marx and Durkheim*, London and Heney: Routledge and Kegan Paul.

Alexander, J. (1983) *Theoretical Logic in Sociology, Vol. 3: The Classical Attempt at Theoretical Synthesis*, London and Heney: Routledge and Kegan Paul.

Alexander, J. (1984) *Theoretical Logic in Sociology, Vol. 4: The Modern Reconstruction of Classical Thought – Talcott Parsons*, London and Heney: Routledge and Kegan Paul.

Alexander, J. (ed.) (1985) *Neofunctionalism and After*, London: Sage Publications.

Alexander, J. (1988) *Action and Its Environments,* New York: Columbia University Press.

Alexander, J. and Sciortino, G. (1985) 'On Choosing One's Intellectual Predecessors: Why Charles Camic is Wrong about Parsons' Early Work', in *Neofunctionalism and After*, Alexander, J. (ed.), London: Sage Publications.

Althusser, L. (1969) *For Marx*, Brewster, B. (trans.), Allen Lane: The Penguin Press, 1969.

Althusser, L. (1971) *Lenin and Philosophy and Other Essays*, Brewster, B. (trans.), London: New Left Books.

Althusser, L. (1974) *Eléments d'Auto-Critique*, Paris: Hachette Littérature.

Althusser, L. (1984) *Essays In Ideology*, London: Verso.

Althusser, L. (1990) *Philosophy and the Spontaneous Philosophy of the Scientists and Other Essays.* London: Verso.

Althusser, L. and Balibar, E. (1970) *Reading Capital*, Brewster, B. (trans.), London: New Left Books.

Anderson, P. (1976) *Considerations on Western Marxism*, London: New Left Books.

Andrews, H. (1993) 'Durkheim and Social Morphology', in *Emile Durkheim: Sociologist and Moralist.* Turner, S. (ed.), London and New York: Routledge.

Antoni, C. (1962) *From History to Sociology: The Transition of German Historical Thinking,* London: Merlin Press.

Archer, M. (1995) *Realist Social Theory: The Morphogenetic Approach*, Cambridge: Cambridge University Press.

Aron, R. (1967) *Main Currents in Sociological Thought 2*, Middlesex: Penguin Books.

Bachelard, G. (1937) *L'Expérience de L'Espace dans la Physique Contemporaine*, Paris: PUF.

Baeher, P. (1990) 'The "Masses" in Weber's Political Sociology', *Economy and Society*, 19(2): 242–65.

Baeher, P. and O'Brien, M. (1994) 'Founders, Classics and the Concept of a Canon', in *Current Sociology*, 42(1): 1–148.

Bailey, K. (1984) 'Beyond Functionalism: Towards a Nonequilibrium Analysis of Complex Social Systems', in *The British Journal of Sociology*, 25(1): 1–18.

Bailey, K. (1994) *Sociology and the New Systems Theory*, New York: New York State University Press.

Bannister, R. (1970) *Social Darwinism: Science and Myth and Anglo-American Social Thought*, Philadelphia: Temple University Press.

Barber, B. (1989) 'Talcott Parsons and the Sociology of Science: An Essay in Appreciation and Remembrance', *Theory Culture and Society*, (6): 623–35.

Barnes, B. (2000) *Understanding Agency: Social Theory and Responsible Action*. London: Sage.

Barrett, M. (1993) 'Althusser's Marx, Althusser's Lacan', in *The Althusserian Legacy*, Kaplan, E. and Sprinker, M. (eds), London: Verso.

Barth, L. (1996) 'Immemorial Visibilities: Seeing the City's Difference, in *Environment and Planning*, 28: 471–93.

Barthes, R. (1975) *The Pleasure of the Text*, New York: Hill and Wang.

Bendix, R. (1960) *Max Weber: An Intellectual Portrait*, Garden City, NY: Anchor Books.

Bendix, R. and Roth, G. (1971) *Scholarship and Partisanship: Essays on Max Weber*. Berkeley, Los Angeles and London: University of California Press.

Benton, T. (1974) 'Claude Bernard's Epistemology: A Reply to P.Q. Hirst', *Economy and Society*, 3 (2): 219–30.

Benton, T. (1977) *Philosophical Foundations of Three Sociologies*, London: Routledge and Kegan Paul.

Benton, T. (1984) *The Rise and Fall of Structural Marxism,* London: Macmillan.

Benton, T. (1992) 'Ecology, Socialism and the Mastery of Nature: A Reply to Reiner Grundmann', *New Left Review*, 194: 55–72.

Benton, T. (1993) *Natural Relations: Ecology, Animal Rights and Social Justice*, London: Verso.

Benton, T. and Craib, I. (2001) *Philosophy of Social Science: The Philosophical Foundations of Social Thought*, Basingstoke: Palgrave.

Benvenuto, B. and Kennedy, R. (1986) *The Works of Jacques Lacan: An Introduction*, London: Free Association Books.

Bernauer, J. (1990) *Michel Foucault's Force of Flight: Towards an Ethics in Thought*, New Jersey and London: Humanities Press.

Bershady, H. (1973) *Ideology and Social Knowledge*, Oxford: Basil Blackwell.

Besnard, P. (ed.). (1983) *The Sociological Domain: The Durkhemians and the Founding of French Sociology,* London and New York: Cambridge University Press.

Bhaskar, R. (1975) *A Realist Theory of Science*, Leeds: Leeds Books.

Black, M. (ed.) (1961) 'Some Questions About Parsons' Theories', in *The Social Theories of Talcott Parsons*, New York: Prentice-Hall.

Black, M. (1962) *Models and Metaphors: Studies in Language and Philosophy*, Ithaca: Cornell University Press.

Blum, A. and McHugh, P. (1971) 'The Social Ascription of Motives', *American Sociological Review*, 36: 98–109.

Bologh, R. (1990) *Love or Greatness: Max Weber and Masculine Thinking – A Feminist Inquiry*, London: Unwin Hyman.

Bono, J. (1990) 'Science, Discourse and Literature: The Role/Rule in Science', in Peterfreund, S. (ed.) *Literature and Science, Theory and Practice*, Boston: North Eastern University Press.

Bourdieu, P. (1977) *Outline of a Theory of Practice*, Nice, R. (trans.), Cambridge: Cambridge University Press.

Bourdieu, P. (1988) *Homo Academicus*, Collier, P. (trans.), Stanford: Stanford University Press.

Bourdieu, P. (1991) *The Political Ontology of Martin Heidegger*, Cambridge: Polity.

Bourricard, F. (1981) *The Sociology of Talcott Parsons*, Goldhanmer, A. (trans.), Chicago: Chicago University Press.

Bowler, P. (1969) 'Malthus and the Evolutionists: The Common Context of Biological and Social Theory', *Past and Present*, 43: 109–45.

Bowler, P. (1976) 'Malthus, Darwin and the Concept of Struggle', *Journal of the History of Ideas*, 37: 631–50.

Bowler, P. (1994) 'Social Metaphors in Evolutionary Biology, 1870–1930: The Wider Dimension of Social Darwinism', in Maasen *et al.* (eds), *Biology as Society, Society as Biology Metaphors*, Dordrecht/Boston/London: Kluwer Academic Press.

Boyd, R. (1993) ' Metaphor and Theory Change', in Ortony, A. (ed.) *Metaphor and Thought*, Cambridge: Cambridge University Press.

Braudel, F. (1972a) 'History and the Social Sciences', in *Economy and Society in Early Modern Europe: Essay from Annales*, Burke, P. (ed.), New York: Harper and Row.

Braudel, F. (1972b) 'Personal Testimony', *Journal of Modern History*, 44: 448–67.

Braudel, F. (1993) *A History of Civilizations*, London: Penguin Books.

Bruce, D. and Purdy, A. (eds), *Literature and Science*, Amsterdam: Rodopi.

Bruun, H. H. (1972) *Science, Values and Politics in Weber's Methodology*, Copenhagen: Munksgaard.

Burchell, G. *et al.* (eds) (1991) *The Foucault Effect*, Chicago: University of Chicago Press.

Burger, T. (1976) *Max Weber's Theory of Concept Formation: History, Laws and Ideal Types*, Durham, North Carolina: Duke University Press.

Buxton, W. (1985) *Talcott Parsons and the Capitalism Nation-State: A Political Sociology as a Strategic Vocation*, Toronto: University of Toronto Press.

Callinicos, A. (1976) *Althusser's Marxism*, London: Pluto Press.

Camic, C. (1979) 'The Utilitarians Revisited', *American Journal of Sociology*, 85: 515–50.

Camic, C. (1992) 'Structure after 50 Years: The Anatomy of a Charter', in *Talcott Parsons Critical Assessments*, Hamilton, P. (ed.), London and New York: Routledge.

Canguilhem, G. (1977) *La Formation du Concept de Réflexe aux XVIIe et XVIIIe Siècles*, Paris: Vrin.

Canguilhem, G. (1994) *A Vital Rationalist: Selected Writings from George Canguilhem*, Delaporte, F. (ed.), New York: Zone Books.

Cannon, W. B. (1939) *The Wisdom of the Body*, New York, Norton.

Cartwright, B. and Warner, S. (1976) 'The Medium is Not the Message', in *Explorations in General Theory in Social Science*, Loubser *et al.* (eds), New York: Free Press.

Carver, T. (1998) *The Postmodern Marx*, Manchester: Manchester University Press.

Castells, M. (1977) *The Urban Question,* Sheridan, A. (trans.), London: E. Arnold.

Clark, T. (1973) *Prophets and Patrons: The French University and the Emergence of the Social Sciences*, Cambridge Mass.: Harvard University Press.

Clarke, S. *et al.* (eds) (1980) *One Dimensional Marxism: Althusser and the Politics of Culture*, London and New York: Allison and Bushby.

Cohen, G. A. (1978) *Marx's Theory of History*, London: Verso.

Cohen, J., Hazelrigg, L. and Pote, W. (1992) 'De-Parsonising Weber: A Critique of Parsons' Interpretation of Weber's Sociology', in *Talcott Parsons: Critical Assessments*, Hamilton, P. (ed.), London: Routledge.

Cohen, P. (1968) *Modern Social Theory*, New York: Basic Books.

Colletti, L. (1975) 'Introduction', in *Karl Marx: Early Writings*, Livingstone, R. and Benton, G. (trans.), London: New Left Books.

Collins, R. (1997) 'A Sociological Guilt Trip: Comment on Connell', *American Journal of Sociology*, 102 (1): 1511–57.

Colomy, P. (ed.) (1990) 'Introduction: The Neofunctionalist Movement', in *Neofunctionalist Sociology*, Brookfield: Aldershot.

Colomy, P. and Rhoades, G. (1994) 'Toward a Micro Corrective of Structural Differentiation Theory', *Sociological Perspectives*, 37 (4): 547–83.

Connel, R. W. (1996) 'Why is Classical Theory Classical?', *American Journal of Sociology*, 102(2): 1511–57.

Craib, I. (1997) *Classical Social Theory*, Oxford: Oxford University Press.

Culler, J. (1981) *The Pursuit of Signs: Semiotics, Literature, Deconstruction*, London and Henley: Routledge and Kegan Paul.

Culler, J. (1986) *On Deconstruction: Theory and Criticism after Structuralism*, Ithaca, New York: Cornell University Press.

Cummings, B. (1998) 'The Korean Crisis and End of "Late" Development', *New Left Review*, 231: 43–72.

Cutler *et al.* (1977, 1978) *Marx's Capital and Capitalism Today: 2 Vols*, London: Routledge and Kegan Paul.

Dahrendorf, R. (1959) *Class and Class Conflict in Industrial Society*, London: Routledge and Kegan Paul.

Davidson, D. (1981) 'What Metaphors Mean', in M. Johnson (ed.), *Philosophical Perspectives of Metaphor*, Minneapolis: University of Minnesota Press.

Davy, G. (1919) 'La Sociologie de M. Durkheim', *Revue Philosophique*, 72: 160–86.

Derrida, J. (1976) *Of Grammatology*, Baltimore and London: Johns Hopkins University Press.

Derrida, J. (1978) *Writing and Difference*, London: Routledge and Kegan Paul.

Derrida, J. (1979) 'Living on: Border Lines' in *Deconstruction and Criticism*, Bloom, H. (ed.), New York: Seabury.

Derrida, J. (1994) *Spectres of Marx*, London and New York: Routledge.

Deutsch, K. (1951) 'Mechanism, Organism, and Society: Some Models in Natural and Social Science', *Philosophy of Science*, 18: 230–52.

Digeon, C. (1959) *La Crise Allemande de la Pensée Française (1870–1914)*, Paris: PUF.

Dreyfus, H. and Rabinow, P. (1982) *Michel Foucault: Beyond Structuralism and Hermeneutics*, Brighton: The Harvester Press.

Dubin, R. (1960) 'Parsons' Actor: Continuities in Social Theory', *American Sociological Review*, 24(4): 457–83.

Durkheim, E. (1966) *Suicide*, Spaulding, J. and Simpson, G. (trans.), New York: The Free Press.

Durkheim, E. (1968) *The Elementary Forms of The Religious Life*, Swain, J. W. (trans.), New York: The Free Press.

Durkheim, E. (1974) *Sociology and Philosophy*, Pocock, D. (trans.), New York: The Free Press.

Durkheim, E. (1978) *Emile Durkheim on Institutional Analysis*, Traugott, M. (trans. and ed.), Chicago and London: University of Chicago Press.

Durkheim, E. (1982a) 'The Rules of Sociological Method', in *The Rules of Sociological Method, and Selected Texts on Sociology and Its Method*, Lukes, S. (ed.), London: Macmillan.

Durkheim, E. (1982b) 'Debate on Explanation in History and Sociology', in *The Rules of Sociological Method, and Selected Texts on Sociology and Its Method*, Lukes, S. (ed.), London: Macmillan.

Durkheim, E. (1982c) 'Social Morphology', in *The Rules of Sociological Method, And Selected Texts on Sociology and Its Method*, Lukes, S. (ed.), London: Macmillan.

Durkheim, E. (1982d) ' Sociology and the Social Sciences', in *The Rules of Sociological Method, and Selected Texts on Sociology and Its Method*, Lukes, S. (ed.), London: Macmillan.

Durkheim, E. (1984) The Division of Labour in Society, Hall, W. D. (trans.), New York: The Free Press.

Eagleton, T. (1993) *Literary Theory: An Introduction*, Oxford: Blackwell.

Eden, R. (1983) *Political Leadership and Nihilism: A Study of Weber and Nietzsche*, Tampa: University Presses of Florida.

Eisenstadt, S. (1985) 'Social Change, Differentiation and Evolution', in *Neofunctionalism*, Alexander, J. (ed), London: Sage Publications.

Ekegren, P. (1999) *The Reading of Theoretical Texts*, London: Routledge.

Elliot, G. (1987) *Althusser: The Detour of Theory,* London: Verso.

Elliot, G. (1998) 'Ghostlier Demarcations: On the Posthumous Edition of Althusser's Writings', in *Radical Philosophy,* 90: 20–32.

Emirbayer, M. (1997) 'Manifesto for a Relational Sociology', *American Journal of Sociology,* 103(2): 281–317.

Engels, F. (1940) *Dialectics of Nature,* London: Lawrence and Wishart.

Engels, F. (1978) 'Letter to Joseph Block', in *The Marx–Engels Reader,* Tucker, R. (ed.), New York and London: Norton and Co.

Fish, S. (1980) *Is There a Text in this Class? The Authority of Interpretive Communities,* Cambridge, MA: Harvard University Press.

Foster, Hal (ed.) (1988) *Vision and Visuality,* Seattle: Bay Press.

Foucault, M. (1978) 'Introduction to the English Translation', in G. Canguilhem, *On the Normal and the Pathological,* Dordrecht: Reidel.

Foucault, M. (1979) *Discipline and Punish: The Birth of the Prison,* Sheridan, A. (trans.), New York: Vintage Books.

Foucault, M. (1991a) 'Politics and the Study of Discourse', in *The Foucault Effect,* Burchell *et al.* (eds), Chicago: University of Chicago Press.

Foucault, M. (1991b) 'Governmentality', in *The Foucault Effect,* Burchell *et al.* (eds), Chicago: University of Chicago Press.

Foucault, M. (1992) *The Archaeology of Knowledge,* London: Routledge.

Foucault, M. (1994) *The Order of Things,* New York: Vintage Books.

Freedman, C. (1990) 'The Interventional Marxism of Louis Althusser', in *Rethinking Marxism,* 3 (3–4): 309–28.

Freud, S. (1991) *The Interpretation of Dreams,* Strachey, J. and Tyson, A. (eds), Strachey, J. (trans.), London: Penguin Books.

Freund, J. (1968) *The Sociology of Max Weber,* Middlesex: Penguin Books.

Frisby, D. and Sayer, D. (1986) *Society,* London: Tavistock Publications Ltd.

Fromm, E. (ed.) (1966) *Socialist Humanism: An International Symposium,* New York: Anchor Books.

Frye, N. (1973) *Anatomy of Criticism,* Princeton: Princeton University Press.

Gadamer, H. G. (1989) *Truth and Method,* London: Sheed and Ward.

GanBmann, H. (1988) 'Money: A Symbolically Generalised Media of Communication? On the Concept of Money in Recent Sociology', *Economy and Society,* 17(3): 285–316.

Gane, M. (1988) *On Durkheim's Rules of Sociological Method,* London: Routledge.

Gerth, H. H. and Mills, C. W. (1995) 'Introduction', in *From Max Weber: Essays in Sociology,* Gerth, H. H. and Mills, C. W. (eds), London and New York: Routledge.

Gerhart, M. and Russell, A. (1984) *Metaphoric Process: The Creation of Scientific and Religious Understanding,* Fort Worth: Texas Christian University Press.

Giddens, A. (1971) *Capitalism and Modern Social Theory,* Cambridge: Cambridge University Press.

Giddens, A. (1976) *New Rules of Sociological Method: A Positive Critique of Interpretative Sociologies,* London: Hutchinson.

Glucksmann, A. (1972) 'A Ventriloquist Structuralism', *New Left Review,* 72: 68–92.

Glucksmann, M. (1974) *Structuralist Analysis in Contemporary Social Thought: A Comparison of the Theories of Claude Lévi-Strauss and Louis Althusser,* London: Routledge and Kegan Paul.

Glucksmann, M. (2000) *Cottons and Casuals: the Gendered Organisation of Work in Time and Space,* York: Sociologypress.

Gordon, J. (1978) *Structures: Or Why Things Don't Fall Down,* Harmondsworth: Penguin Books.

Gould, M. (1989) 'Voluntarism versus Utilitarianism: A Critique of Camic's History of Ideas', *Theory Culture and Society,* 6: 637–54.

Gouldner, A. (1970) *The Coming Crisis of Western Sociology,* New York: Basic Books.

Green, B. S. (1988) *Literary Methods and Sociological Theory*, Chicago and London: University of Chicago Press.

Gregory, F. (1977) *Scientific Materialism in Nineteenth-century Germany*, Dordrecht and Boston: Reidel.

Gregory, D. and Urry, J. (eds) (1985) *Social Relations and Spatial Structures*, London: Macmillan.

Guiton, J. (1968) *Regards sur la Pensée Française: 1870–1940: Leçons de Captivité*. Paris: Beauchesne.

Gutting, G. (1989) *Michel Foucault's Archaeology of Scientific Reason*, Cambridge: Cambridge University Press.

Habermas, J. (1984) *Communication and the Evolution of Society*, McCarthy, T. (trans.), Cambridge: Cambridge University Press.

Habermas, J. (1987) *The Philosophical Discourse of Modernity*, Lawrence, F. (trans.), Cambridge, Mass.: MIT Press.

Habermas, J. (1989) *The Theory of Communicative Action, Vol. 2: The Critique of Functionalist Reason*, McCarthy, T. (trans.), Cambridge: Polity Press.

Hall, S. (1970) 'Rethinking the Base and Superstructure Metaphor', in *Class, Hegemony and Party*, Bloomfield, J. (ed.), London: Lawrence and Wishart.

Hamilton, P. (1983) *Talcott Parsons*, London: Tavistock Publications.

Hamilton, P. (ed.) (1992) *Talcott Parsons: Critical Assessments*, 4 Vols, London and New York: Routledge.

Harré, R. (1970) The *Principles of Scientific Thinking*, London: Macmillan.

Harré, R. and Madden, E. H. (1975) *Causal Powers*, Oxford: Basil Blackwell.

Harré, R. and Martin-Soskice, J. (1982) 'Metaphor in Science', in D. Miall (ed.), *Metaphor: Problems and Perspectives*, Brighton: Harvester.

Harvey, D. (1985) *The Urbanization of Capital*, Baltimore: Johns Hopkins University Press and Basil Blackwell.

Hejl, P. (1994) 'Importance of the Concepts of "Organism" and "Evolution" in Emile Durkheim's Division of Social Labor and the Influence of Herbert Spencer', in Maasen, S. *et al.* (eds) *Biology as Society, Society as Biology Metaphors*, Dordrecht/Boston/London: Kluwer Academic Press.

Heller, A. (1976) *The Theory of Need in Marx*, London: Allison and Busby.

Heller, A. (1981) 'Paradigm of Production, Paradigm of Work', *Dialectical Anthropology*, 6: 71–9.

Heller, A. and Fehér, F. (1991) *The Grandeur and Twilight of Radical Universalism*, New Brunswick: Transaction Publishers.

Helmholtz, H. (1995) *Science and Culture: Popular and Philosophical Essays*, Cahan, D. (ed.), Chicago and London: University of Chicago Press.

Hennis, W. (1988) *Max Weber: Essays in Reconstruction*, London: Allen and Unwin.

Hesse, M. (1966) *Models and Analogies in Science*, Notre Dame: University of Notre Dame Press.

Hindness, B. (1977) *Philosophy and Methodology in the Social Sciences*, Hassocks: Harvester Press.

Hindness, B. and Hirst, P. (1975) *Pre-capitalist Modes of Production*, London and Boston: Routledge and Kegan Paul.

Hirsh, Jr. E. D. (1967) *Validity in Interpretation*, New Haven: Yale University Press.

Hirst, P. Q. (1973a) 'Morphology and Pathology: Biological Analogies and Metaphors in Durkheim's Rules of Sociological Method', *Economy and Society*, 2(1): 1–34.

Hirst, P. Q. (1973b) 'Claude Bernard's Epistemology', in *Economy and Society*, 2(4): 431–64.

Hirst, P. Q. (1975) *Durkheim, Bernard and Epistemology*, London and Boston: Routledge and Kegan Paul.

Holmwood, J. (1996) *Founding Sociology? Talcott Parsons and the Idea of General Theory*, London and New York: Longman.

Holmwood, J. and Stewart, A. (1991) *Explanation and Social Theory*, London: Macmillan.

Holton, R. and Turner, B. (1988) *Talcott Parsons on Economy and Society*, London: Routledge.

Hughes, S. H. (1959) *Consciousness and Society: The Reorientation of European Social Thought 1890–1930*, London: Macgibbon and Kee.

Iggers, G. G. (1968) *The German Conception of History: The National Tradition of Historical Thought from Herder to the Present*, Middletown, Connecticut: Wesleyan University Press.

Ingarden, R. (1973) *The Literary Work of Art*, Evanston, IL: Northwestern University Press.

Iser, W. (1989) *The Act of Reading: A Theory of Aesthetic Response*, Baltimore: Johns Hopskins University Press.

Jakobson, R. and Halle, M. (1956) *Fundamentals of Language*, S-Gravenhage: Mouton.

Jakubowski, F. (1976) *Ideology and Superstructure*, Booth, A. (trans.), London: Allison and Busby.

Jay, M. (1994) *Downcast Eyes: The Denigration of Vision in Twentieth-century French Thought*, Berkeley: University of California.

Johnson, W. (ed.) (1981) *Philosophical Perspectives on Metaphor*, Minneapolis: University of Minnesota Press.

Kalberg, S. (1994) *Max Weber's Comparative-Historical Sociology*, Cambridge: Polity Press.

Kalberg, S. (1997) 'Max Weber's Sociology: Research Strategies and Mode of Analysis', in *Reclaiming the Sociological Classics*, Camic, C. (ed.), Oxford: Blackwell.

Kaplan, A. and Sprinker, M. (eds) (1993) *The Althusserian Legacy*, London: Verso.

Kay, L. (1995) 'Who Wrote the Book of Life? Information and the Transformation of Molecular Biology, 1945–1955', *Science in Context*, 8: 609–34.

Keller, E. F. (1995) *Refiguring Life Metaphors of Twentieth-century Biology*, New York: Columbia University Press.

Kelly, A. (1981) *The Descent of Darwin*, Chapel Hill: The University of North Carolina Press.

Knorr-Cetina, K. (1980) 'The Scientist as an Analogical Reasoner: A Critique of the Metaphor-Theory of Innovation', *Communication and Cognition*, 13, 2(3): 183–208.

Knorr-Cetina, K. (1981) *The Manufacture of Knowledge*, Oxford: Pergamon Press.

Kontopolos, K. (1993) *The Logics of Social Structure*, Cambridge: Cambridge University Press.

Kuhn, T. (1959) 'Energy Conservation as an Example of Simultaneous Discovery', in *Critical Problems in the History of Science*, Clagett, M. (ed.), Madison: Univeristy of Wisconsin Press.

Kuhn, T. (1970) *The Structure of Scientific Revolutions*, Chicago: University of Chicago Press.

Laclau, E. and Mouffe, C. (1994) *Hegemony and Socialist Strategy*, London: Verso.

Lakoff, G. and Johnson, M. (1980) *Metaphors We Live By*, Chicago: Chicago University Press.

Larrain, J. (1979) *The Concept of Ideology*, London: Hutchinson and Co.

Latour, B. (1990) 'Postmodern? No, Simply Amodern! Steps Towards an Anthropology of Science', *Studies in History and Philosophy of Science*, 21: 145–71.

Law, J. and Hetherington, K. (2001) Allegory and Inference: Representation in Sociology, online at *www.comp.lancs.ac.uk/sociology/reskhjl1.html*

Leatherdale, W. H. (1974) *The Role of Analogy, Model, and Metaphor in Science*, Amsterdam: North Holland Publishing Company.

Lecourt, D. (1975) *Marxism and Epistemology*, Brewster, B. (trans.), London: New Left Books.

Lefebvre, H. (1974) *La Production de l'Espace*, Paris: Anthropos.

Lehmann, J. (1993) *Deconstructing Durkheim: A Post-Post-Structuralist Critique*, London: Routledge.

Lemert, C. (1995) *Sociology after the Crisis*, Boulder, CO: Westview Press.

Lenoir, T. (1988) 'Practice, Reason, Context: The Dialogue Between Theory and Experiment', *Science in Context*, 2(1): 3–22.

Levin, S. (1981) *Metaphoric Worlds*, New Haven and London: Yale University Press.

Levine, D. (1981) 'Rationality and Freedom: Weber and Beyond', *Sociological Inquiry*, 51(1), 5–25.

Lewis, P. (1996) 'Metaphor and Critical Realism', *Review of Social Economy*, LIV (4): 487–506.

Lipietz, A. (1993) 'From Althusserianism to "Regulation Theory"', in *The Althusserian Legacy*, Kaplan, E. and Sprinker, M. (eds), London: Verso.

Lockwood, D. (1959) 'Some Remarks on the "Social System"', *British Journal of Sociology*, 7: 134–46.

Lockwood, D. (1964) 'Social Integration and System Integration', in *Explorations in Social Change*, Zollschan and Hirsch (eds), Boston: Houghton Mifflin.

López, J. and Potter, G. (2001) *After Postmodernism: An Introduction to Critical Realism*, London: Athlone Press.

López, J. and Scott, J. (2000) *Social Structure*, Buckingham: Open University Press.

Love, N. S. (1986) *Marx, Nietzsche and Modernity*, New York: Columbia University Press.

Löwith, K. (1993) *Max Weber and Karl Marx*, London and New York: Routledge.

Luhmann, N. (1976) 'Generalized Media and the Problem of Contingency', in *Explorations in General Theory in Social Science*, Loubser *et al.* (eds), New York: Free Press.

Luhmann, N. (1982) *The Differentiation of Society*, Holmes, S. and Larmore, C. (trans.). New York: Columbia University Press.

Luhmann, N. (1995) *Social Systems*, Bednarz, J. (trans.), Stanford: Stanford University Press.

Luhmann, N. (1998) *Observations on Modernity*, Stanford: Stanford University Press.

Lukes, S. (1992) *Emile Durkheim*, London: Penguin Books.

McCanles, M. (1978) 'All Discourses Aspire to the Analytical Proposition', in *What Is Literature?*, P. Hernadi (ed.), Bloomington: Indiana University Press.

McLellan, D. (1973) *Karl Marx*, New York: Macmillan.

Maasen, S. (1994) 'Who is Afraid of Metaphors?', in S. Maasen *et al.* (eds), *Biology as Society, Society as Biology Metaphors*, Dordrecht/Boston/London: Kluwer Academic Press.

Maasen, S., Mendelhson, P. and Weingart, P. (eds) (1994) *Biology as Society, Society as Biology Metaphors*, Dordrecht/Boston/London: Kluwer Academic Press.

Major-Poetzl, P. (1983) *Michel Foucault's Archaeology of Western Culture: Towards a New Scientific History*, Chapel Hill: University of Carolina Press.

Man, P. de (1979) *Allegories of Reading*, New Haven: Yale University Press.

Marsden, R. (1999) *The Nature of Capital: Marx after Foucault*, London: Routledge.

Marx, K. (1977) *The Philosophical and Economic Manuscripts*, London: Lawrence and Wishart.

Marx, K. (1978a) '1859 Preface', in *The Marx–Engels Reader*, Tucker, R. (ed.), New York and London: Norton and Company.

Marx, K. (1978b) 'Theses on Feuerbach', in *The Marx–Engels Reader*, Tucker, R. (ed.), New York and London: Norton and Company.

Marx, K. (1978c) 'The Grundrisse', in *The Marx–Engels Reader*, Tucker, R. (ed.), New York and London: Norton and Company.

Marx, K. (1983) *Capital: 3 Vols.*, London: Lawrence and Wishart.

Marx, K. (1996) 'The Eighteenth Brummaire of Louis Bonaparte', in *Marx: Later Political Writings*, Carver, T. (ed.), Cambridge: Cambridge University Press.

Marx, K. and Engels, F. (1978) 'The German Ideology', in *The Marx–Engels Reader*, Tucker, R. (ed.), New York and London: Norton and Company.

Melden, A. (1961) *Free Action*, London: Routledge and Kegan Paul.

Miles, S. (2001) *Social Theory in the Real World*, London: Sage.

Mills, C. W. (1959) *The Sociological Imagination*, New York: Oxford University Press.

Mitchell, S. (1994) 'The Superorganism Metaphor: Then and Now', in Maasen, S. *et al.* (eds), *Biology as Society, Society as Biology Metaphors*, Dordrecht/Boston/London: Kluwer Academic Press.

Mitzman, A. (1970) *The Iron Cage: A Historical Interpretation of Max Weber*, New York: Alfred A. Knopf.

Mommsen, W. J. (1989) *The Political and Social Theory of Max Weber*, Cambridge: Polity Press.

Morgan, M. (1994) 'Evolutionary Metaphors in Explanations of American Industrial Competition', in Maasen, S. *et al.* (eds), *Biology as Society, Society as Biology Metaphors*, Dordrecht/Boston/London: Kluwer Academic Press.

Morse, C. (1961) 'The Functional Imperatives', in *The Social Theories of Talcott Parsons*, New York: Prentice-Hall.

Mouzelis, N. (1995) *Sociological Theory: What Went Wrong?*, London: Routledge.

Münch, R. (1987) *Theory of Action: Towards a Synthesis Going Beyond Parsons*, London: Routledge and Kegan Paul.

Némedi, D. (2000) 'A Change in Ideas: Collective Consciousness, Morphology and Collective Representations', in *Durkheim and Representations*, Pickering, W. S. F. (ed.), London: Routledge.

Nerlich, B. and Clarke, D. (2001) 'Mind, Meaning and Metaphor: the Philosophy and Psychology of Metaphor in 19th-century Germany', *History of Human Sciences*, 14(2): 39–61.

Nisbet, R. (1952) 'Conservatism and Sociology', *American Journal of Sociology*, 58: 167–75.

Nisbet, R. (1965) *The Sociology of Emile Durkheim*, New York: Oxford University Press.

Nisbet, R. (1969) *Social Change and History*, Oxford: Oxford University Press.

Noppen, J. P. van, de Knop, S., Jongen, R., Nitelet, B., Nysenholc, A. and Shibles, W. (1985) *Metaphor: Bibliography of Post-1970 Publications*, Amsterdam and Philadelphia: John Bengamins Publishing Co.

Noppen, J. and Hols, E. (1990) *Metaphor II: A Classified Bibliography of Publications, 1985–1990*, Amsterdam and Philadelphia: John Bengamins Publishing Co.

Norris, Christopher (1991) *Spinoza and the Origins of Modern Critical Theory*, London: Basil Blackwell, 1991.

Oliga, J. (1996) *Power, Ideology and Control*, New York and London: Plenum Press.

O'Neil, J. (ed.) (1973) *Modes of Individualism and Collectivism*, London: Heinemann.

Ortony, A. (1979) 'Metaphor: A Multidimensional Problem', in *Metaphor and Thought*, Ortony (ed.), Cambridge: Cambridge University Press.

Parker, D. (1997) 'Why Bother with Durkheim? Teaching Sociology in the 1990s', in *The Sociological Review*, 45(1): 122–46.

Parsons, T. (1949) *The Structure of Social Action*, New York: Free Press.

Parsons, T. (1960) 'The Pattern Variables Revisited', *American Sociological Review*, 25: 467–83.

Parsons, T. (1961) 'The Point of View of the Author', in *The Social Theories of Talcott Parsons*, Black, M. (ed.), New York: Prentice-Hall.

Parsons, T. (1964) *Essays in Sociological Theory*, New York: The Free Press.

Parsons, T. (1967) *Sociological Theory and Modern Society*, New York: Free Press.

Parsons, T. (1971) *The System of Modern Societies*, Englewood Cliffs, NJ: Prentice-Hall.

Parsons, T. (1977a) *The Evolution of Societies*, Jackson, J. (ed.). New Jersey: Prentice-Hall.

Parsons, T. (1977b) *Social Systems and Evolution of Action Theory*, New York: Free Press.

Parsons, T. (1991) *The Social System*, London: Routledge.

Parsons, T., Bales, R. and Shils, E. (1953) *Working Papers in the Theory of Action*, New York: The Free Press, 1953.

Parsons, T. and Platt, G. (1973) *The American University*, Cambridge: Harvard University Press.

Parsons, T. and Shils, E. (1951) *Toward A General Theory of Action*. New York: Harper and Row.

Parsons, T. and Smelser, N. (1957) *Economy and Society*, London: Routledge and Kegan Paul.

Pearce, F. (1984) *The Radical Durkheim*, London: Unwin Hyman.

Pearce, F. and Woodiwiss, A. (2001) 'Reading Foucault as a Realist', in López, J. and Potter, G. (eds) *After Postmodernism: An Introduction to Critical Realism*, London: Athlone Press.

Pickering, W. S. F. (1992) 'The Origins of Conceptual Thinking In Durkheim: Social or Religious', in *Emile Durkheim: Sociologist and Moralist*. Turner, S. (ed.), London and New York: Routledge.

Pickering, W. S. F. (ed.) (2000) *Durkheim and Representations*, London: Routledge.

Porpora, D. (1987) *The Concept of Social Structure*, New York: Greenwood Press.

Postone, M. (1996) *Time, Labor and Social Domination: A Reinterpretation of Marx's Critical Theory*, Cambridge: Cambridge Univeristy Press.

Postone, M. (1997) 'Rethinking Marx (in Post-Marxist World)', in *Reclaiming the Sociological Classics*, Camic, C. (ed.), Oxford: Blackwell.

Potter, G. (1998) 'Truth in Fiction, Science and Criticism', *Journal of Literary Semantics*, 27(3): 173–89.

Potter, G. (1999) *The Bet: Truth in Science, Literature and Everyday Knowledges*, Harlow: Ashgate.

Potter, G. (2000) *The Philosophy of Social Science: New Perspectives*, Harlow, New York: Prentice-Hall.

Prigogine, I. and Stengers, I. (1985) *Order out of Chaos*, London: Flamingo.

Privitera, W. (1995) *Problems of Style: Michel Foucault's Epistemology*, Albany: State University of New York Press.

Rabinbach, A. (1992) *The Human Motor: Energy, Fatigue, and the Origins of Modernity*, Berkeley: University of California Press.

Rabinow, P. (1994) 'Introduction: A Vital Rationalist', in *A Vital Rationalist: Selected Writings from George Canguilhem*, Delaporte, F. (ed.), Goldhammer, A. (trans.), New York: Zone Books.

Rasch, W. (2000) *Niklas Luhmann's Modernity: The Paradox of Differentiation*, Stanford: Stanford University Press.

Readings, B. (1991) *Introducing Lyotard: Art and Politics*, London: Routledge.

Resnick, S. and Wolf, R. (1993) 'Althusser's Liberation of Marxian Theory', in *The Althusserian Legacy*, Kaplan, E. and Sprinker, M. (eds), London: Verso.

Rex, J. (1961) *Key Problems in Sociological Theory*, London: Routledge and Kegan Paul.

Rex, J. (1971) 'Typology and Objectivity: A Comment on Weber's Four Sociological Methods', in *Max Weber and Modern Sociology*, Sahay, A. (ed.), London: Routledge.

Richards, I. A. (1936) *The Philosophy of Rhetoric*, London: Oxford University Press.

Robertson, R. and Turner, B. (eds) (1991) *Talcott Parsons: Theorist of Modernity*, London: Sage.

Rocher, G. (1974) *Talcott Parsons and American Sociology*, London: Nelson and Sons.

Rorty, R. (1979) *Philosophy and the Mirror of Nature*, Princeton: Princeton University Press.

Rose, J. (1986) *Sexuality in the Field of Vision*, London: Verso.

Rossi, I. (1983) *From the Sociology of Symbols to the Sociology of Signs*, New York: Columbia University Press.

Roth, G. and Schluchter, W. (1979) *Max Weber's Vision of History: Ethics and Methods*. Berkeley, Los Angeles and London: University of California Press.

Rubenstein, D. (1977) 'The Concept of Action in the Social Sciences', *Journal for the Theory of Social Behaviour*, 7: 209–36.

Runciman, W. G. (1972) *A Critique of Max Weber's Philosophy of Social Science*, Cambridge: Cambridge University Press.

Russet, C. (1966) *The Concept of Equilibrium in American Sociology*, New Haven: Yale University Press.

Sapir, E. (1949) *Selected Writings in Language, Culture and Personality*, Berkeley: University of California Press.

Savage, S. (1981) *The Theories of Talcott Parsons: The Social Relations of Action*, London: Macmillan Press.

Scaff, L. (1989) *Fleeing the Iron Cage: Culture, Politics and Modernity in the Thought of Max Weber*, Berkeley: University of California Press.

Schmaus, W. (1994) *Durkheim's Philosophy of Science and the Sociology of Knowledge*, Chicago and London: The University of Chicago Press.

Schmidt, A. (1971) *The Concept of Nature in Marx*, London: New Left Books.

Schroeder, R. (1992) *Max Weber and the Sociology of Culture*, London: Sage.

Schwanenberg, E. (1990) 'The Two Problems of Order in Parsons' Theory', in *Functionalist Sociology*, Colomy, P. (ed.), Aldershot: Edward Elgar.

Schwinn, T. (1998) 'False Connections: Systems and Action Theories in Neofunctionalism and Jurgen Habermas', *Sociological Theory*, 16(1): 75–95.

Scott, J. (1996) *Stratification and Power: Structures of Class: Status and Command*, Cambridge: Polity Press.

Scott, J. (2001) *Realism, Complexity, and Structure: In Search of Ontological Depth,* paper presented at the joint meeting of the National Centre for Social Research (EKKE) and the Association of Greek Sociologists (SEK).

Scott, J. F. (1963) 'The Changing Foundations of the Parsonian Action Schema', *American Sociological Review*, 28: 716–35.

Sciulli, D. and Gerstein, D. (1985) 'Social Theory and Talcott Parsons in the 1980s', *Annual Review of Sociology*, 11: 369–87.

Sica, A. (1988) *Weber, Irrationality and Social Order*, Berkeley and London: California University Press.

Smith, C. (1998) T*he Science of Energy: A Cultural History of Energy Physics in Victorian Britain*, London: Athlone.

Smith, S. (1984) *Reading Althusser*, Ithaca and London: Cornell University Press.

Soja, E. (1989) *Postmodern Geographies*, London and New York: Verso.

Spivak, G. C. (1976) 'Translator's Preface', in *Of Grammatology*, Derrida, J., Baltimore and London: Johns Hopkins University Press.

Stauth, G. and Turner, B. (1988) *Nietzsche's Dance: Resentment, Reciprocity and Resistance in Social Life,* Oxford: Basil Blackwell.

Stehr, N. and Grundmann, R. (2001) 'The Authority of Complexity', *British Journal of Sociology*, 52 (2): 313–29.

Szacki, J. (1979) *History of Sociological Thought*, Westport: Greenwood Press.

Thompson, E. P. (1978) *The Poverty of Theory and Other Essays*, London: Merlin Press.

Thompson, J. B. (1989) 'The Theory of Structuration', in *Social Theory and Modern Societies: Anthony Giddens and his Critics*, Held, D. and Thompson, J. B. (eds), Cambridge: Cambridge University Press.

Tiles, M. (1987) 'Epistemological History: The Legacy of Bachelard and Canguilhem', in *Contemporary French Philosophy*, Griffiths, P. (ed.), Cambridge: Cambridge Univeristy Press.

Tiryakian, E. (1978) 'Emile Durkheim', in *A History of Sociological Analysis*, Bottomore, T. and Nisbet, R. (eds), New York: Basic Books.

Traugott, M. (ed.) (1978) 'Introduction' in *Emile Durkheim on Institutional Analysis*, Chicago and London: Chicago University Press.

Turner, B. (1981), *For Weber*, London: Routledge.

Turner, B. (1982) 'Nietzsche, Weber and the Devaluation of Politics: The Problem of State Legitimacy', *The Sociological Review,* 30: 367–91.

Turner, B. (1986) 'Parsons and his Critics: On the Ubiquity of Functionalism', in *Talcott Parsons on Economy and Society*, Holton, R. and Turner, B. (eds), London: Routledge. 1988.

Turner, B. (1991) 'Neofunctionalism and the New Theoretical Movement: The Post-Parsonian Rapprochement between Germany and America', in *Talcott Parsons: Theorist of Modernity*, Robertson, R. and Turner, B. (eds), London: Sage.

Turner, B. (1995) 'Preface to the New Edition', in *From Max Weber: Essays in Sociology*, London: Routledge.

Turner, B. (1999) *Classical Sociology*, London: Sage.

Turner, J. (1974) *The Structure of Sociological Theory*, Homewood Illinois: The Dorsey Press.

Turner, J. and Maryanski, A. (1979) *Functionalism*, Menlo Park California: Benjamin/ Cummings.

Turner, S. (ed.) (1993) *Emile Durkheim: Sociologist and Moralist*, London and New York: Routledge.

Venuti, L. (1998) *The Scandals of Translation*, London and New York: Routledge.

Vergata, A. (1994) 'Herbert Spencer: Biology, Sociology, and Cosmic Evolution', in Maasen, S. *et al.* (eds) *Biology as Society, Society as Biology: Metaphors*, Dordrecht: Kluwer Academic Press.

Wallwork, E. (1972) *Durkheim, Morality and Milieu*, Cambridge: Harvard University Press.

Watkins, J.W.N. (1973) 'Ideal Types and Historical Explanation', in *Modes of Individualism and Collectivism*, O'Neill, J. (ed.), London: Heinemann.

Wearne, B. (1987) *The Theory and Scholarship of Talcott Parsons to 1951: A Critical Commentary*, Cambridge: Cambridge University Press.

Weber, M. (1949) *The Methodology of Social Sciences*. E. Shills and H. Finch (eds), New York: The Free Press of Glencoe.

Weber, M. (1951) *The Religion of China*, Glencoe: The Free Press.

Weber, M. (1975) *Roscher and Knies: The Logical Problems of Historical Economics*, New York and London: The Free Press.

Weber, M. (1978) *Economy and Society*, Roth, G. and Wittich, C. (eds), Berkeley and London: California University Press.

Weber, M. (1992) *The Protestant Ethic and Spirit of Capitalism*, London: Routledge.

Weiner, N. (1954) *The Human Use of Human Beings: Cybernetics and Society*, New York: Avon.

Weiner, N. (1961) *Cybernetics*, Cambridge: MIT Press.

White, H. (1973) *Metahistory: The Historical Imagination in Nineteenth-century Europe*, Baltimore and London: The Johns Hopkins University Press.

Whitehead, A. N. (1967) *Science and the Modern World*, New York: Free Press.

Williams, R. (1961) 'The Sociological Theory of Talcott Parsons', in *The Social Theories of Talcott Parsons*, Black, M. (ed.), New York: Prentice Hall.

Williams, R. (1977) *Marxism and Literature*, London: Oxford University Press.

Winch, P. (1970) *The Idea of a Social Science*, London: Routledge and Kegan Paul.

Wittgenstein, L. (1967) *Philosophical Investigations*, Oxford: Blackwell.

Woodiwiss, A. (1990) *Social Theory after Postmodernism*, London: Pluto.

Woodiwiss, A. (1993) *Postmodernity USA: The Crisis of Social Modernism in Postwar America*, London: Sage.

Woodiwiss, A. (1997) 'Against "Modernity": A Dissident Rant', *Economy and Society*, 26(1): 1–21.

Woodiwiss, A. (2001) *The Visual in Social Theory*, London: Athlone Press.

Woodiwiss, A. and Pearce, F. (2001) 'Reading Foucault as a Realist', in *After Postmodernism: An Introduction to Critical Realism*, López, J. and Potter, G. (eds), London: Athlone.

Wrong, D. (1961) 'The Oversocialized Conception of Man in Modern Sociology', in *American Sociological Review*, 26: 183- 193.

Zeitlin, I. (1994) *Ideology and the Development of Social Theory*, New Jersey: Prentice Hall.

Index